More praise for *Pilobolus: A Story of Dance and Life*

"A highly readable, insightful journey into the history, creative process, and fascinating personalities of America's most inventive dance/theatre company."—**Steven Banks**, playwright, actor, and *New York Times*–bestselling writer

"Pranzatelli lovingly captures the enchanted, ingenious world of Pilobolus: the open-hearted spirit of discovery; the fearless commitment to exploration; the irreverent, unquenchable creativity of the artists who have shaped and reshaped this remarkable project over the decades." —**Trish Sie**, filmmaker, *Sitting in Bars with Cake*

"A thorough, insightful, expressive, and very readable account of a singular dance troupe. While chronicling Pilobolus's journey through the decades, and astutely spotlighting relevant people, dynamics, and context, this book gives a sense of the troupe's vitality, in part through eloquent description and analysis of specific dance works and overall aesthetic." —**Celia Wren**, theatre and dance writer

"Pranzatelli has written the saga of a creative 'chosen family,' and it is both appealing and a real page-turner."—**Elizabeth Zimmer**, coeditor of *Envisioning Dance on Film and Video*

PILOBOLUS

UNIVERSITY PRESS OF FLORIDA

Florida A&M University, Tallahassee
Florida Atlantic University, Boca Raton
Florida Gulf Coast University, Ft. Myers
Florida International University, Miami
Florida State University, Tallahassee
New College of Florida, Sarasota
University of Central Florida, Orlando
University of Florida, Gainesville
University of North Florida, Jacksonville
University of South Florida, Tampa
University of West Florida, Pensacola

PILOBOLUS

A STORY OF DANCE AND LIFE

Robert Pranzatelli

UNIVERSITY PRESS OF FLORIDA

Gainesville · Tallahassee · Tampa · Boca Raton
Pensacola · Orlando · Miami · Jacksonville · Ft. Myers · Sarasota

The author gratefully acknowledges the *Paris Review:* portions of chapters nine and fourteen appeared, in different form, as part of an essay published by the *Paris Review Daily* in 2019.

Library of Congress Cataloging-in-Publication Data
Names: Pranzatelli, Robert, author.
Title: Pilobolus : a story of dance and life / Robert Pranzatelli.
Description: 1. | Gainesville : University Press of Florida, 2024. |
    Includes bibliographical references and index.
Identifiers: LCCN 2023037525 (print) | LCCN 2023037526 (ebook) | ISBN
    9780813080499 (paperback) | ISBN 9780813073255 (ebook)
Subjects: LCSH: Pilobolus Dance Theatre—History. | Dance companies—United
    States—History. | Modern dance—United States—History. | BISAC:
    PERFORMING ARTS / Dance / History & Criticism | PERFORMING ARTS / Dance
    / Modern
Classification: LCC GV1786.P54 P73 2024 (print) | LCC GV1786.P54 (ebook)
    | DDC 792.80973—dc23/eng/20230925
LC record available at https://lccn.loc.gov/2023037525
LC ebook record available at https://lccn.loc.gov/2023037526

The University Press of Florida is the scholarly publishing agency for the State University System of Florida, comprising Florida A&M University, Florida Atlantic University, Florida Gulf Coast University, Florida International University, Florida State University, New College of Florida, University of Central Florida, University of Florida, University of North Florida, University of South Florida, and University of West Florida.

University Press of Florida
2046 NE Waldo Road
Suite 2100
Gainesville, FL 32609
http://upress.ufl.edu

CONTENTS

List of Illustrations   ix

PART ONE

ONE • First Person   3

TWO • Dartmouth   16

THREE • Quartet   40

FOUR • Tall Ladies   60

FIVE • Broadway   73

SIX • Reinventions   97

PART TWO

SEVEN • Among the Gnomen   117

EIGHT • Pools of Light   134

NINE • Combinations   155

TEN • Differences   179

ELEVEN • Dreams and Silhouettes   190

PART THREE

TWELVE • Shadows   205

THIRTEEN • Partners   221

FOURTEEN • Branches   236

FIFTEEN • Life   251

Acknowledgments   261
Pilobolus Dancers through the Years   263
Bibliography of Sources   265
Index   273

ILLUSTRATIONS

All illustrations are the copyrighted work of the photographers indicated and are used by permission.

Covers and frontispiece: John Kane / Silver Sun Studio

Front cover, "Nude Mushroom" a.k.a. "Embrace": Renée Jaworski, Jenny Mendez, and Manelich Minniefee, 2005.

Back cover, "Bow and Arrow": Jun Kuribayashi and Matt Del Rosario, 2012.

Frontispiece, "Walking Creature": Rebecca Anderson, Becky Jung, and Darryl Thomas, 1995.

——

Images of the early Pilobolus, 1971–72: Jonathan Sa'adah

Page 30, *Pilobolus* silhouette, from *Pilobolus* (the original piece) as seen in 1972.

Page 45, Robby Barnett and Robb Pendleton backstage (Robby applying makeup) in Center Theater, 1972.

Page 46, Jonathan Wolken (*upper image*), Lee Harris (*lower image*), early Pilobolus rehearsals, Dartmouth College.

Page 47, Robb Pendleton, early Pilobolus rehearsals, Dartmouth College (*upper image*), Robby Barnett, Hanover, New Hampshire, 1971 (*lower image*).

Pages 48–49, Four images of the Pilobolus work *Ocellus,* 1972.

Page 50, Pilobolus, *Ocellus,* 1972: Robb Pendleton (*aloft*), Jonathan Wolken (*front*), Robby Barnett, and Lee Harris.

——

Images through the years: John Kane / Silver Sun Studio

Page 96, Martha Clarke photographed by John Kane, circa 1990.

Page 116, "Gordian Knot": Matt Kent and Rebecca Anderson, 2000.

Page 144, "Spiral": From center: Josie Coyoc, Rebecca Anderson, Benjamin Pring, Gaspard Louis, Matt Kent, Otis Cook, 2000.

Page 145, "Mandala": Benjamin Pring, Otis Cook, Rebecca Anderson, Josie Coyoc, 2000.

Page 156, "Thighstand": Renée Jaworski and Matt Kent, 2003.

Page 169, "Candle": Josie Coyoc and Matt Kent, 2005.

Page 170, "Scorpion Lift": Josie Coyoc and Matt Kent, 2005.

Page 170, "Scorpion 2": Josie Coyoc and Matt Kent, early 2000s.

Page 171, "Pendulum": Renée Jaworski and Jennifer Macavinta, early 2000s.

Page 172, "Position to Celebrate" (original), six dancers, 2004.

Page 204, "Shadowland Transformation 2": Molly Gawler, 2008.

Page 213, "From the Cave": Jeffrey Huang, Christopher Whitney, Jenny Mendez, Matt Del Rosario, Annika Sheaff, Andrew Herro, 2009.

Page 222, "Tangle": Jeffrey Huang and Jenny Mendez, 2009.

Page 240, "David": Renée Jaworski and Andrew Herro, 2007.

Page 241, "Bow and Arrow": Jun Kuribayashi and Matt Del Rosario, 2012.

Page 241, "Fan": Jun Kuribayashi, Shawn Ahern, Andrew Herro, Matt Del Rosario, Winston Dynamite Brown, Nile Russell, 2011.

Page 250, "Tower": Jeffrey Huang and Christopher Whitney, 2009.

Page 284, "Barn (Milking Parlor, Northville)": Andrew Herro and Matt Del Rosario, 2009.

PART ONE

ONE

First Person

A November night in 1997, at the Shubert Theater in New Haven, Connecticut: four male dancers appear on a bare stage; they too are bare except for black trunks and the light projected on their skin by theatrical design. With agile strength and expressive subtlety, they make even the most grueling of their gymnastic, acrobatic achievements appear fluid; their bodies seem lighter than air, and they radiate vitality as they quietly and powerfully enact a strange vision of male social interactions, ostracism, inclusion, bonding, and love.

The clockwork-smooth choreography with its remarkable lifts, carries, and inversions becomes part tribal ritual, part abstract storytelling. When three of the men gang up on the fourth, he gets twisted into a human pretzel, so contorted and hunched that he walks on one hand and one foot, unsteadily, only to thump his head on the floor. It is comic, poignant, and physically inventive all at once, as is a later sequence, in which one of the men lies on his side, asleep, as his three comrades, standing in a row, each slip one of their feet under him in unison, lift his body, and rock him tenderly as if in a cradle. Yet the wit turns elegiac as the music swells and the lifts seem to partake of a triumphal yet heartrendingly valedictory sensibility. In the piece's final moments the men are left in a seated-kneeling position, staring ahead: whether into the void or at divine grace, into mystery or at mortality, in prayer or stoic enlightenment, we do not know. We do know, however, that we, like them, have been brought face to face with something profound.

As I sat in the dark of the audience, I found myself yearning to merge into the vision on stage. The dancers, two of them light-skinned and two of them dark-skinned, had fashioned themselves, or had been fashioned, into something that, while elusive, had many levels of meaning amid its quality of transcendence; and in their mixture of discipline and ingenuity, they seemed to possess a kind of enlightenment. The piece, called *Gnomen*, was, for me, revelatory—in its conflation of male physicality, mystery, and emotional resonance, wrapped in the aura of ritual, and its vision of male failings and male beauty and the mingling of the two.

It had been the fourth of five works on the evening's program. The fast-paced surreal finale that followed, entitled *Day Two*, used all six of the company's dancers, four men and two women, for a turn into a more trippy mysticism, a compressed epic of creation-myth-charged-by-Eros infused with intense visual inventiveness, set to a rousing polyrhythmic accompaniment in the music of Talking Heads and Brian Eno; after it, the troupe returned for an invigorating variation on closing bows that doubled as a comic encore: the dancers propelled themselves in a seated position, with legs extended, across a wet stage like exuberant kids on a slide, before mischievously splashing a few nearby audience members as if with a sprinkle of *joie de vivre.*

During the downpour of applause that followed, many in the audience looked happily astonished, and someone marveled aloud at what it must be like to be those dancers, given the intense physical trust required of such an ensemble. I wondered: Did it create an indescribable bond, a one-of-a-kind brotherhood? How much did these dancers really like one another; how close were their friendships; were any of them lovers? Did they regard themselves strictly as professionals, or as a fraternity, a family? On stage they become a fantasy, perhaps a radically different one for different observers: an athletic fantasy, an emotional, artistic, or sexual fantasy, or a social or moral fantasy that demonstrates the virtues of mutual effort and respect. In any case, a fantasy with Utopian tones and tendencies, activating latent yearnings in the applauding observer. And I thought, if this is what it is to run away and join the circus (no pitching of hay, no ringmaster with a bad mustache), if this is the new, cool circus—then the impulse to run away is entirely understandable.

I stood in the balcony with the crowd, in a state of awe and discovery, but what, exactly, had I discovered? I had accepted a free ticket earlier that day, knowing nothing about this troupe, and had walked in completely unprepared for their work's otherworldly quality, its masterful eccentricity. It felt as if the dancers were conduits of a new energy I needed to absorb, a foreign radiance in which glinted a tantalizing force, one perhaps related to my dreams.

White towels draped around their shoulders, the dancers reemerged and sat at the edge of the stage to take questions. One recent addition, a young man with longish dark hair, had an especially open, welcoming quality. Among all the performers that night, he had most stood out to me: I had been delighted by both his comic skills and frankly insane endurance in the slapstick *Walklyndon* earlier in the evening (in which his colleagues had very literally walked all over him), but even more by the way his comedic abilities coexisted easily with, and when necessary yielded to, other aspects of his performances, not least the artful physical demands required of *Gnomen* and *Day Two*. Now he conveyed an almost puppyish enthusiasm: "We're based right here in Connecticut, and we love to have visitors, so you should come visit us," he said, not merely to the person whose question he was answering but to the entire audience, as if inviting the mob of us to pop by the troupe's rural headquarters in the hills to the west. The suggestion seemed heartfelt but terribly impractical, and I recall thinking *wouldn't that be cool* and *wouldn't it be cool to know someone like that* but also *how would that work?* before dismissing the idea as hopeless. What did I have in common with any of these dancers? Why would any of these jock-like kids have the slightest interest in my friendship? I was already a comparatively old thirty-three. This seemed, at best, an invitation to social awkwardness.

The young man, whose name was Matt, answered another question, explaining the group's choreography with a phrase along the lines of "We just come up with ideas for cool stuff and then see if we can figure out a way to do it"—which struck me as rather lame. He had, however, done an awfully good job of spewing water like a fountain as he slid across the stage a while earlier, like a Tarzan boy with his long curly dark hair and near-naked body. Definitely cute, and a sweet guy, sure, but—I wondered. He had been credited as a co-creator of *Gnomen*. To what degree was he an artist, as opposed to someone whose qualities and skills were well utilized by other artists? I couldn't tell, but I liked him. He had been central to one of the best nights I'd ever had in a theater.

2

They were called Pilobolus Dance Theatre, or simply Pilobolus. On that mid-1990s night the company was in its twenty-fifth season and already long praised for its wit, style, sensuality, and innovative approach to human physicality. It had originated as an all-male trio in a Dartmouth dance class in 1971 and soon expanded to an all-male quartet and then to a sextet that included two women. It was this last configuration that achieved fame in the 1970s, with a Broadway run. The *New Yorker*'s Arlene Croce had declared Pilobolus not a dance company but a "brilliant acrobatic-mime troupe" that consisted of, in her view, "six of the most extraordinary people now performing." A couple of decades later, and after much further evolution, Pilobolus was still thriving.

Eager to learn more, I made use of a relatively new resource called the internet. The troupe itself didn't seem to have done much with it yet, but a man who had found Pilobolus as revelatory as I had—and whose name and writings I can no longer locate—had posted an essay entitled "The First Time I Saw Pilobolus." In his case the inspiration had much to do with the occasional nudity and frequent near-nudity of the male dancers, not in a prurient sense (though, as a gay man, he was certainly attracted to their handsome, ideal physiques) but because seeing these men interact in a nonsexual but intimate way, without much clothing and with neither shame nor homophobia, was for him profoundly affirming and liberating. His essay articulated an important aspect of the performance I'd seen.

I remained interested in Pilobolus, and several years later, in May 2002, I saw them at a Saturday matinee in New Haven. The selection of pieces was different and so were most of the dancers, except for *that guy again:* Matt, still full of energy, still remarkable, and now listed in the program as "dance captain." I imagined he must have moved up in status—even though, in the only piece that I recognized from a few years earlier, he was still being stepped on by everyone else.

Afterward, in another round of online searching, I discovered that Pilobolus had begun publishing an annual wall calendar. It contained no performance shots; instead, many of the set-ups used a simple white background with the dancers in brightly colored leotards or a minimum of clothing (dance belts, for an essentially nude look), with nothing to distract from the playfulness and sheer physical beauty of their inventive poses (two dancers partnering, with one partner upside-down; several dancers combined to form a larger creature; two dancers demonstrating a seemingly impossible, or highly improbable, lift; and so on). As the years rolled along, the calendars kept the Pilobolus energy subtly pulsing in the background of my life.

More than a decade after I had first seen them perform, I learned of a weeklong Pilobolus summer workshop, open to nondancers as well as dancers, taught in their studio in western Connecticut. It sounded exhilarating and, to me, terrifying. But I saw that it would be taught by the husband and wife team of Matt and Emily Kent. Yes, *that* Matt.

3

On Monday, July 14, 2008, the first morning of the workshop, a Pilobolus staff member greeted each of the two dozen or so participants, many of them twenty years younger than myself and most of them female, as we arrived, and checked off our names. I milled around, as did others, discreetly checking out the surroundings—the spacious Washington Club Hall with its hardwood floors and barn-high ceiling—and, more discreetly, checking out my instructors. Matt, in a t-shirt and sweatpants, his hair now short, sat on the floor hunched over an Apple laptop like a mad scientist oblivious to the room around him. Emily stood calmly nearby with an infant in her arms, and occasionally spoke with the few people in the room who already knew her. I had never seen her before. In her early thirties, with long brown hair, and, like her husband, wearing a t-shirt and sweatpants, and in fantastic shape, what struck me most was her face, not simply because it was pretty but because she bore a kind of family resemblance to a girl with whom I had once been hopelessly in love, while also a close friend and confidant, in my teens. I suddenly had the secret thought that Matt had excellent taste. I also sensed that he and Emily were a simpatico pair, an intuition that grew more certain when we all sat on the floor and circled up to introduce ourselves.

Each of us in turn was to state our name, where we lived, our profession, and what we expected from the workshop. About halfway around the circle, one young woman stated only the first three items, and was asked: "And your expectations?"

"Oh, zero," she said, a bit emphatically, to assert that she had arrived with an open mind. "I have zero expectations."

"We can meet those expectations," Emily said with playful assurance.

The line got a laugh. She had delivered it exactly the way certain of my dearest friends from my college days would have, with a slight emphasis on the word *meet*.

I like her, I thought, and suddenly felt that she and Matt might be of my tribe.

The entire group, even at this early moment, seemed to connect, and it felt as if I were rejoining a group I'd been in before, reconvening. After a few words about the coming week, Emily asked us to stand and then told us to "start walking"—all of us, in any direction, or all directions, as she and Matt called out instructions. They told us to use different speeds (slower, faster), to go through the middle of the space as well as around the outer edges, to avoid touching, to brush against each other or bump lightly, to make eye contact or not, and to try other, different kinds of movement— to learn to be aware of oneself, others nearby, then the group as a whole and one's own choices within the larger group's evolving choices from mo- ment to moment. With everyone gradually picking up on the same gesture or behavior and then letting it transform, by the end of this ever-morphing exercise we were dancing en masse, a group already bonded and unified. Again I had the sense of being right where I belonged, having reconvened with old friends or old souls.

Throughout the morning we did other exercises that also evolved into improvisations, and as the day proceeded we improvised without music and with music added. We created short pieces in groups of four, with no soundtrack, then Matt would select from his iTunes and throw the music on and we would have to adapt to it as we performed. At one point he used a terrific jazz track that I identified, with amazement, as a jazz remake of Nirvana's "Smells Like Teen Spirit." When asked, Matt told us the name of the band, but by the end of the day I had forgotten it. Before leaving I walked up to him and asked again. "The Bad Plus," he said, and mentioned that they had also recorded a version of "Heart of Glass."

"Ah, now you've said the magic words," I replied, and told him of my longtime Blondie obsession. As we spoke briefly about cover versions, I saw that on the subject of music Matt glowed; and a little while later, alone in my room at the inn where I was staying, I realized that there had been a moment when his face had taken on a familiar look—but how could that be possible, given that we had never met before? I struggled to place it, and finally realized that it was the look my friend John Kulka gets when he's pleased with something I've said—a certain friendship-related satisfaction—a detail I found intriguing, particularly as Matt and John don't really resemble each other.

I had approached the workshop with some trepidation, despite my enthusiasm. A lifelong nonathlete as well as a nondancer, I tended to associate physical challenges with failure, misery, and ridicule. What I had seen of Matt suggested he was a nice guy, but how did I know what he'd be like as an instructor? A few months prior to the workshop I had watched a documentary film about Pilobolus entitled *Last Dance,* which I had loved, but it revealed some of the tensions and arguments between artistic directors. Matt, one of the dancers, wasn't directly involved in the arguments but was described, in the film and one of the accompanying short features on the DVD, as "crazy" and "intense." These adjectives seemed meant in a mostly positive way, but again, how was I to know?

I had become aware of his formidable resumé in an online bio note (sample sentence: "He has performed on stilts, on trapeze, on circus silks, and of course on other dancers"). Now, on the first day of the workshop, I had begun to see that the intensity of his husky voice, large biceps, and overall demeanor had its match in the quickness of his perceptions and the fast pace and high energy that animated him, but what seemed most unusual was his focus. Often an extraordinarily energetic person has a slightly out-of-control quality, and the perpetual motion can be exhausting to be around, yet Matt's boundless energy seemed to have its own built-in discipline, as if he knew exactly how to channel it. That martial arts had played a role in his life helped to explain this, but I'd never met anyone like him. Instead of finding his intensity draining or intimidating, I found I *got* energy from being around him, a gift of vitality.

By the second day I began to realize that the trappings of the workshop, the surrounding details—doing yoga in my room at the Heritage Inn; my related morning rituals; my tote bag with towel, bottled water, granola bars, and one or two other useful items; my daily arrival, entering Club Hall each morning and stretching, and doing more yoga on the hardwood floor (we used no mats, a choice that surprised me but to which I soon grew attached); my return, for the first time in decades, to the habit of going barefoot for hours at a time; lunches in the pleasantly shady little café across the way—were also a vital part of the experience, and made me feel as if this were not only a workshop but a life.

4

In many ways Monday and Tuesday would be my best days, the freshest and most exhilarating. On the second day it hit me with a little *frisson* that Club Hall was the same space Pilobolus used as its studio, seen in the film *Last Dance,* and I could connect images from the documentary with the space I was in.

By midday Tuesday I felt pretty terrific. For several of us, lunch at the café across the street included a bucolic visit with Matt and Emily, open and generous with their thoughts and stories, traces of their Georgia-bred hospitality in the summer air as we ate beneath the trees. After more workshop activity, by late afternoon it was time to get on a bus for our trip into New York to see Pilobolus at the Joyce Theater. There I found that I observed the dances with a new viewpoint, noticing not only the breathtaking "don't try this at home" moments but also the small ones, seeing elements of things we had tried in the past two days. Whole sections of *Day Two* looked like they could have evolved from a "follow the leader" exercise like one we had done, and I saw that the piece's power came not simply from its physically difficult aspects but from how interesting the ideas and images were, and how well assembled.

On Wednesday, Matt had to be in New York to direct a television commercial, so Emily was joined by a guest instructor, Renée Jaworski, a veteran Pilobolus dancer turned artistic associate and rehearsal director. I recognized Renée from my Pilobolus calendars: her broad smile, twinkling eyes, medium-length haircut, the strength and bearing that allowed her to merge feminine and tomboy energies or toggle between different aspects of each.

As a workshop instructor she seemed tougher than Matt and Emily, not in personal manner but in the level of physical activity she encouraged, the running around she had us do, the extent to which she left us panting for breath. She also had us try exercises that seemed maddeningly beyond our grasp. A modified follow the leader with numerous extra challenges left me baffled as to how anyone, even a Pilobolus dancer, could possibly do it. (On the other hand, everyone in the room except Renée had gone into New York the night before, stayed late to meet the dancers, and taken a long bus ride back to northwestern Connecticut in the middle of the night. After a tantalizingly brief sample of sleep, simply keeping our eyes open seemed ambitious.)

In any case, all this was in the morning; in the afternoon we would see a different side of Renée. As for Emily, as on previous days, she occasionally stepped away to nurse her newborn, Owen, but otherwise remained present. During one of the breaks she chatted with a few of us and told an anecdote about Matt slipping twice on a sweaty stage during a performance. When she got to the part of the story where he slipped, Emily said, "He did one of these" and executed a perfect pratfall, then bounced back up instantly and continued the story uninterrupted: "He came around again and—" and she did another, and again bounced back up. It was brilliant, and she seemed not to think anything of it. At lunchtime, she ate with a few of us in the shade of the tree in front of Club Hall, again in the serene summer air.

In the afternoon, when it came time to break into groups and work on our pieces-in-progress, Renée made the rounds to observe and give advice. My group consisted of several women, ranging from young to middle-aged, and myself. We had come up with the idea of using me as a centerpiece around which the others would move. I would start crouched on the ground, my head down and arms pulled in, as compressed as possible, and gradually "open" and slowly rise like a plant or tree growing, as the women, holding hands, circled me. I realize it sounds horrendous, like a parody of bad theatre, but it was a beginning. We thought of it only as a place to start.

When Renée stopped by, we presented it to her with disclaimers and very little confidence, but she responded with choreographic insight and nurturing warmth, and advised us that we indeed had something good to work with. She told us to slow it down and think of "sweet custard dripping" to give it the right sensibility as we continued to work on it.

At the end of the day, a dark-haired young dancer named Julie with whom I'd struck up a rapport drove me back to the inn. During the ride we compared thoughts. We both were very taken with Matt and Emily, but Julie had preferred Renée's approach in the morning exercises, with its (to me) seemingly unattainable goals, because Renée was, she said, "more what I'm used to" from a dance instructor. Julie's dance training had conditioned her to expect physical challenges and a certain level of exhortation to push oneself harder. As I would learn, trained dancers often prefer to be given a goal, no matter how difficult. Nondancers, by contrast, even those who feel hopelessly limited physically, can sometimes excel in the areas of invention, improvisation, or the subtler aspects of theatrical performance. In a Pilobolus workshop, especially at the introductory level, the two groups can help each other. Dancers trained to obediently reproduce movement rather than invent it may find themselves at a disadvantage; when expected to invent, they may freeze, at which point they can turn to the nondancers next to them, who in turn may require help, or workarounds, for the physical elements. Many attendees find themselves partnering with exactly the person who they might have thought would offer them nothing.

On Thursday Matt was back but Emily was gone, having flown home to Georgia for the funeral of her grandfather. Matt was on his own. One morning (was it Thursday or Friday?) he realized with a start, as our workshop day was about to begin, that he had forgotten to change from his street clothes (blue jeans, polo shirt) to his workout clothes. "Hold on! This will only take me a minute," he assured the two dozen of us seated on the floor. Then he spun around, and standing with his back to us peeled off his clothes at top speed and did a quick change, as the rest of us, bemused, found the "boxers or briefs" question rather decisively answered by the black briefs flattering his dancer-perfect rounded butt. Having already been shown a clip of him performing naked, I suppose no one in the workshop should have been fazed; I certainly wasn't, but given his role as DJ to our improv exercises I couldn't resist calling out: "I think we should have music for *this*"—and he shot me a devilish grin and did a little striptease flourish with one of his arms.

5

Thursday afternoon and most of Friday were devoted to working on our final group pieces, in my case the "tree piece." Our group dynamic became difficult as we all had different ideas and floundered. We kept adding material but none of the additions worked. We had been told that a small contingent from the Pilobolus office down the street might stop by to see our final performance on Friday afternoon, which added to the pressure; that the visitors might include one or more of the founding artistic directors increased the pressure further. Yet I wasn't terribly worried about any of that. My frustration was that even with the clock conspicuously ticking, I couldn't get my group to listen to each other instead of breaking off into separate, simultaneous, counterproductive conversations.

Friday turned into the first truly steamy-hot day of the week. And then, suddenly, time ran out. Midafternoon arrived and with it our guests, our audience. As they were ushered in, perhaps a dozen people at most, I recognized a few of them from the film *Last Dance*. Here they were, a decade further along: Jonathan, still mustachioed, curly-haired, and smiling mischievously, but a little grayer, loosely dressed for the heat, strolling in like a self-proclaimed guru who owns the place; Robby, tall, bald, silent, veering off to sit in a corner as far away as possible, as if he might climb out a window to escape into the green hills while no one was looking; Matt's former dance partner Rebecca, the Pilobolus poster girl of the 1990s, her sweet, earnest, bleached-blonde aura transposed to a slightly less girlish, more thirtysomething register; and, of course, Renée, here to see how our pieces had turned out. Also present were several faces unfamiliar to me, including Itamar, the company's executive director, who did look like he might work in an office, and smiled amiably as he sat on the floor to the left of Jonathan, who had placed himself front and center in lotus position though not necessarily Buddha-like. Matt encouraged Robby to join them, Robby demurred ("I'm fine here"), and Matt sat to Jonathan's right. Had there been an argument? I admired Jonathan and Robby as the creators of *Gnomen* and other works, but I'd also seen them argue in *Last Dance* and had gotten a sense of Jonathan's combative personality. Matt, briefing him in a whisper in advance of the performance, seemed visibly nervous. On that hot afternoon, seated on that hardwood floor, Pilobolus struck me as a high-functioning but highly dysfunctional family.

As each small group took its turn, my group and I were eager to get it over with. At the last moment, in hushed tones, we conferred and agreed to drop every disastrous idea we had tried in the preceding two days, and instead revert to the basic "tree piece" from Wednesday afternoon. It was the only thing we had that wasn't completely mortifying. However, every other group was getting selected to perform before we did. After each performance, Jonathan would ask for comments and then deliver his opinion and related lessons with an air of mild pontification—but he wasn't mean, and everything he said was spot-on. At one point, I forget in what context, he referenced Dr. Seuss and Bartholomew Cubbins, and as one of the few people in the room familiar with the word "Oobleck" I found myself smiling.

Finally, finally—we were the last group to go!—it was time for me to be a tree. We had decided to slow the piece down even more than ever, the slowest we could possibly make it, which meant that my slow-motion rise, already excruciating for my thighs (and a study in discovering muscles I never knew were waiting to be made sore), would need to be even more dragged-out. That was OK with me, as this was the last time I would ever perform the thing, and this was the performance that would count. I decided to pour on all the thigh masochism and spiritual emoting of transcendent-tree-blossoming that I could possibly pour, and I sensed that the rest of our group was also in do-or-die mode.

We gave it all we had. And then it was time to hear the verdict from the Lawgiver.

"I heard that this group had some difficulties. Is that true? You had some difficulties agreeing?" Jonathan began. A couple of us mumbled something along the lines of "er . . ." None of us wanted to discuss it.

"Of course that *never* happens in Pilobolus," Jonathan added dryly. He then told us what he thought of the piece.

"Of the pieces we've seen, this one has the least movement, the least amount of dance, it is the shortest, and it is perfect. It is a perfect moment."

We were stunned.

He went on. He called the piece "beautiful" and said, "It is a lesson in simplicity." He talked about the "less is more" philosophy, and his own formulation of it, which he called "the sushi principle" ("Less, perfectly served, is often just right").

And then he turned to me: "Do not think ill of this piece. You may think you were just standing there, but you were doing far, far more." He concluded with a phrase that had a distinctly Jonathan ring to it: "Let consternation turn to lumination."

And before we knew it, the guests were gone. Renée sat with us and led us through a rapid recall of things we had learned from the week (ideas about leading and following, making decisions in the moment, and other concepts), we were handed Pilobolus t-shirts, people were saying their goodbyes. Renée was amused when I told her that I had recognized her from my Pilobolus calendars, we had a nice moment, and then she too was gone. The room, the day, had become sweltering, everyone dripping with sweat, but it seemed like the sweat was not punishment but some kind of proof. People were heading out to their cars, Julie was frantically copying a list of email addresses by hand, the room and the week itself seemed to be spinning apart like petals blown from a flower, and unbeknownst to me a seed from the moment rested within me, as if it knew it would later blossom into a long paragraph or two. At the time, however, my sole concern, which suddenly made me insecure, was whether I would connect with Matt again before he rushed off to catch his flight to Georgia. As he was frantically packing his things, I cautiously approached. I knew I'd been a paying customer here, and just because you take a workshop doesn't mean you can expect the instructors to want to be your friends. I felt like a geek. But I complimented him again, told him how much *Gnomen* had meant to me, he said it was one of the things of which he was proudest to have been a part, I asked a bit sheepishly if we might stay in touch, he said absolutely, he gave me his card, I thanked him and left him to his frantic packing. Meanwhile Julie, my ride, was still copying the list as fast as she could, so she could return the original to Matt. I stood a little ways off, by myself, so as not to hover. And then, when Matt was finally ready to head out, he did something I didn't expect. "OK, Rob," I heard, and he swung toward me and embraced me in a brief, beautiful, sweaty hug, as he left. The place was empty. Julie and I were the last to leave, and we made sure we closed the door correctly behind us.

TWO

Dartmouth

1

May 1971. A sense, even indoors, of spring: the floriferous, one-time-only spring of the final weeks before college graduation. In a large, open space that resembles a gymnasium, three boyish men perform, twice in succession, an odd little dance (but is it a "dance" or something else?) eight minutes long, for no audience other than the camera and its operators; and then they stand around and banter through a loose, six-minute interview. They, and life, the world, all its possibilities, are young, and even in black and white footage the brightness is in the air, in their eager laughter and playful camaraderie, a bit giddy. The only hint of a shadow is a passing reference to the risk, faced by one of them, of being drafted.

The ringleader, Robb Pendleton, has, with his darkly bearded face, the darkest looks as well as the most muscular bearing, and the most to say, the most energy, from the start. ("I'm from Lyndonville, Vermont. Lived there all my life. Twenty-two years up on Lochlyndon Farm. And I go to school at Hanover, New Hampshire. And I hope to go back on the farm and work in my garden, plant Swiss chard, dance, play music, be in some sort of environment which is clean, healthy, plenty of space. I want to get a group of creative people up there, and hopefully something affirmative, I'm sure affirmative, will develop this summer. We have eight more weeks of school.") Stephen Johnson is more bookish, bespectacled, cleanshaven with neatly parted hair, modest, soft-spoken, a good-natured science major from Memphis who already knows he will likely become a doctor. ("We were in Alison Becker's dance class fall term together at Dartmouth, and she asked us to work on putting together a program for a 12:30 Rep at Dartmouth, which is a noon concert sort of thing. And the three of us decided we would like to work together in preparation for this concert.") Jonathan Wolken, thinner and taller, with a lighter beard than Robb, comes across as somewhere between the two, less in command than Robb but quick to articulate his thoughts when given the chance. He's the one concerned about the draft but he overflows with enthusiasm for this new phenomenon, dance, that "started out as a little nugget" and then "expanded, drove everything out of my life."

Even if one might not guess that Robb Pendleton is an English major, he speaks the most fluently on artistic creation and its prerequisites, remarking that the trio were rescued from "academic bullshit" when "suddenly Alison flew in out of some cloud." He mentions the additional influence of Alwin Nikolais who "came up in November" and Claudia Melrose, who followed, both of whom further inspired them. Now they are a group. "We can work intimately. We're all very close. That's what you need, you know. You have to lose your inhibitions in order to explore anything. And that's how we got into this dance. We sort of lived with each other, we ate dinner together . . ."

At this they all laugh, Jonathan adding "Lost weight together . . ." and Robb continuing, "Cooked organic . . . yeah, we lost twelve pounds together . . ." Jonathan: "Ate spinach and rice and vegetables . . ." Robb: "That's the type of thing which will free us, or free anybody into exploring some type of dance." Jonathan adds that he doesn't think he could work in New York: "You've got to be up where you can go out and sit under a pine tree somewhere and gather your thoughts together" and Robb agrees: "That type of isolation is good. If people with a lot of energy are isolated, in a place like Hanover, there's not all this goddamn pressure from outside to copy anything . . ."

They discuss the title of the piece.

JONATHAN: It was really going to be called *Lentil Snoop*.

ROBB: That was our working title. *Lentil Snoop*. Because—

JONATHAN: Well, we all ate lentils together—

ROBB: And we all snooped around on the stage.

The piece, however, is called *Pilobolus*. Stephen explains "It's the name of a phototropic fungus." To which Robb adds, "This is our science major." Jonathan, who came up with the name, clarifies: "Anyway, it is the name of a fungus, but it means 'felt'—it derives from the verb 'to feel.' We only found that out afterwards when someone actually went and looked it up. I picked it out because it was just a beautiful word."

To this, Stephen adds a sincere, appreciative "Yeah . . ." and Robb quips "It's something organic in this abstract, cold, dehumanized dance" and they all laugh. In fact, this piece that a videographer has just taped twice (first, from a distance, then closer) bears little resemblance to what the word *dance* has traditionally evoked, but although "abstract" it's certainly not "cold": their working title *Lentil Snoop*, which sounds like a British comedy show, or a skit in one, reveals the comic sensibility half-hidden amid their gymnastic athleticism. In the piece, the three men wear aviator headgear (Stephen wears goggles), close-fitting tank top shirts, and tights. It begins with Robb and Jonathan standing back to back, and Stephen hanging upside down, his knees bent over Robb's shoulders, his ankles secured under Jonathan's arms. Stephen raises himself up; the others gradually lower to the ground; at a certain moment, Jonathan leaps out from underneath, as if launching himself, then begins a leaping, running display of odd energy, and a strange alternative reality begins to be evoked; a sense of manic motion in sudden and madcap runs and leaps; the men bend and connect in unexpected configurations that make various shapes and patterns. Weird, vaguely ominous music floats throughout, with an interlude of funny vocals in the middle: five and a half minutes in, Robb and Stephen carry Jonathan stretched out straight between them, face down, with Jonathan's legs over Robb's shoulders and his arms extended to Stephen's shoulders, and they begin marching in a circle, making silly sounds, including squawks from Jonathan. The sequence lasts less than thirty seconds but has a disproportionate effect, a breath of fresh, comic air. In this and in their banter after the performance they seem a sweet, healthy, funny trio of boy-men. How could anyone imagine that the twenty-two-minute video from this long-ago spring day would become a meaningful time capsule in the history of dance?

2

Months earlier, in the fall of 1970, at the age of twenty-four, Alison Becker—who would become Alison Becker Chase when she married her then-boyfriend Eric Chase—had arrived at Dartmouth College in Hanover, New Hampshire, to take up a position as choreographer in residence and assistant professor of dance. Born and raised in St. Louis, she had danced from the age of four through her late teens, earned an MA in Dance from UCLA, and had trained with Merce Cunningham, Mia Slavenska, and Murray Louis. One of her other influences, the pioneering *New York Times* dance critic John Martin—who, after decades as a leading advocate for modern dance in America, had spent five years teaching at UCLA—had given her a piece of advice: stay away from New York, at least for a while, and go to a smaller, less intense environment to allow oneself time to develop. She had thought it a wise suggestion.

Slender, dark-haired, and beautiful, she could have passed for a student, though female students were scarce at Dartmouth. The last of the Ivy League holdouts against coeducation, the school allowed a small number of female transfer students to take classes, visiting for just one semester, but women were still not admitted, and this highly intelligent, progressive-minded young dance teacher had stepped into a world in which student banners hung from windows, angrily proclaiming *Better Dead Than Co-Ed.* The school's defiantly sexist, rowdy frat culture would serve as inspiration, a few years later, for the film *Animal House,* cowritten by one of its own alumni. Yet Dartmouth had other sides to its culture, and like colleges and universities across the country it was in the throes of change.

Several years earlier, in November 1962, the college had opened an impressive performing arts center that would serve as both a cultural hub and the headquarters for an ambitious arts education program. The Hopkins Center represented a major statement by the college, reinforced by the choice of Wallace Harrison as designer. Harrison's previous architectural projects had included Rockefeller Center and the Corning Museum of Glass; he would go on to design the Metropolitan Opera House and oversee the creation of Lincoln Center, as well as the United Nations Headquarters. When Alison visited Dartmouth, the Hopkins Center, set amid a beautiful campus of lush greenery and fresh air, tempted her. She had wanted to start her own company, but the head of the UCLA dance department, Alma Hawkins, had, with a more practical view, sent her on job interviews; Alison had already interviewed at Boston University and was scheduled to interview next at Antioch College in Ohio. When she mentioned the latter to her contacts at Dartmouth, they asked that she not accept an offer from Antioch without talking to them again first. So she headed to Antioch, but prior to her interview she called Dartmouth to tell them, with sly matter-of-factness, that Antioch seemed quite interested. Dartmouth quickly hired her. They had determined that a modern dance class should be offered, and that she should be the person to create one. In this she had been preceded by Ray Cook, who taught a dance class that focused on movement for actors; Alison's course would be the first to focus on dance for its own sake. But given the school's predominant student demographic—a not very diverse collection of white-boy jocks—who would sign up for it? The answer: those who were required to take an arts or humanities class to graduate and thought this would be an easy one; those with a crush on the lovely young instructor or attracted by the few female transfer students who also took the class; and those who fell into both categories.

Dartmouth gave her plenty of room to do as she wished, though they did ask that she also become involved in theatre productions, an area in which she had no background and felt she had to catch up. Whether in theatre or dance, however, she knew early on that a director could dominate or nurture, and faced with the choice to be a dictator or a catalyst, she chose the latter. Nonetheless, at first, trying to teach dance to her atypical collection of students seemed, in her phrase, "a relative disaster." She tried, for a couple of days, to teach technique, and saw that it wouldn't work; and she knew that if she criticized these boy-men they would simply shut down. She quickly developed a new strategy. She would show them how to *make* dances. To coax them past their formidable performance anxieties she had them play, improvise, invent; and then she gave them assignments to compose dance pieces. She wanted them to not only get used to performing, but "to bringing in pieces of choreography every day, the way a writer gets used to writing every day."

It was a brilliant solution. Among her own interests in dance, she had found herself primarily drawn to choreography from college onward, and now she could tap both her knowledge and the teachings of her mentor Merce Cunningham, who prized innovation, invention, process, and collaboration—all a perfect match for her students, coming of age amid communes, long hair, and rebellious social experiments, eager to shatter traditional forms. Soon, her class itself became an experiment, energized and dynamic, all the more so because her students had not seen modern dance and had no preconceptions. She encouraged them to draw on their own ideas. In the case of one of her first students, Michael Tracy, for example, that meant ideas derived from wrestling and gymnastics. Indeed, many of the students borrowed from sports and adolescent male horseplay, to amazing effect.

The male-oriented, sports-oriented mentality of the school made for a highly competitive environment, in academics and all other areas, and the spirit of competition spilled into the dance class in an interesting way. With Alison's encouragement, as the students grew excited by one another's clever inventions they would borrow, swap, and improve on the ideas, trying to top each other and raise the stakes. Better still, the results, made and performed by athletic but technique-free bodies, often had a remarkable freshness and naturalness. With no traditional dance vocabulary and no ingrained habits to overcome, her students could easily avoid cliché. They were making a new vocabulary, their own—and having fun.

Because the Hopkins Center, affectionately known as the Hop, had no dance studio, the class was held in Webster Hall. A handsome old auditorium and concert hall built at the turn of the twentieth century, it somehow felt much older, perhaps in part because it had fallen into relative disuse. At the time, it still had a raised stage with hardwood floors and a cyclorama, and mildly raked audience seating divided by a middle aisle, as well as balconies and side windows—and on that stage Alison's class was held. As Steve Johnson recalled, "It was fantastic, a big auditorium. Old wooden seats. A stage, big. Alison would beat a little drum to give you a count for your steps. A perfect environment." (More than a quarter-century later, in 1998, the building would be redesigned to house the Rauner Special Collections Library, which includes among its many archives those of a certain world-famous dance company.)

Michael, a sophomore, had been born in Florence, Italy while his parents were there studying art, for their PhDs; his father had been a navy pilot in World War II, and had become an artist, then an art professor at the University of Connecticut, and finally, to support his five children, the head of Xerox's graphics department during that company's boom. Michael had always loved athletics: diving, wrestling, gymnastics, soccer—and had also studied piano and violin in his childhood and teens, respectively, then become more interested in theatre. Having, like others, been attracted to Dartmouth by the Hopkins Center, he soon became what was known as a "Hop rat," a student who spent all his time at the Center. His fellow students in the same section of Alison's course included Robert Morgan Barnett, known as Robby Barnett, an art major entering his junior year. Born and raised in the Adirondack Mountains, the son of author and *Life* magazine correspondent Lincoln Barnett, Robby had grown up in a distinctly literary household. Despite his major, however, he had no grand ambition to be an artist; he thought he might teach art for a while after graduation, to pay off his student loans while deciding what else to do with his life.

As the academic year progressed Alison got an even better grasp of her innovative teaching. Among her students in another class section were sophomore Lee Harris, a self-described "hick from Wyoming" with the heart of an engineer and a passionate interest in computers (a rather futuristic subject in 1970); pre-med senior psychology major (and pole-vaulter) Steve Johnson, born in Seattle and raised there through sixth grade, until his Southern family relocated to Memphis, right across the street from Graceland (he found it to be "like going to Mars" but he adjusted); and senior Jonathan Wolken, a philosophy and science major (and fencer). Jonathan had a hippie-friendly country-flavored side: he folk-danced and played the banjo. He was not, however, from the south, but from Pittsburgh, descended from immigrants from Lithuania. He had only dim memories of his mother, who had died very young, when he was four. As a small child, Jonathan and his older sister Ann felt, as Ann later said, "alone in the world" due to "this tremendous loss. You can't even talk about it, you can't even wrap your mind around it, but it exists in some primitive way inside of you." She and her father called Jonathan "Buster" as a child, and she felt protective of him. Their mother had been an artist, a painter, and Ann would become a painter as well, but Jonathan did not think of himself as an artist, simply as a person of many interests. Nor was he an athlete, really, except that in high school he had gotten a ten-speed bike and had bicycled all over his extraordinarily hilly hometown.

Most of the male students flirted with Alison, or wanted to, and some wanted to imagine themselves, romantically, as her gallant protector. A few, even then, recognized the misogyny around them. Lee Harris had gone to coed public school in Casper, Wyoming, and "found it weird to be on a campus that was all guys" where "it was not at all unusual to hear women talked about in objectified terms." He knew of a female student who was harassed by a male professor, and as for the attitudes of other male students, it seemed to him that single-sex education "turned out some pretty twisted people." Steve Johnson recalls that many of the frat parties really did resemble their future depiction on film: "The parties at Alpha Delta were like they were straight out of the movie *Animal House*." Needless to say, given the era, in a class full of male college athletes—what Alison later called "a total roomful of testosterone cases"—one also found a certain low-grade homophobia. Some of the guys wore jeans, terrified that their parents would refuse to pay their tuition if they discovered they wore tights; others made Alison laugh, with remarks like "God, if my father could see me running around in panty hose."

Whether goaded on by a desire to prove their masculinity, outdo their friends, impress their instructor, or plunge into the adventurous spirit of the times, the students created with a youthful bravado that grew more extreme. In one legendary performance, Steve Johnson, drawing on his skills as a pole vaulter, bounded down the theater's central aisle without a pole but with great speed and giant strides, took a superheroic flying leap onto the six-foot-high stage, and slid all the way to the back, rolling into a handstand against the cyclorama.

Perhaps the most striking student, however, was another senior, Robb Pendleton, the unusually athletic English major. He had humor mixed with a strange intensity, and Alison noticed that he also had a somewhat cheeky penchant for altering the assignments.

3

For Robb, life was in a constant state of reinvention, for reasons that ran deep and dark. He had grown up on a dairy farm in northern Vermont, the work of his father, his hero, whose dream "to create the perfect Holstein Friesian milking cow" became that of his favorite son as well. "My father believed it was perfectly fine to pull me out of school anytime one of our Holsteins was to be seen by the vet or about to give birth," he later said. But one hot July day in 1962, his father, at the age of fifty-three, took his own life, leaving his wife to struggle and his six children abandoned. Rob—his name spelled with a single "b" back then—was thirteen. With the family farm largely shut down afterward, he and his siblings "made up our own sports." He became an athlete: in high school, at Lyndon Institute, a boarding school in Lyndon, Vermont, he was on the track team, and captain of the ski team. After he broke his leg in a downhill ski accident he felt it would be intolerable to repeat the necessary training to regain his level of ability, so he switched to Nordic (a.k.a. cross-country) skiing and jumping, but suffered a bad concussion while jumping. His sports-related accidents narrowed his focus but not his intrinsic drive for physical self-expression, his guiding spirit. His senior year he won the Vermont State Championship in cross-country skiing. He connected with an Austrian ski team in Oregon, who became a surrogate family of sorts, "wild and daring and full of mountain energy," his coaches like surrogate fathers. He would continue to need parent figures; his mother would descend into her own tragedy of mental illness and cancer and die several years after his father had.

Rob came to Dartmouth in the fall of 1967 to train with his hero, Al Merrill, known as "the Silver Fox," the coach of the US Olympic cross-country ski team, who had seen him win the Vermont State Championship and recommended him to the Ivy League school on the basis of his athletic ability. Rob had lived the clean, pure, focused life of an athlete, and after he graduated from high school he had run, each day, fifty miles; all to prepare for his role on the ski team at Dartmouth. On his second day on campus, after having moved into his dormitory, Lord Hall, and set up his bookshelves, he went out to play soccer on Leverone Field as part of the ski team's fall training. He played goalie, and in a terrible accident, another player—his roommate—kicked him and broke his leg, the same leg that had been broken before, in high school. It was a catastrophe: his ski career shattered along with his leg, a double explosion.

Dartmouth had the best ski team in the country, and Rob had arrived with a star reputation; the news of his injury was traumatic for others going out for the ski team—such as Steve Johnson, who was then also a recently arrived freshman, and had been a serious ski racer and jumper himself, though not a champion. In the months ahead he would realize that he wasn't really competitive for the Dartmouth ski team, a disappointment that combined with academic worries to send him toward depression until, in January, he received a letter from the track coach, saying that Dartmouth needed another freshman pole vaulter. The invitation pulled him out of his blues and back into shape, both physically and mentally, helped his academics, and led him to become a successful varsity pole vaulter.

For Rob, however, the trauma and loss were deeper and less easily remedied. His leg in a large cast, he lay for weeks in Dick's House, Dartmouth's health service building, and he soon learned that his mother was fighting a losing battle with breast cancer. It must have seemed as if nothing would be left of his life and identity, that his world had entirely collapsed. When asked decades later what got him through this period, he gave a clear and unhesitating answer: he had been saved by love; specifically, by a kind, compassionate young woman named Alice Kitchel.

He and Alice had both grown up on farms, in adjacent towns in Vermont's Northeast Kingdom, Lyndonville and Barnet. They went to separate schools (Lyndon Institute and St. Johnsbury Academy) that were huge sports rivals, with the oldest high school football rivalry in the country. In high school she hadn't known him, but had heard about him, as he was a celebrated athlete—and she was, at her school, the head majorette. She was a year ahead of him, and after high school, she went to Wellesley, where she would major in art history.

It wasn't until the summer after her freshman year of college and Rob's senior year of high school that they met, when Alice accompanied two friends, Sandy and Mark, on a visit to the Pendleton farm, which had a pond nearby. That day Alice liked Rob a lot, liked his sense of fun, his abundant energy; but she didn't think any more of it until, a couple of weeks later, he called to ask her out, and they went to a show. It turned out that Rob's and Alice's fathers had had some things in common. They had known each other from farming in the same area; Alice's father ran a dairy, owned Burke Mountain Ski Area, and by the time Alice and Rob met, had become a state senator; he had come from a rather wealthy family in Connecticut, and Nelson Pendleton (Rob's father) had been heir to the Pendleton family wool fortune.

After his disastrous start at Dartmouth, Alice came to see Rob on weekends, from Wellesley, two and a half hours away. Rob's dying mother was at a hospital in St. Johnsbury, so eventually Alice drove herself and Rob up to visit. His mother suffered a great deal of pain, and died in December. At the same time that he had to absorb this tragedy, at school he also felt lost. "Being a star athlete had been his identity," Alice recalled. "He no longer had that 'ticket'—socially, financially, psychologically. He was searching for a new identity." Who was he, who could he be?

He floundered, as if ruined. He had, however, a person next to him who could help. As a small child, painful shifts in her family's emotional dynamics had tested Alice's sense of self, and like many who are forced to navigate such difficulties early in life, she had been left with the gift of greater understanding and empathy for others. She instinctively knew how vital it was to rescue or reassemble an identity, as Rob searched for a way to reassemble his. What's more, because she hadn't found Wellesley to be a good fit for her, she enjoyed visiting Dartmouth as often as possible. Accustomed to the conservative attitudes of the era, she didn't find the all-male campus as daunting as some women did, and by her own account she thoroughly enjoyed being there.

As Rob, on crutches, tried to find a new place for himself, and tried to get into the campus fraternities, he would take Alice with him, an attractive companion to help open social doors. Alice saw, as he did, the proper match for him: "Rob gradually got excited about intellectual pursuits, and that was why Foley House was perfect—a nonfraternity, it was where the nerds were, where people wanted to talk about books." She recalls that she and Rob "didn't go much to the jock houses. He got excited about the intellect and this became his new identity." As he found his way forward, his latest shifting of shape took on a whimsical outer manifestation: he began to spell his name "Rhob" rather than Rob.

As their college lives proceeded, Alice and Rhob continued to spend a lot of time together and had plenty of fun. Although he had abandoned his sports aspirations, he taught her to cross-country ski. They would go down to New York to nightclubs. (She loved to dance, but, ironically, in those days he didn't.) Even quotidian activities took on new vividness in the light of Rhob's energetic approach to life as, all around them, the late 60s continued to transform their world. By the spring of his sophomore year, the country had experienced the assassination of Senator Robert Kennedy, the violent chaos of the Democratic national convention in Chicago, and the ever-increasing horror and tragedy of the war in Vietnam; the presidency of the United States had shifted from LBJ to Nixon; and student protests and uprisings had shaken campuses across the country. It was also the era of the Beatles' White Album, the newly founded *Rolling Stone* magazine, and, since the 1967 "Summer of Love" in San Francisco, a romanticized, flowers-in-your-hair notion of the West Coast as a mecca for hippies, harmony, new ideals, and new energy. Now, on the verge of the summer of 1969, Rhob and Alice decided to go west for their own summer in San Francisco.

Rhob had grown his hair out, long, ready for Haight-Ashbury. Alice swapped cars with her mom, trading her Volkswagen bug for her mom's Volkswagen squareback, and she and Rhob drove out with a friend named LeGrand, a Mormon who had to get home to Salt Lake City, where Rhob and Alice stayed for a week and felt, predictably, very out of place. When they proceeded to their own destination, however, they experienced a near-miraculous stroke of luck: they drove into San Francisco, a complete unknown to them, and within their first hour connected with someone from Dartmouth who offered them a place to stay. Their hosts, a couple, had a one-bedroom apartment with a Murphy bed in the living room, and generously gave Alice and Rhob the bedroom. There would be other additions, with a number of young people piled into the apartment by the end of the summer.

Alice had arranged to take some classes at Stanford, to which she commuted. Rhob looked for work and did odd jobs, but with a recession on, jobs were scarce and times were hard. He did a little roofing but quickly discovered that working on roofs in San Francisco was a lot different than back home—he wasn't used to these heights—and he soon became uncomfortable with the dangers of the work. He did what he could find (unloading wood, picking apricots) but at times they were hungry, without money to buy food. Alice, starting to feel desperate, cast about for ways to help. One day she went to an audition for models, from which she was discourteously dismissed, and when she left, humiliated, a guy who had witnessed the scene dashed out after her to offer an alternative. The job, working in a less-than-savory bar, was decidedly not one to add to her resumé, but she took it as a stopgap measure.

In late July she and Rhob attended an encounter group (at that time still a brave new phenomenon of the 1960s, a workshop meant to open up honest emotional expression and strip away psychological defenses). They had been experiencing some strains in their relationship and thought it might help. There Rhob had what he would later regard as one of his first meaningful experiences in the dynamics of collaboration, which he found revelatory. Afterward, they went to the Berkeley Student Union, to watch with others as, televised live, Neil Armstrong placed his left foot on the surface of the moon and made his historic declaration: "That's one small step for man, one giant leap for mankind." But the summer's destabilizing aspects had begun to take a toll on Alice's enthusiasm, a decline that worsened when the horrific news of the Tate-Labianca murders made headlines in early August. Alice, like millions of Americans, found the story extremely unnerving, and only more so because it had happened in Los Angeles, less than six hours away, and the murders were as yet unsolved, the killers—Charles Manson and his followers—unidentified and still at large. By summer's end Alice was eager to return home to the Northeast, any romantic notions of the West Coast having been replaced by the thought *Enough of this crazy place.*

Back at Dartmouth that fall, Rhob felt he had been transformed by the summer, his eyes ablaze, ready to initiate intense eye contact with everyone he met and to proselytize on the virtues of nudity. He later realized that his near-messianic zeal had gone too far, scaring people away. As for Alice, she didn't perceive this as a turning point for Rhob because she felt he had always been intense. He had, however, become increasingly interested in theatre, a discipline in which intensity is prized alongside intellect and physicality.

They continued to see each other throughout the new academic year. It was his junior year and her senior year, and, as she continued to prefer Dartmouth to Wellesley, it made her happy that she could arrange to spend the last half of it, the first few months of 1970, at Dartmouth, where she and Rhob lived together off-campus in the house of a professor who was away. Their summer in San Francisco, however, had confirmed Rhob's desire to embrace the "free love" ideals of the time, which went hand in hand with certain aspects of the "encounter" movement. He would later explain that there was, in his view, a brief cultural window of true sexual freedom in which casual, fleeting sexual encounters between strangers had extraordinary profundity built on a willingness to absorb rather than deny human sexual energy. In short, an entire society's inhibitions seemed to be crumbling, and he thoroughly approved. Yet despite the power and significance of the sexual revolution, free love wasn't to everyone's taste, and Rhob's belief in it wasn't shared by Alice. She knew herself well enough to know, quite simply, "I just wasn't made that way."

It became more and more obvious to her that their relationship wasn't working. She had found life with him "exciting, exhilarating, sometimes confounding," filled with the pleasures of "always being a part of, or getting ready for, an event, a happening." His energy animated the days: "Whether it was about something mundane, breakfast for example, or a trip to New York, a flat tire, a concert, everything was a fantastic event full of wonder and colored by Rhob's intensity and vivid and elastic imagination." Yet she wanted monogamy, and that's not what she now had. As she later explained, "I fought against it, and eventually realized that he was not going to change. I would have to either accept him as he was so that we could continue in some way, or bow out. I knew I couldn't accept it and stay, so I bowed out."

She broke up with him in May. To her surprise, he was devastated. As she had been the one upset by their situation, it hadn't occurred to her that he could have loved her so much while not willing to commit to her exclusively. She graduated, and a little over a year later she went to Scotland, then to Europe for three years, and only heard about him distantly. They each would remember the other as their first love. Alice would go on to become both a visual artist and an art therapist, and later a life coach, and would continue to put her empathy to good use, helping others.

As for Rhob—or Robb, as he next became—it would be only a few months before his world would shift again. That fall, as he entered his senior year, Alison Becker would arrive at Dartmouth to teach dance, and he would soon be, like many of his classmates, smitten with his lovely professor.

4

That winter Alison noticed that one of her students, a guy named Danny, was a loner, either by temperament or because he was an African American on an overwhelmingly white college campus at the dawn of the 1970s. She suggested to Robb and Stephen that they work with him, to coax him into a collaboration. She told them to make a trio to show at the "12:30 Rep," a lunchtime performance series held in a small black box theater in the bottom of the Hopkins Center, which anyone could attend for free. The three were assigned to come to Webster Hall at seven o'clock in the evening to work on the piece. Jonathan, though not a part of the assignment, was intrigued, and he asked Robb to let him come along. At seven o'clock Robb and Stephen met as arranged, with Jonathan tagging along, but Danny didn't show up. A half an hour later he still wasn't there.

After an hour, Stephen decided they needed to do something. "Let's warm up," he suggested, and proceeded to show Robb an exercise the track team used, called a "backover," in which two individuals stand back to back, with arms linked, and then one bends forward to lift the other off the ground and stretch the spinal column. Robb found it "kind of funny to look at" and the three began to experiment, "taking two people on our back rather than one." In the mirror, the resulting mandala-like shape had an oddly poetic quality, and the next day they brought it into class. It would become part of the short dance—only about seven or eight minutes in its original form—that Robb, Jonathan, and Steve would make. The three men worked with silhouette, weight sharing and leveraging, and unusual combinations of body contact. As Jonathan put it: "We managed to combine our bodies, climb over each other, flip, swing, fly, lift, flop each other around in different ways." (The "backover" got used within the piece shortly before the brief section of marching and funny sounds, though the piece would later be altered through subsequent revisions.)

Steve had been a good football player in high school and had loved the "flying bodies" in football; he also loved ski jumping, and this, along with his pole-vaulting, pointed to a pattern: he loved airborne bodies in space. As for Robb, Steve felt that "the energy he put into the piece was partly displaced from his athletic career," energy that had been sublimated after he switched to theatre. When he discovered dance "he quickly became very fit, and stayed that way." Jonathan had "a really good scientific mind" and Steve found it to be "a hugely collaborative experience with bright, interesting guys." The three men had never socialized before. Robb was in Foley House, so the trio would gather there for dinner, joined on occasion by Alison.

All three wanted to include an element of lightheartedness in the piece, and from the goggles Steve wore—stolen from the woodworking shop in the Hopkins Center—to the rest of their offbeat costuming and quirky choreography, they assembled their ideas. Among their discoveries along the way would be a broader and deeper one: to stand onstage as an individual could be daunting, but physically clinging together for support decreased their insecurity and increased their sense of unity, of strength in numbers. As a unit, they could overcome their fears.

When it came time to name the piece, they toyed with the goofy title *Lentil Snoop* until Jonathan proposed a more esoteric name: *Pilobolus*. It came, in a way, from his father, who had grown up wanting to be a scientist and had become one—a photobiologist, a type of biophysicist—working, eventually, in an independent research laboratory to which he would take his son; over the years, almost inevitably, Jonathan had begun to imagine that he too would become a scientist. During his college summers he had progressed from lab assistant to doing actual research, which he found exciting, and he had studied a phototropic (light-loving) fungus called Phycomyces, closely related to a similarly light-loving fungus his father had worked on in younger days, of which his father had shown him pictures: *Pilobolus crystallinus,* or, Pilobolus. Only over time would Jonathan fully realize the name's appropriateness. As he told an interviewer three and a half decades later: "It turns out ironically that the metaphor is apt. It's a wonderful thing—a living, growing, intelligent thing. It has good memory, has amazing energy, it grows, bends, twists toward the light, and when it's good and ready it loses the entire top of its body, its entire head, and throws it some rather impressive distance."

The piece, performed in class, greatly impressed everyone. Alison found it, in its entirety, startling and "a bit mad" (in the best way). One can easily see why. Alongside the bravery and athleticism of the lifting and balancing, the unanticipated comic elements draw a smile or a laugh and mark the unmistakable presence of human idiosyncrasies in the seemingly abstract work; they dispel pretense, and recast the experimentation in a humbler, more playful light. The silent admission that the visually innovative piece is all a schoolboy romp, which in so many ways it was, is surprisingly winning.

Toward the end of the winter term, Alison's students presented a 12:30 Rep showing, and included, as planned, *Pilobolus*. Robby Barnett, who had taken Alison's advanced class, attended the showing. "It absolutely floored me," he recalled, decades later. "I had never seen anything like it. And neither had anybody else . . . It was imagination, it was intimacy, it was unself-consciousness, it was an ability to move slowly and let an image resonate from a shape as well as from movement. It was *not* obsessively concerned with arm waving and moving around, but with the creation of images. It was sort of an abstract linking of images that was almost like Tarot cards. You know, how you put things on the table, and you move them around until there's some kind of resonance that happens when they're next to each other and you just feel that these things ought to be aligned. Somehow they magically found that. And I think everybody who ever saw that piece recognized it. It changed my life."

5

That spring, Alison received an invitation to a symposium to be held in New York. Colleges in New England were invited to bring dance students to attend a seminar on technique with Murray Louis, and then to perform one piece of student choreography as part of a showing in which he would critique the works. Alison loved the idea. Louis wasn't simply one of her mentors, he was one of the greatest modern dancers and choreographers, and what's more, she knew it would be fun to take the students to New York City and for them to meet students from other colleges. In keeping with her nondictatorial teaching method, she asked the class to decide which piece to bring to the showcase, and the selection finally came down to a choice between two works: a whimsical solo by Michael Tracy, about a squirrel who wakes up and visits a pond, or the trio by Robb, Steve, and

Jonathan. Because the latter involved three people rather than one, the students opted for *Pilobolus*. (At least, this was Alison's recollection. Steve Johnson recalled Michael's solo as having "interesting movement on the ground, with sounds from insects and sounds from a pond" but he doesn't recall the class being given a choice. His memory is that "Alison asked a couple of coeds to bring their piece and they declined" so she then asked the trio, as an alternative. Either way, the precariousness of fate is evident: *Pilobolus* almost wasn't chosen.)

Lee Harris was among those who attended the symposium: "It was your typical modern dance master class. Murray Louis was fantastic in that situation." When it came time for the student showcase, the group from Dartmouth were last on the roster, either because they had arrived late or for some other forgotten reason, and they watched as the participants from other colleges performed. Alison had taught her students to recognize cliché, and they whispered to her throughout the show, noting how terrible the pieces were. Something like twenty pieces were unveiled, one after the next, and before long Jonathan was, as he later recalled, "sort of jumping up and down . . . thinking, *God, this is boring. This is terrible. These guys know—what? What is this? This is just eh . . .*" Steve knew that his two partners were "really keyed up for this performance. They wanted to pursue a future in dance—and not go to Vietnam." When their turn came, they took to the stage knowing that they had something unlike any of the others; and they brought down the house.

The other Dartmouth students were sitting, along with Alison, behind Murray Louis, up front, close to the stage. As Lee recalled, "It blew everyone away. Murray Louis was speechless, then became very effusive." Amid the wild audience response, he turned around and said to Alison, "My God, that was fabulous. Whatever you're doing, you're doing a great job." He was, in fact, an ideal judge for the work, as he particularly valued the quirky and surprising. "Comedy has to be in the nature of the choreographer," he would say a few years later. "It has to be a deep-rooted philosophy about living. It has to be an essential ingredient, a leavening agent in the dough of life."

Stunned by what he had seen, he turned from praising Alison to next praise Robb, Steve, and Jonathan, and he encouraged them to continue making new work. He also asked them to stay over, to remain in New York for a few days. He brought them to his and his partner Alwin Nikolais's studio, The Space, on West 36th Street. A converted church in the Garment

District that had been made into a number of studios, it contained a large potential performance space in what had once been a gymnasium within the church. There, two days after the symposium, they filmed *Pilobolus*— Louis and Nikolais had their own video team. During these New York days, he also took the three of them to dinner one night, along with two of his associates, and at some point he made them an offer. He suggested that if in the coming months they could assemble a program, he would arrange for them to give a full performance, a showcase in New York, at The Space—and he would invite his New York friends and prominent critics to see them. "It was incredibly exciting," Steve said, half a century later, and he still recalled the effect, in that instant, on Robb and Jonathan. "You could see their eyes light up, and that was where their future was determined."

6

Later that spring, Robb, Jonathan, and Steve graduated from Dartmouth, with their respective degrees in English literature, philosophy, and psychology, and Steve helped Robb move all his belongings up to the Pendleton family's enormous, derelict but still lovely farm, Lochlyndon, in northern Vermont. Steve left, but Jonathan moved to the farm with Robb to continue their theatrical experimentation. Communes and related experiments were everywhere in Vermont; the Vietnam War was on, and in the US the counterculture consciousness—and the solidarity of young people and older individuals who opposed the war—was strong. Jonathan sought an alternative not only to the war, but to the conventional lifestyles that had long prevailed in American society. His desire for the life of a scientist had faded. Working in his father's biophysics lab "on beautiful summer days in a climate-controlled atmosphere watching people in the distance play tennis," he had often thought wistfully of trading places with those who were clearly having more fun.

"Pilobolus grew up really as kind of a graduate school of make-believe," he later explained. "We made it up as we went." He and Robb spent that first summer stretching, eating the yogurt that Jonathan made, eating "weeds and soy breads," working outdoors, and thinking up new creative endeavors. In the spirit of the times, they decided to call themselves the Vermont Natural Theater, and by late summer they had organized an outdoor program that involved taking an unsuspecting audience on a three-mile stroll around the farm. Robb would drape a sheet over himself and run ahead of his family's cattle—of which there were fifty—piquing their curiosity and causing them to pursue him: "On one ridge there was the audience, and on the other was myself and the black and white Holsteins . . . These black and white forms would come running toward the audience, a stampede of milking Holsteins. That was very new and exciting!" And also silly; he would later refer to this choreographic adventure, with his penchant for shameless puns, as "cowography." Some audience members were also treated to a meal of Jonathan's highly regarded hot buttery baked soy logs.

By fall, Robb and Jonathan saw that their "natural" theatre company had no future. They had paid a visit that summer to Steve, at a camp for the blind where he was working before he would leave for med school, and in their mini-reunion the three men had performed *Pilobolus* for the other camp staff and the blind campers (who, although they couldn't see the choreography, listened to the strange music). Now, as the new school year beckoned Steve to pursue his studies, Jonathan and Robb drifted back to Dartmouth, the birthplace of their earlier success. In light of Steve's departure they needed a new collaborator or two, a problem with a ready solution: Lee Harris, now entering his junior year, and Robby Barnett, entering his senior year.

Lee, beyond his identity as a brilliant computer nerd (Jonathan recalled him as "living in a cave underneath the computing center, some lightless little hovel of a room" and enthusiastically showing his friends "early precursors of video games"), had more to his background than his "hick from Wyoming" modesty suggested. Active in clarinet in junior high, he had played in bands and orchestras; and when, after his sophomore year of high school, he had broken his neck in a car wreck (his fault) and been told not to play football or wrestle, his parents had sent him to a cotillion program; soon he had also gotten involved in theatre at his high school, with a great drama teacher, danced in the spring musical "paired with a gorgeous senior," continued to be active in the drama program through dancing rather than singing, and learned some tap dancing and done quite a lot of it. At Dartmouth, he had wandered into the computer center and immersed himself completely, but when he needed a humanities course to fulfill a requirement he took Ray Cook's modern dance class, which had a ballet "layer" in terms of the exercises. Next he had gotten a job at the computer center during the summer—and then Alison had arrived, at the beginning of his sophomore year, and he had taken her class. He also had some diving technique, and with his help, Robb and Jonathan re-created and re-formed *Pilobolus* (the dance), with Lee taking over Steve's role.

As for Robby Barnett, he had, in Robb Pendleton's estimation, a wild physical presence comparable to Nijinsky, like a figure in the trees, a creature to be captured. In fact, Robby had, at the time, moved not merely off-campus but nearly off-century. Next to an old graveyard in Norwich, Vermont, he had found an abandoned shack that he and a group of friends "patched up": "I fumigated it to get the wasps out of the chimney and I patched up the roof and put some plastic over the windows, and I squatted in this cabin through the fall and into the early winter." Or as Jonathan put it, "No electricity, no water, like a hermit. We went out and got him." Contrary to the romantic notion of stalking Robby in the wild, however, the "capture" took a more socially conventional form. That September, not long after the new school year had begun, Robb ran into Robby in the parking lot of the local movie theater, the Nugget Theater in Hanover. "Hey, we'd like you to join us!" Robb declared, full of enthusiasm. There wasn't much of anything to join yet, no real company, but after some thought Robby decided *Why not? Why don't we fool around?*

Robb and Jonathan sent a promotional packet, with photos of the four of them, to various New England colleges in the hope of getting gigs. A student event coordinator at Smith College named Donna Goodman called them. There had been a cancellation, and they needed an opening act—for Frank Zappa and the Mothers of Invention (or simply The Mothers, as they were often called at the time). Stunned, they eagerly accepted, and in October, in John M. Green Hall at Smith College, Pilobolus opened for Zappa. They had only one piece, the trio *Pilobolus,* now performed by Robb, Jonathan, and Lee, so Robby watched from the audience. Around him, he could feel the crowd's reaction progress from chilly reception to energetic applause, a transformation that struck him forcibly and became a turning point that inspired the group to continue with new determination. For Robb Pendleton, likewise, opening "for 3,000 screaming Smith girls" with "Zappa himself calling it not 'modern dance' but 'The Theatre of the Very Far Out'" made a heady and lasting impression. "We just couldn't believe it! The next day we sat on the gravestones next to Lord Hall. Zappa had asked us to go to Des Moines to open for him, but we had to decline due to a math exam the next day. I thought *What just happened to us? Maybe we could get something going here.*" Jonathan too loved Zappa, with an admiration that would abide, and there would be talk of working with him in the future, though it never came to pass. Still, their one shared public appearance had been monumental for the fledgling quartet, and the idea of Pilobolus as the dance equivalent of a rock band began to take shape.

In the weeks that followed that lightning-stroke of good fortune, the group did one or two additional performances, which the sands of time have blurred in memory. It may have been an informal show at Hampshire College at which they shared a bill with poet Diane di Prima, whose *Memoirs of a Beatnik* had appeared a couple of years earlier. That, and an even more casual college performance, with flashlights in a dormitory commons room during a power failure, began what would become the group's New England college barnstorming period.

Over the Thanksgiving break, the four men went back up to the Pendleton family farm in Lyndonville, and using a school squash court as a choreographic space they created a new piece, a slapstick skit-as-modern-dance hybrid. The initial concept, according to Lee, was "chance encounters on the street and what could happen," and the result, a parade of struts and collisions by naively fumbling characters, evoked circus clowns and vaudevillians. They named it *Walklyndon,* a punning reference to both Lochlyndon, the family farm, and, stretching the pun further, to Jonathan's penchant for cooking in a wok (if one pronounces "walk" and "wok" similarly). Black and white footage of an early version shows the four of them, in sleeveless shirts and what look like swim trunks, performing it on stage and getting laughs, but without the piece yet polished to its best comic effect; it ends with the four players exiting via a group tumble in which they are linked together in pairs that suggest a human wheel. That idea—a forerunner of a four-man linked tumble known within Pilobolus as the "gerbil wheel"—would eventually be used well in other pieces, but in *Walklyndon* it would be replaced by a much funnier, low-man-running-away punchline. The revised *Walklyndon* would also benefit from goofier attire—bright yellow unitards—that, along with clockwork comic timing, would lend it a "Dr. Seuss meets Monty Python" sensibility and sharpen it into a perpetual crowd-pleaser, one that elicits loud laughs from adults and squeals of delight from children.

During that Thanksgiving break they also improvised another, more private bit of whimsy. They had made for themselves an enormous, mouthwatering Thanksgiving dinner, with all the traditional elements, from turkey and mashed potatoes to apple and pumpkin pies. The night before, a heavy snowstorm had deposited eight to ten inches of snow, and now, the picturesque vision of both the candlelit table set with the feast and the fresh-fallen snow on the ground inspired a strange idea—to which, as Lee recalled, "Everyone said, 'That would be fun.' We walked some distance from the house and then approached it as if it were 'a house in the woods.'" As Robby recalled, "We went outside. We got incredibly stoned, and walked around the house and peered in through the windows and said, 'Wow. Look at this. Somebody's just made Thanksgiving dinner. This is so cool. I can't believe it.'" So, pretending they had discovered, like travelers on a cold day, an empty house with a dining room table mysteriously and magically set with a lavish Thanksgiving meal for them, they exulted in their good fortune, and went in and thoroughly enjoyed it.

Robb and Jonathan had stayed in touch with Murray Louis after their presentation at the college symposium in New York the prior spring. During the summer, Jonathan had called and asked Murray if he really would give them a show, and assured him that they wanted to do it. Robb and Jonathan would make the long drive down to New York to visit The Space, feeling it the center of the action, where they needed to be. They had received no firm commitment in the summer, but in the fall Murray called with his answer: yes.

At the end of December, Pilobolus made its New York debut. The program included the trio *Pilobolus* revised and extended to eleven minutes, with Lee continuing in Steve's former role; it now opened with the mandala shape, placed a greater emphasis on the otherworldliness of its sensibility, and still included a few touches of humor (though different ones than in the prior version). The staging also made use of a spotlight to project large shadows of the trio, behind and above their movement on stage. The piece met with a great round of applause, and Robby quickly hopped into view, performing his brief solo *Geode*—a suitably athletic addition, which also benefited, at certain moments, from his giant shadow projected by the spotlight. The performance, intense and dramatic, with leaps, gyrations, stillness, falls, and a sense of contrasts and change, lasted two or three minutes before it segued into *Walklyndon*.

The twenty minutes of Pilobolus movement pieces were then followed by *twenty-five* minutes of musical performance by Robb & Jonathan (minus Robby and Lee), which included sixteen minutes of conga drumming in tandem and then, with another segue, a banjo performance by Jonathan. In this half of the show, as in the first, large shadows of the performers were projected onto the wall behind them. At the end, after all four men took their bows, Robb Pendleton turned to the audience and added, helpfully, that there was "some cider and food" upstairs.

Although *New York Times* dance critic Anna Kisselgoff, in her December 31 review, dismissed the musical performance as "country raga on a banjo and some jar thumping" that should perhaps "have been left behind at the campus coffeehouse," her review was otherwise a rave. She called the group's accomplishments in light of their relative dearth of dance training "astounding" and Robby's solo "extraordinary." These were young men who "displayed amazing physical fearlessness, humor, inventiveness, and unselfconsciousness."

Alison read the review with amazement and delight, stunned that in such short order these young men—still kids, really—had won the attention of the *New York Times*. They had achieved a wild, improbable leap forward, and were poised for more.

THREE

Quartet

In January 1972, Dartmouth welcomed a new artist in residence, a sculptor named Philip Grausman. Robby, a senior art major, became one of his students, and an avid one: he considered him a great art teacher, the best he had ever encountered.

The sculptor's wife, Martha Clarke, had come from a somewhat privileged, culturally rich background. She had grown up in Pikesville, Maryland, a suburb of Baltimore, in a family steeped in music and the arts, her father a jazz composer turned attorney, her grandfather a violin collector who hosted a string quartet recital in his home each week while little Martha watched *The Lone Ranger* ("four old men fiddling Brahms away in the next room every Thursday night of my entire childhood"). The experimental filmmaker Shirley Clarke, her aunt, had suggested naming her Martha, after Martha Graham, and as it turned out, dance—as well as drawing and horses—was among the things she loved from early on. Having begun to study dance and art at the age of six, she had had a total immersion in dance from about age thirteen and had performed her own solo work when she was only fifteen. From her early teens her resumé reads like a Who's Who of modern dance: Helen Tamiris had cast her at age thirteen; Louis Horst, José Limón, Alvin Ailey, and Merce Cunningham had been among those who taught her at the American Dance Festival at age fifteen and sixteen; Horst had then gotten her into Juilliard after her junior year of high school, the first student admitted without a high school diploma, where he continued to teach her; Antony Tudor, whom she revered to the point of adoration, also taught her at Juilliard, and had a lasting influence on her through his recognition of the psychology of acting in dance, the need for each movement to have an underlying motive; and Anna Sokolow, another choreographer of dramatic power, after teaching her at Juilliard hired her into her company. Martha had graduated in 1965 at age twenty, and soon after, she had married Phil.

Her time in Anna Sokolow's company proved difficult, in keeping with Sokolow's reputation as a strict choreographer who demanded of her dancers a soul-baring intensity. "I didn't particularly like Anna because she was tough," Martha later explained. "I used to have nightmares about her actually, but I deeply respected her as an artist." At age twenty-three, Martha turned to her husband and said, "I don't like working with Anna Sokolow. *We never laugh.*" She chose to leave the company and to abandon her career as a dancer.

She and Phil then moved to Italy. After their return she gave birth to their baby, David, in New York. In 1969 they moved to Connecticut. Now, at twenty-seven, she had arrived at Dartmouth with not only husband and child, but also a restless need to find a channel for her dormant creative impulses. Seeking a direction and, perhaps, an ally, she called Alison Chase. Martha years later summed up their first meeting with a single word, emphatically stated: *"Laughter."* The diametric contrast to Sokolow couldn't have been more delicious. "She was beautiful and talented. She was really happy to have me up there. The fact that a professional dancer had come to Hanover—we bonded immediately. Very positive. We *really* hit it off." She and Alison would "put on leotards and tights and warm sweaters" and go over to the beautiful old church, with its blue carpet, and "stretch and talk." They soon started to work together, making duets.

Martha also soon met her husband's art student, Robby, and struck up a friendship with him as well. She would come by the studio with little David in tow, and sit and chat, while Robby, at a high-easel drafting table with a big sheet of paper on it, worked on an elaborately detailed large-scale doodle. Though he had no particular plan to be an artist, he had a strong interest in graphic arts and an active intellect that Martha appreciated; and of course this longhaired, talkative young man whose company she enjoyed was one-quarter of the recently formed, all-male troupe Pilobolus.

For most artists starting out, whether an individual or a group, the biggest initial challenge is to build up a sufficient quantity of strong material. Like a rock band still on its way to its first album deal, Pilobolus remained

acutely aware that they could only fill about twenty minutes of stage time—
particularly after the show in New York, in which they had padded their
otherwise dynamic program with forgettable music. Fortunately, an idea
for another piece soon presented itself. It isn't clear who had suggested a
nude photo shoot, but according to Robby it happened that the four young
men took their clothes off and rolled around Pilobolus-style for a private
set of pictures that in turn triggered the idea of doing a piece based on
sculpture. Lee recalls that the underlying concept was "the idea of a Grecian
frieze, a bas-relief. The bodies are in a single plane, two-dimensional." The
result, which they called *Ocellus,* would become another key early work.
Abstract, nonnarrative, a communal display of four stripped but muscular
human bodies in contact and partnership with one another, it also marked
a shift from the playfulness of the prior pieces into a certain gravitas, or at
least a more straight-faced brand of artistic experimentation, and allowed
the group to present a more varied program.

Its making reinforced the underlying assumptions of what would become the Pilobolus creative process. With no preconceived idea other than
a basic theme, the four men made things up as they went along, evaluating
their ideas collectively throughout, trying to commit each worthwhile bit
to memory and then repeat it successfully and add another little bit, as they
inched forward. As it had with *Walklyndon,* but this time for a work with a
radically different tone and style, the process delivered a remarkable result.
The method would have a profound influence on Pilobolus's future, and,
for Lee, a lifelong influence on his way of working in business management. "What made Pilobolus work was that when we were working, egos
got checked at the door," he said, "and the only thing that mattered was
what would delight the audience." In those early days, "There was never an
argument. It was always a discussion of what was best. We always started
with an organizing principle." That principle might be chance encounters
(*Walklyndon*) or a Grecian frieze (*Ocellus*), but it only served as a starting
point. Lee compares the process to four people standing at a blank canvas,
with each given a pot of paint and a brush, to paint an agreed-upon picture: "But if you all go at once it will be a mess, so you have to make decisions together, step by step." One of the rules: there could be no trade-offs,
compromises, or deal-making—as in "If you let me do my idea, I'll let you
do yours"—because that only weakens the result. Instead, they weighed
each choice as a group. "That's how the dances got put together and why
they were compelling. A clarity came through." The group approach would

extend to critiquing each other's solos as well: "Anyone doing a solo was subject to everyone else's criticism." Together they proceeded.

As they did so, their work began to be documented through photographs taken in several sessions by Jonathan Sa'adah, a friend of Robby Barnett's. The two had attended rival prep schools (Robby had gone to Deerfield, Jonathan Sa'adah to Choate) and had met and struck up a friendship during their freshman year at Dartmouth. It made sense for Pilobolus to invite an artful photographer to travel with them, and Sa'adah, who had never photographed them before, would capture them in the studio as well as in early gigs on small stages. His images, in black and white, convey the youth and soulfulness of the four men, the originality of their early pieces, and especially the dynamism of *Ocellus*—and, though unpublished and almost entirely unseen for half a century, they encapsulate quite magnificently a fleeting but crucial moment in the company's genesis.

2

That winter of 1972, the foursome—Robb, Jonathan, Robby, and Lee— bought a house together on Turnpike Road in Norwich, Vermont, just across the Connecticut River from Hanover, New Hampshire. At the time, Norwich had a population slightly under two thousand. The home purchase had largely been engineered and financed by Robb, as he had a trust fund. (According to Lee, "Nobody else had any money at all," and living there saved Lee from paying room and board at college.) The two-story house had four small bedrooms upstairs and four small rooms downstairs, including the kitchen. They had a cast iron potbelly stove to add heat. Their life there was totally communal, in the tradition of a 1960s-style commune. The house had acres of land that felt somewhat overgrown and unloved— it was in a field with a pond nearby—but they maintained a garden, and, on the other side of a little valley (and hence less conspicuous), a massive harvest of marijuana: "Jonathan's little marijuana plantation." They were only a few blocks past Dan & Whit's general store, where they would buy bulgur wheat, tofu, and other healthy food. On a typical evening, Jonathan and Robby would cook and they would all eat a meal, talk about their performing, smoke a joint, do an ice cream run back to Dan & Whit's, have ice cream, and go to bed.

As the house didn't include a room that could be used as a rehearsal space, they would drive into town to rehearse, usually at Webster Hall, which had mirrors (which, at the time, they considered necessary for rehearsals, though years later Pilobolus would banish the use of mirrors). Another on-campus rehearsal space was Rollins Chapel, across the street from Webster Hall. Robb—who, even decades later Lee would still regard as "the most intense individual I ever met in my life, bar none"—would arrive at rehearsals early and spend long periods of time massaging his damaged toes or feet; he would work his body for hours on end; he would look straight into another person's eyes with his unusually focused, tightly wound energy. He had a boundaryless, "anything goes" approach to life. What he offered in intensity, Jonathan offered in enthusiasm. The two men each had both elements, but with the proportions inverted: in Robb intensity dominated, and in Jonathan enthusiasm, as when, for example, Jonathan would talk with Robby Barnett about food and cooking and go on animatedly about the things that excited him. Yet beneath it all, Robb and Jonathan's hidden common denominator remained early loss and the void it left to be filled. What Jonathan's sister Ann called the "total devastating loss" of her and Jonathan's mother, a loss "that never went away," had parallels to the tragedies in Robb's personal history; and, as Ann later observed, "It was always there, and it fueled the energy, the passion of this dance company."

That winter Robby and Lee were at Dartmouth (Robby as a senior, Lee as a junior), but Robb and Jonathan had their days free—so their job was to get up each morning, drink lots of coffee, and get on the phones to try to line up gigs, mostly school-sponsored gigs in New Hampshire, lecture-dance presentations in a cafeteria-auditorium or in the gym, for which Pilobolus would be paid perhaps fifty or seventy-five dollars. With Anna Kisselgoff's *New York Times* review as an endorsement, their own energetic, fast-talking determination, and a willingness to reply to any request with an eager *Yes, we'll do that,* they soon succeeded in landing a series of gigs with the New Hampshire public schools through the spring.

As their touring increased and the end of Lee's junior year approached, Alison suggested that Lee apply for a senior fellowship in dance so he wouldn't have to go to class during his senior year, and with Robby about to graduate, they would all be free to tour. That's what Lee did, and it worked. His senior year would be pure Pilobolus. He had an old red Volkswagen that he had bought from Alison ("for $75 or something, I don't recall the exact amount"). Later the group bought an Audi 80 with Robb's trust fund, added a roof rack, and used it as their tour car.

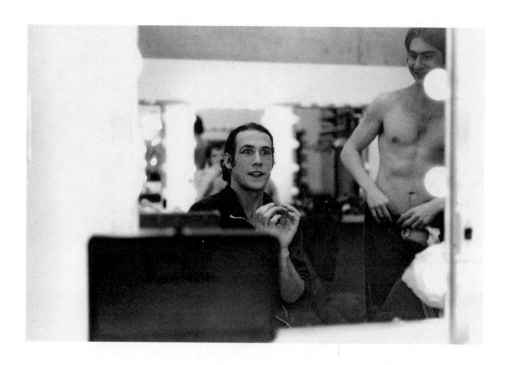

Photographer Jonathan Sa'adah captured the original four-man incarnation of Pilobolus in images that have remained almost entirely unseen until now but have the power of an indelible lived experience. *Above*: Robby Barnett and Robb Pendleton backstage, as Robby applies makeup, in Center Theater, 1972. On the next two pages, Jonathan Wolken, Lee Harris, Robb, and Robby in individual portraits from 1971 and 1972, the latter year a period of intense evolution in the studio, and, on the following pages, the four men in the Pilobolus work *Ocellus*, 1972.

Jonathan Wolken

Lee Harris

Robb Pendleton

Robby Barnett

In the meantime, they continued the push to create new work. That spring Lee built a set in a wood shop at Dartmouth that included a giant box on legs out of which he dropped like a spider, in a piece called *Anaendrom.* The underlying theme of "kinetic energy" inspired *Spyrogyra.* At the same time, they continued to toy with the other pieces in their repertoire. Then, a setback: not long after Robby graduated, he and Jonathan were playing around in the chapel, trying a stunt that involved running and jumping, and Robby fell and shattered his wrist, breaking the radius in four places at the joint. It would require months of recovery. Robb and Jonathan burst into Michael Tracy's biology lab to ask him—to the bewilderment or disdain of the surrounding pre-med students—if he would abandon school to join their dance company. He turned them down, or said he would think about it after finishing his degree. Because they had a show scheduled, the group had to find a more immediate substitute; they did, but Robby's curly-haired replacement broke his nose in a body collision during *Spyrogyra.* After that, Pilobolus stayed on the sidelines for a while.

In the fall of 1972, Dartmouth finally went fully coed, the last Ivy League school to do so. Women at Dartmouth would be subjected to taunts, threats, and harassment of various kinds, much of it drunken, and "Better Dead Than Co-Ed" banners would continue to fly from some of the dormitories for years to come, but no amount of boorish behavior would reverse the forward motion.

3

"The dance world seemed not to possess terminology to deal with a clump of four men twisted together like proteins," Robby would later write, "and we attracted a lot of curious attention. And incredibly, the possibilities seemed to open in front of us as we explored the opposing and mirrored sides of this new world, the first a purely physical one where weights and balances and the forces of tension and release yielded continually surprising ways of moving, and second a sort of parallel kingdom of psychological suggestion where, because we were constantly in physical contact with each other, the resonance of touch flickered through all our interactions inside this other domain governed by emotion and implication."

In grappling with those possibilities, however, the quartet first had to make their way through the awkward trials and errors of any young artist learning to navigate questions of aesthetic choice, emphasis, and discretion. This phase can be seen in three short videos taped in color for the Maryland Center for Public Broadcasting, each an in-studio performance of a single work: *Pilobolus, Spyrogyra,* and *Ocellus.* In this version of the namesake piece *Pilobolus,* performed in bright (red, yellow, green) skin-tight costumes and headpieces, with Robb wearing goggles, the choreography has been somewhat altered, and the music has become not only more dramatic but melodramatic, self-consciously suggestive of science fiction films to the point of cliché: an eerie, silly, lunar soundscape. The brief interlude of comic vocal effects has been replaced by goofy but less endearing synthetic sounds. The focus, in keeping with some of the other early Pilobolus pieces, has moved to the presentation of a human kaleidoscope of inventive shape-shifting, but the overall effect is narrower. Yet while less appealing than the prior version, it blends in more with the tone of the two pieces presented alongside it as the four men begin to develop a group identity based on an unbelievably flexible, endlessly surprising display of movement. Though there is still humor in the group's hatha-yoga-gone-overboard quirkiness, the mischievous, collegiate comic touches of the original trio are largely suppressed, the comedy having been channeled into *Walklyndon* (not present in these videos), and it's hard to find the line of demarcation between play and straight-faced abstraction, or to locate the overall intent. Occasionally a leap or spin has a flourish that seems like an unintentional parody of ballet. Still exploring, the four men have yet to root out the gestures that might seem unoriginal or affected, because they have yet to acquire the experience and discernment to say, "That's not Pilobolus."

Nonetheless they were on a roll, and their communal lifestyle had much to do with it. Their best ideas "were always formed by being bounced around four heads," as Robb Pendleton would tell the *New York Times* a few years later. "It freed us to experiment. You know, it's the same when a kid won't break a window by himself, but he will do it if he's with others."

Although they may not have broken any windows, that scofflaw spirit also informed one of the group's less enlightened habits: shoplifting groceries. With almost no income, they augmented their homegrown meal ingredients with illicitly obtained canned goods to keep themselves fed. Martha would recall Jonathan's "dirty blue down coat, very puffy," its pockets and puffiness compatible with smuggled cans of tuna. Padded down coats with zippers inside were useful in those days before electronic security codes and surveillance cameras thwarted what some considered a common form of youthful bad behavior, less shocking in a counterculture community than to the mainstream.

Likewise the relaxing—or expansion and redefinition—of the parameters of relationships, whether in or out of marriage, reflected the countercultural liberation of the time; and in the midst of that unstated, unspecified openness, another dimension of the house's 1960s-commune ethos soon emerged. Alison and Martha, although they didn't live there, began to appear occasionally, and then more frequently, and soon it became apparent to both Jonathan and Lee that two parallel affairs were taking place. For Martha, her affair with Robby had a "home-away-from-home" quality; they shared a dark sense of humor and, as she put it, "a sweet perversity." The other affair, between Alison and—should we call him Rob? Rhob? Robb? No, none of the above. Around this time, in a final shift of identity, he abandoned his former name in all its spellings, to take his grandfather's name and become *Moses* Pendleton. The affair between Alison and Moses would have a more complex underpinning, both tender and turbulent.

"For the four of us," Martha later said, "it was part of the creative impulse, and in the nature of the overt physical proximity of our work. And we were creatures of the time we were living in." The affairs, she felt, had the effect of "intensifying things"—and the intensity got into the pieces that Pilobolus made.

To Moses, for whom intensity and sexual freedom were a given, the lack of inhibition that lovers feel in touching and playing with each other's bodies and the making of the body-combination creations of Pilobolus were all intertwined, and both natural and undeniable. He recognized—and required—passion as the center of his life and art.

4

In April 1973, Pilobolus, still a male quartet, appeared again at The Space, presenting seven works on a Sunday afternoon, and were again reviewed extremely positively in the *New York Times*. Dance critic Don McDonagh called the effect of their presentation "extraordinary" and "astonishing" and noted that their "visual impact . . . easily transcends stunt muscularity."

Pilobolus had to cancel its spring tour, however, when Moses broke a toe. By the summer they were performing again, with a new ingredient added. Alison and Martha had made some short pieces together, and Martha had also made a duet with Robby, *Aubade.* Pilobolus still didn't have an overabundance of material, and the two women thought it would be nice to have their pieces on a Pilobolus program, to give them a test run; what's more, Alison, after three years teaching at Dartmouth, was eager to pursue her primary ambition to create choreography; and the four romantic friends—Robby, Martha, Moses, and Alison—had been hanging out together more and more. The group did one or two appearances in which the men performed their Pilobolus pieces and the two women presented their duets and joined an expanded *Walklyndon.* Despite a strong feeling that the two women's pieces were too "un-Pilobolus" for the program and that they would need to alter their approach, the combination wasn't bad, and when Pilobolus received a commission from the American Dance Festival they decided to create their first official six-person piece, *Ciona.* It wasn't entirely new, as the men already had two abstract movement quartets, *Spyrogyra* and *Ciona,* which they merged into the new six-person *Ciona.*

When they performed it and other pieces at the American Dance Festival that summer, they acquired an important new fan who they immediately liked a lot: the festival's director, Charles Reinhart. To his eyes, Pilobolus was that once-in-a-decade phenomenon, an act that "makes you catch your breath because they are so totally innovative." He saw immediately that they were creating, from their fresh, innocent approach, "a new artistic direction based on what they knew, which was athletics, science, and bodies." His embrace of their work heralded the beginning of a long and mutually devoted relationship between Pilobolus and the American Dance Festival, one that would continue uninterrupted through the decades.

By now it had become abundantly clear that the women wanted in. Although Pilobolus was only just beginning, Martha, like Alison, could see their special qualities, their irreverent freshness and sense of fun, and now, a gradual broadening of artistic possibilities. Although Martha disliked *Ciona,* she loved that Pilobolus didn't come from a dance background. To her, they offered an antidote to the self-seriousness of modern dance that had put her off. "Alison and Pilobolus pulled me back to movement," she explained. "The joy of just goofing around was both a rediscovery and a liberation."

Jonathan and Lee were initially opposed to the addition of the women. Pilobolus had worked hard to establish itself, with an unusual identity as an all-male quartet, athletic in what was then a decidedly male way, hetero-sexual men in an art form in which the stereotype of male dancers as gay still prevailed. Taking a step away from what made them unique seemed dangerous. Their mentors Alwin Nikolais and Murray Louis warned them against it, saying that Pilobolus was like the Beatles and would lose its iden-tity if women joined. And for Jonathan and Lee there had to be another danger as well, even if unstated or only half-realized: the power dynamic. One voice in four is more influential than one voice in six, and if four of the voices belong to two pairs of lovers who are all close friends one can easily imagine a range of unpleasant possibilities.

As Jonathan later explained, "We turned our back and—" (he snapped his fingers) "—and instantly they were there . . . And it was an issue, a huge issue, among us as to what should happen . . . Mo and Robby had become more involved with Alison and Martha; they were in a relationship . . . that was exciting in their lives." He and Lee saw, however, that both women brought obvious attributes in terms of knowledge, skills, abilities, and ideas (and, a reality not to be underestimated, they were also lighter-weight ob-jects to lift). And given that Moses and Robby liked the idea, and Alison had been their teacher, they didn't have much choice but to give it a try. The group decided to bring the women with them on their summer tour to Edinburgh and see what happened.

The first or second time Murray Louis had seen Pilobolus perform, he had said "You guys need to take this on the road. In five years you'll be touring Europe." This estimate proved to be too long by three years; they were already, in the summer of 1973, embarking on their first international tour, having connected with Jan Murray (the cousin of the Canadian singer Anne Murray), who, as the dance critic for *Time Out* magazine in Lon-don, got them a performance at the Roundhouse theater. They had also booked themselves into the Fringe Festival in Edinburgh, and so they flew to Scotland to perform a frantic three-week run with cobbled together, do-it-yourself staging, lighting, and publicity. "We were on a pretty small stage in a primary school," Lee recalled, but the shows were very well attended; they received a rave review in the *Daily Telegraph* and won the Scotsman Award at the festival; Princess Margaret came to see them and they did a photo onstage with her ("unbelievably great publicity"). After the UK tour, Alison and Martha returned home and the four men proceeded to Israel to perform again as a quartet ("a great visit but very hot" according to Lee;

Robby would retain "vivid memories of sitting on a soccer field, sort of under the brow of the Golan Heights") then flew to Amsterdam, where the next morning they learned, to their horror, that Israel and Egypt had just gone to war and that they had only narrowly escaped being trapped in the midst of it. Next, the foursome received a telegram from Alison and Martha with happier news: the Bordeaux Festival had a hole in its schedule and wanted Pilobolus to perform for three nights. The quartet flew home, from which they would fly to France as a sextet, with Alison and Martha.

How exactly the women became a permanent part of the company is a question that elicits various tales, anecdotes, and memories with no decisive answer: there are stories of a pitch made while everyone sat together on a waterbed; a Sunday afternoon on which the two ladies brought a garbage can filled with ice and a bottle of cold duck or other cheap wine to a theater and got their four future colleagues a little drunk (and, of course, the guys smoked some of Jonathan's well-harvested crop, in which Martha never indulged); and, less dramatically, Robby's recollection that they never quite *asked,* it just gradually happened, a little at a time. Was it "because" of the affairs? No, the men saw the possibilities that adding the women presented, in terms of variation, color, new theatrical and dramatic themes, and the wealth of insight and experience they brought. Romance was there, yes, but also, as Martha aptly put it, "There was great compatibility, a great deal of laughter, a great deal of the headiness of youth, and it was an awfully appealing proposition."

And then there was the Bordeaux Festival. The first night the theater was full, the crowd enthusiastic; the second night's performance, the theater even more full; and by the third performance the house was so totally full that the management had to shut the doors. The word was out. At the end of the last piece, the crowd went wild. "Electrifying," as Lee happily recalled. It was the turning point, and Pilobolus began "really taking off."

5

By the fall of 1973, Alison and Martha had become part of Pilobolus, and rose to the work's arduous physical challenges with stunning commitment. They would take on roles previously handled by the men and carry a man when needed (though Martha would slip a disc doing so), and, importantly, they added a new theatrical sensibility, with a heightened level of dance expertise that contrasted with the men's untrained athleticism. Or, in Martha's words: "We had a finish, they were cruder, and the combination has become the signature of Pilobolus."

Although their arrival had initially caused Lee some concern, once he began working with them he quickly saw that the creative process did not suffer at all. He had always recognized and appreciated Alison's gifts as a teacher of choreography; and as for Martha, Lee felt that "Out of everybody, out of the six, Marty was the most normal. Much more even, smart, level-headed, maybe because she had a kid to take care of. She had a great laugh. Definitely a very *steady* individual."

Lee, however, decided to leave Pilobolus at the end of that year, and, because he had initially voiced concerns about the two women joining the group, it was long thought, even within Pilobolus, that he had left because of them. In reality, that was never the reason. He had seen that Pilobolus was on a fast-moving trajectory toward massive success, and though rightly proud to be a part of it, he also had begun to have a terrible time with constant fatigue in his legs. It was, in his words, "pretty intense," and the physical challenges were clearly only going to ramp up with more and more touring. This came alongside a parallel emotional challenge, due to another change wrought by success: originally Moses and Jonathan had done the marketing and publicity, and Lee had taken care of other practicalities (finances, stage management, lighting), but by the time Alison and Martha joined, Pilobolus had an outside accountant and other help, so Lee didn't need to do those things, didn't need to be in the theater before everyone else, and found himself left on his own. Robby and Martha would go off together, Alison and Moses would go off, Jonathan would go make friends, and Lee would wonder "What do I do?" Unlike Moses and Robby, he didn't have a girlfriend, and he wasn't as socially self-sufficient as Jonathan. It wasn't that he felt like the odd man out—he liked everyone and felt that he belonged—but out on the road, which is where he knew Pilobolus would spend most of its time as its popularity continued to snowball, there wasn't much to sustain him. As he put it: "It's a weird freakin' life. Every week you're in a different place." During a tour to California he realized this wasn't how he wanted to spend his life, and he decided to return to the other subject that had engrossed him during his days at Dartmouth, where he had once immersed himself in the computer center. He would leave Pilobolus to pursue the burgeoning field of computing. In December, he moved out of the house.

His natural successor was Michael Tracy. Michael had turned them

down before but, having completed his major in social work and graduated magna cum laude from Dartmouth several months earlier, he might
now be persuaded. He had been in Alison's first classes—alongside Robby
Barnett, with whom he had collaborated on a piece—and had also clowned
around and collaborated with Moses (then, of course, still known as Robb)
on kooky projects, including an outdoor, dawn hour "tree dance" as a final
assignment for their eccentric chemistry professor. An illusionistic game
of popping in and out of shadow like a pair of squirrels among the surrounding pine trees, its creation had involved much playfulness and laughter. Like Moses, Michael had a strong athletic side paired with a love of
theatre, and Pilobolus would enable him to combine the two. After a bit of
hesitation, he said yes.

Lee counted Pilobolus lucky to get Michael: "He was just what they
needed, and he was exactly my size." Michael would take over Lee's spot
in Pilobolus and in the shared house. Only one adjustment needed to be
made. While all of the guys had long hair, Michael had *very* long hair;
his blond locks extended below his shoulder blades, almost waist-length,
certain to be problematic amid the topsy-turvy kineticism of Pilobolus.
Martha, who had already assumed the role of company barber, cut it for
him; and with that rite of passage complete, Pilobolus had recruited the last
of its founding members.

6

Martha took her little son David, starting at age four, with her on tour while
his dad remained to teach at Dartmouth. David, with cherubic innocence,
became part of the Pilobolus show. The box for *Anaendrom,* from which
Lee had dropped onto the stage like a spider, now contained Alison with
little David, who would sometimes pee ("Alison, I peed in the box") and
the two of them would shift to whichever side or corner was tilted slightly
higher and therefore drier. The piece ended with the box flipping and Alison dropping on all fours with David clinging to her like a baby monkey.
She would set him down and he would hop around until, at the edge of
the stage, he could open his mouth in which had been concealed a piece of
rubber—a rubber flower from a bathing cap—and flip this strange tongue
in and out. Audiences, taken completely by surprise, loved it. They hadn't
expected to see a small child in Pilobolus. (David eventually had a little
cup offstage in which he could pee. Once, when Moses strode offstage and

grabbed what he thought was his usual cup of water and chugged it, he got an even bigger surprise than the audience.) In another role, added to *Walklyndon,* in a nod to the 1970s phenomenon of "streaking" David ran naked across the stage as fast as he could. The joke had a few variations: one night the musical comedian Peter Schickele, better known as his fictional alter ego P.D.Q. Bach, streaked in place of David; on another occasion, a sheepdog took on the job—but, in a reversal of the streaking theme, the dog wore the same brightly colored boxer shorts as the members of Pilobolus. During rehearsals, David played with a yo-yo; he watched the shows again and again; his earliest memories would include Lee, prior to his departure, with "long shaggy hair" in a solo walking around the stage smoking a cigarette like "performance art" (all the more so because Lee, in fact, was not a smoker). David liked to be around the audience and hear people talking about the show afterward. And he liked hearing the applause. He didn't fully understand it, but he felt connected to it. For the next few years, as he traveled with Pilobolus, with his mom—to Paris a dozen times (where, to celebrate his sixth birthday, Pierre Cardin would throw a party for him in a restaurant, with Jerome Robbins in attendance), to other parts of Europe and the world, to Japan repeatedly—at dinners and in the company of new acquaintances the adults would encourage him to sing. He especially sang "Second Hand Rose"; he sang it to everyone, even to silk merchants in Kyoto, at an elegant dinner in a Japanese inn. At home his teachers were amazed by his travels, perhaps a little envious, and a bit amused. Of course, he had to bring a mountain of homework with him on each tour; Robby would help him with it, especially with science; sometimes the other guys would help too. To David, an only child, they were almost like older siblings, all of them fun, and when he took bows with Pilobolus, when they all held hands, in the early years he would be lifted, like a brightly shining bulb on a string of lights, between the adults on either side: a sweet little boy with his feet off the ground.

FOUR

Tall Ladies

1

In January 1974 Pilobolus performed a program of eight pieces in New York, at a benefit for the Skowhegan School of Painting and Sculpture held at the Hunter College Playhouse, and again received an enthusiastic review from Don McDonagh in the *New York Times.* Among the pieces were Robby's solo *Geode;* his duet with Martha, *Aubade;* and Alison and Martha's duet *Cameo,* which was seen as perhaps too traditional and not sufficiently fresh and Pilobolus-like. McDonagh, for a second time, singled out for particular praise *Anaendrom,* which had by now been expanded from a quartet to a sextet to include Alison and Martha (with little David and his synthetic tongue as a surprise seventh element).

In the summer Pilobolus toured Europe again, performing in Germany, Italy, Finland, and Holland, and while in Amsterdam began to create a new piece that would be completed in the US. *Monkshood's Farewell,* with its medieval theme, inspired in part by the paintings of Hieronymus Bosch, would consist of six interrelated vignettes and mark the group's biggest evolutionary leap yet. Its creation would also begin their southern migration, from Hanover—where, for lack of an alternative, they had continued to use the stage in Webster Hall, breaking into the building with a credit card—down to western Connecticut, to which Martha and Phil had returned after Phil's residency at Dartmouth. (The couple had settled there in 1969 in a lovely area that Robert Redford, an old friend of Phil's, had enthusiastically recommended.) Alison and Eric had settled in Connecticut, too. Martha located a rehearsal space, a beautiful dance studio at Wykeham Rise, a private school for girls, situated on more than two dozen acres in the rolling green landscape of Washington, Connecticut. As it was summer, the men of Pilobolus could stay in the dormitories while everyone worked on *Monkshood* in the studio.

It would be their happiest collaboration. Although they had created *Ciona* as a sextet by revising and expanding prior material, they had never made an entirely new work as a six-person troupe, and now fresh energy and ideas abounded. "Robby was the real intellect of the company," Martha recalled. "He had talked about medieval herbs and flowers. Moses was a natural comedian. He and I were the silliest." For the first time the group began to reference images and characters that were not simply gymnastic: "*Monkshood* had the codependent bodies making an image, plus a theatricality of a slightly literary flavor that depicted the atmosphere of another time. Theatricality at a different level of shape-making."

The first and perhaps most popular of those comic images is the sight of two sets of three dancers piled on one another to form a pair of opposing knights in a medieval joust. Other odd, funny, striking images follow; the second sequence begins with the two women "walking" with each of their feet on the back of a different crawling man; the third brings us Moses's fantastic solo in which he balances on one leg for a jaw-dropping amount of time (two and a half minutes in the filmed version later shown on *Dance in America,* but almost four minutes in some of the earlier live performances—in at least one archival film of a live show he maintains his one-legged solo for three minutes and forty-five seconds, while continuing to do a number of other things with the upper half of his body). There are also four hunchbacks, Martha's "St Vitus's Dance / village idiot" routine, and more. Robby would remember laughing with the others while working on the portrayal of the hunchbacks. They all were having fun. Toward the end of the process, Murray Louis and Alwin Nikolais—Murray and Nik, to Pilobolus—were performing at the University of Connecticut, and Robby recalls the group going to see them, then returning to the studio excited to work on the last section of *Monkshood.* Afterward they went to a state park, Mount Tom, for a swim, deeply satisfied to have completed what was then, at thirty minutes in length, their longest and most fully developed piece. Its making would remain for Martha the purest pleasure of her collaborative work with Pilobolus: "A young flower in bloom. It had innocence, in the making of it."

The floral metaphor is apt, because the group decided to give each of the six sections its own name, like chapter titles, and derived those names largely from a book of English wildflowers. Martha had the book, and the naming process was another part of the fun. Hence, for example, the segment in which we see the two women walking in their peculiar fashion is called "Celandine and Hellebore Encounter the Foetid Goad of Passion" and another is called "Hedgemustard's Rhume." Moses's solo bears the nonfloral but entirely compatible title "From Haunts of Coot and Hern" and reveals his background in English literature: "I come from haunts of coot and hern" declares the first line of Tennyson's poem "The Brook"; it refers to coots and herns, or herons, birds associated with large bodies of water and who, not coincidentally, are known to stand on one leg. As for the title of the full piece, when it made its debut at the American Dance Festival on July 28 the program listed it as *Monkshood's Delight,* but it would soon be retitled *Monkshood's Farewell* when someone suggested that *Monkshood's Delight* sounded like a dessert. Regardless, it was one of the brightest successes of that year's festival, a crowd-pleaser that quickly became, and remained for the next several years, a signature piece for the company.

In those glory days, its humor and skit-like quality, alongside the expanded and much-improved six-person *Walklyndon,* further propelled Pilobolus's appeal. The 1970s were a strong decade for comedy, always a cherished genre, and a comic element seemed welcome nearly everywhere. Television, by now ubiquitous, served up countless sitcoms, among them such cultural landmarks as *All in the Family* and *M*A*S*H,* as well as variety shows increasingly devoted to sketch comedy, and old films that revived interest in the Marx Brothers and other comedians of the past. The British comic geniuses Monty Python reached US audiences in 1974, and the following year saw the advent of *Saturday Night Live.* Stand-up comics Steve Martin, Lily Tomlin, and Richard Pryor and filmmakers Mel Brooks and Woody Allen were all in their heyday, and one of the most influential institutions in the history of American humor, *Mad* magazine, reached its commercial height. Even in music, perhaps thanks to the recent memory of the Beatles and their charmingly funny interview style, it behooved pop stars to traffic in playful quips. With all of these comic models, the average social interaction in everyday life had become more joke-infused too. In 1970s America, it often felt as if everyone and everything should be funny.

Pilobolus, of course, offered other dimensions as well. As *Chicago Tri-*

bune theatre critic Richard Christiansen wrote a few years later, *Monkshood's Farewell* "includes humorous jousting and earthy peasant dances in its six sections, but its final image of men struggling forward into the light is the one that helps make this work such a vivid evocation of the Medieval spirit." Pilobolus had found a surprising combination of the comic, the intellectual, and the physical, and even if the result sometimes looked to dance purists like a novelty act, most critics and audiences recognized it as a legitimate artistic innovation and experienced it as a revelatory joy.

2

Among the places that Pilobolus members stayed during their first Connecticut summer visits, perhaps the most memorable was the home of the photographer Nell Dorr. About eighty at the time, she had had a long and distinguished career marked by lasting achievements, such as her books *Mother and Child* (1954) and *Of Night and Day* (1968), and her inclusion in the Museum of Modern Art's famously innovative group exhibition *The Family of Man*, which opened in New York in 1955 and subsequently toured the world for eight years. Now she lived in a large barn, built against a hill, on Nettleton Hollow Road in Washington. Martha knew her as a friend, and soon Robby had met her through Martha. He weeded Nell's gardens during his first summer after college, in 1972, and lived with her the next couple of summers.

Nell was a great fan of Walt Whitman. She walked around in her bare feet, in stark contrast to her best friend, screen legend Lillian Gish, who would come to visit and keep her slippers next to her bed so she could place her feet in them directly; she informed Robby that her bare feet had never touched the ground. Nell and Lillian would fight with each other, and Robby would sometimes find them squabbling or glaring, like a pair of cats, but their friendship had endured since childhood.

Robby and Jonathan made the audio tape for *Monkshood's Farewell* at Nell's house. Her grandson Chris Ashe, a big guy with long blond hair and a big beard, was at the time their company manager and had a tape recorder; they used it to tape sounds off of vinyl records (Martha had one called *Sounds of the Swamp*, especially useful for Moses's one-legged solo) and they painstakingly cut and spliced the tape with razors to edit it, in the exhaustingly labor-intensive low-tech manner of the day.

That same summer of '74, a last vestige of an earlier Pilobolus reached a new, wider public. On July 1, the PBS television station WNET, Channel 13 in New York, aired Ed Emshwiller's film *Pilobolus and Joan,* featuring folk singer Joan McDermott and the original all-male Barnett-Harris-Pendleton-Wolken quartet, who collectively portray a cockroach turned into a man, in a comic reversal of Kafka's "Metamorphosis." Writing in that day's *New York Times* to alert readers to the broadcast that night, John J. O'Connor noted: "In one extraordinary sequence simulating a sex dream, human limbs and appendages are used to build layers of sensual textures and movements on the screen." He adds that although McDermott is "good," Pilobolus is "sensational" in the film, "using dance, gymnastics, and acrobatics to concoct an incredibly original and memorable creature" and praises them as "almost startlingly inventive and energetic."

Dance critic Deborah Jowitt agreed. As she later wrote: "Nowhere is the image of male bonding, which underlay almost all Pilobolus work until recently, clearer" than in this film that "asks us to accept that Pendleton, Barnett, Wolken, and Harris are a single insect who's trying to think and act like a man and understand the human world. . . . Emshwiller's dazzling camera effects turn their dances into the splitting and rejoining of a single organism, into a slow-motion, erotic blossoming of flesh."

Of the making of the film, Lee Harris would only recall the four of them wearing their tights and dashing from one location to the next during "an absolutely antic day in New York City with Ed Emshwiller filming. He had seen something and wanted to film us."

3

The men of Pilobolus, having come down to Connecticut to spend the summer of 1973 working on *Ciona* and then the summer of 1974 working on *Monkshood,* began to see the advantages of a permanent move to the state, and specifically to Litchfield, a county in the northwestern area, in the foothills of the Berkshires. Martha already lived there, Alison wasn't very far, and in 1975 the others moved down as well. It wouldn't make sense to stay in Vermont, as their relentless touring schedule now required closer proximity to airports; yet they all wanted to stay as far from the city as they reasonably could. Their strong preference for a rural setting would remain one of the few things on which they would all unwaveringly agree.

In Washington, Connecticut, they would find their ideal home base. Bucolic, idyllic, with a classic New England rural small-town feel; "out in the boondocks" by the standards of Northeasterners accustomed to a certain population density, but within easy reach of necessities. Having already been conditioned to New England's intense differentiation of the four seasons, a landscape where summer is summer, and winter is harsh, where autumn brings a symphony of color followed by the crispness of October air and of fallen leaves, no major adjustment would be needed. The green hills of northwestern Connecticut; the sense of farm and forest; the winding, hilly roads, the many curves. The *old* homes—the use of stone—and stone walls. Driving along, and getting stuck behind a farm tractor on the road ahead. Horses grazing in a field. The joyful omnipresence of fresh air.

Quiet but often massive wealth, tucked away discreetly like a recluse, gave the area a secret cachet, but the twin elements of money and resident celebrities in low profile did not detract from the natural beauty of the countryside (and perhaps helped to preserve it). Robby and Moses rented a little farmhouse; Jonathan and Michael found lodging elsewhere. Pilobolus would eventually arrange to use Club Hall, a local social hall, for rehearsals. Serving as the Pilobolus studio during the week, it would host weddings and other events on evenings and weekends. They would rent the first floor of an old house not far away, owned by the hardware store next door to it, to use as their informal office space.

In the preceding months they had continued their ascent. On the evening of September 1, 1974, Pilobolus had performed *Ciona* and *Monkshood's Farewell* at the New York Dance Festival at the Delacorte in Central Park, and had received a standing ovation in the rain, followed by a third rave review from Don McDonagh in the *New York Times,* who noted that "The blend of casual muscularity and wit that is the Pilobolus special formula obviously delighted an audience of relative strangers to its work." In the spring of 1975, that contagious delight was about to take another giant leap forward—or, rather, straight *up*—and carry American dance with it.

4

From the opening moments of *Untitled* (1975), it is clear that the world of Pilobolus has acquired a decidedly new sensibility. Instead of dancers in unitards, or near-naked men wearing only dance belts, the piece begins with Alison and Martha costumed as a pair of elegant young ladies in long dresses and hats suited to a nineteenth-century summer day; they look as if they've stepped out of an Edwardian painting of a picnic. Using their earlier duet *Cameo* as a template—the piece that was considered insufficiently Pilobolus-like—they seem ready to enact a parodic, playful dance of youthful innocence. Or so it seems, until their movement begins to verge on the airborne, and suddenly, up they go, to nearly twice their height, and stay there, having turned into giantesses. This startling transformation happens live on stage through a device that is hilariously easy for the audience to comprehend, as one glance at the hairy male ankles and bare feet now protruding from beneath those elegant hemlines indicates. The "tall ladies," as they are affectionately known within Pilobolus, continue their dance until they give birth, so to speak, to the men under each of their costumes, who roll out onto the stage buck naked, possibly babies or possibly lovers. That the two proper young ladies had handsome naked men under their skirts (literally and, perhaps, metaphorically?) is a great bawdy joke, but part of the brilliance of *Untitled* is the decision to refrain from playing to that joke or making the rest of the piece into a comedy. Instead, it heads off into uncharted, even more ambiguous territory, with a kind of half-story made of montage: two other men, fully clothed as gentlemen suitors, show up to pay court; there is a fight; there are various literal and abstract tableaux; and there is a sense, when the two ladies seem to repose in rocking chairs, that we have witnessed scenes from a life in another age—an age that would never have produced a theatrical work resembling this one, in which the traditional and the modern, the audacious and the demure, and the refined and the bluntly sexual, have collided in a way that is startling not for its contrasts but for its ability to all coalesce according to some internal logic (or illogic) that leaves the audience with the sense of having had an unforgettable, unnamable dream, meaningful but elusive, impossible to quantify. From a piece that was too "dancey" for Pilobolus, and a comic stroke seemingly too gimmicky for serious art, emerges a breakthrough.

That breakthrough, even more than most Pilobolus achievements, came out of not only collaboration but conflict. It began when Alison, who had been working on a solo, demonstrated her work-in-progress to Moses, and he had a lightning-strike of comic inspiration: to hide under her dress and, at the close of the solo, lift her up, turning her into a giantess. Alison was thrilled. An ingenious ending for her solo! Moses too knew he had hit upon something brilliant, and he couldn't resist showing the move, separately, to Martha—without telling her that it had already been "given" to Alison. Martha's eyes lit up. She knew a theatrical gem when she saw one, and she wanted Moses to do this new move of his for her; it would be the perfect addition to the duet she and Robby were making. Moses knew instantly that he had stirred up trouble, as he later admitted: "I thought *Oh no, now I've pitted them against each other.*" That became painfully apparent when Martha called Alison to regale her with an enthusiastic account of the wonderful new move Moses had given her. One can only imagine the arctic silence with which this news must have been greeted, and the bitter words that may have followed in their dispute over who would get to become the giantess. Moses knew that he and Robby had to find a solution. In those days, the two of them had a habit of lazing on air mattresses on a pond, sunning themselves and trading thoughts. In this supine philosophical state they assessed the crisis and saw only one way out: Alison and Martha must *both* become giantesses, together, with Moses and Robby doing the respective lifting. Neither the solo-turned-duet that Alison wanted nor the duet-turned-trio that Martha wanted, but a quartet. Not that it was an easy sell. In Martha's words, "It became a quartet with some tears and anger."

Jonathan and Michael were still in Europe, where they had stayed following the group's recent tour. Pilobolus had a terrific agent in that territory, a woman whose cheerful smile, orange hair, and glasses made an endearing pumpkin face while with polyglot brilliance she booked them all over Europe. While in Copenhagen, the need to create a new piece for the upcoming American Dance Festival had prompted Moses, Alison, Martha, and Robby to head home and get to work, but Jonathan and Michael had decided to stay, and join them later. With those two still on holiday, and thus unavailable to further complicate an already contentious situation, Moses and Robby decided to move fast, and the two couples set to work to make the new piece. Soon after they finished—or thought they had—the others returned. Jonathan strode into the studio and declared, with characteristic bluster (as if he alone possessed a serious work ethic), that it was time to get down to business and make the new piece, only to be brought up short by the news, delivered with perhaps too large a dollop of satisfaction, that it had already been made. That sparked a clash so great that, by some accounts, Alison and Martha demanded that Jonathan and Michael be thrown out—of the studio, of Pilobolus—saying that they refused to work with them. Again it fell to Moses and Robby to salvage the situation.

The key to a resolution proved also to be a key to the piece: the group took the aversion that the women felt toward the intrusion of their colleagues and gave it to the tall ladies, who do not welcome the sudden appearance of two uninvited men as suitors. The unwanted "suitors," Jonathan and Michael, choreographed a fight scene between themselves that got attached to, and further altered, the existing structure, and somehow it all worked. While inwardly a curved mirror of the interpersonal dynamics between the six members of Pilobolus, outwardly the piece had layers of resonance, with the male intruders a contrast to the two naked men who might be the women's babies or lovers or—as Moses brilliantly observed—a cryptic representation of the women's own male energies or a projection of themselves.

When it came time for the group to name the piece, according to Michael, they conceived and wrote down one hundred titles. One was *Rowan Oak,* which evokes both a mythical tree and the novelist William Faulkner (it's the name of Faulkner's former home in Oxford, Mississippi) and, by extension, the antebellum South and its gardens, its ladies, its mint juleps sipped on front porches. As each idea was tossed into the running, however, it would spark yet another vehement debate. They couldn't agree, and so the piece became *Untitled,* a name that, ironically, proved appropriate to its strange, unquantifiable nature.

Their most theatrical work yet, *Untitled* would also be the first in which they would dance to live music, a score by Robert Dennis that perfectly underlined the period sensibility. For its premiere that hot summer at the American Dance Festival in New London, Connecticut, they had several exhausting days of rehearsals with live orchestra to learn the music cues, not having heard the score until their arrival there. On August 1, opening night, they were nervous. Moses and Robby, hidden under the dresses, had not been completely nude in rehearsals, but would appear completely nude onstage. As it turned out, when they did, at the moment when the two men emerged into visibility, the musicians in the orchestra—who had never seen them naked, until the live performance—stopped on a dime, with jaws dropped, stunned into total silence. As was the audience. And then, from the awkward quiet, a tapping sound: Robert Dennis tapping, to urge the musicians on. Once the orchestra "recovered" everyone continued. The piece carried on, to its end, and then there came another shock: a delirious, over-the-top standing ovation.

5

Tales of conflict tend to breed conflicting accounts, and there's no consensus on certain stories about Pilobolus and its possible near-collapse circa 1975: whether, for example, Moses, Robby, Alison, and Martha decided Pilobolus should call it quits around the time of *Untitled* and prepared a "farewell speech" for a performance at the Brooklyn Academy of Music, but were talked out of it; whether the two couples felt they might prefer to work without Jonathan and Michael; and at what point various internal dynamics changed. It seems certain, however, that the growing success of both their art itself and their popularity as a group, and the attendant rise in encouragement from outside, provided an incentive to remain a sextet, and to remain Pilobolus.

The repertoire continued to grow and flourish with smaller works as well. Jonathan had developed a solo that in many ways distilled and concentrated the aesthetic of the abstract works made by the earlier, all-male Pilobolus. With Robby's *Geode* as its forerunner, *Pseudopodia* turns that sensibility into a brief, rolling-and-tumbling tour de force. In its brevity and deceptive simplicity it embodies what Jonathan would later term "the sushi principle," a concept with which he would explain to future generations of Pilobolus dancers and workshop attendees that less is more. In Jonathan's words:

> In the crush of ideas and individual efforts in our work lives and certainly in our creative lives, we are challenged to hear our own voice over the din of others. For most of us our early formative school years set in motion a process of competitive achievement that sticks with us and colors our habits. We rush forward with answers, we create a blizzard of ideas, we avoid the understated approach by covering with mass quantities of . . . just about everything.
>
> The sushi principle reminds us that there is an alternative—a spare and simple approach that appeals to the mind and attracts the eye.
>
> We can see this principle at work on the stage, especially during an improvisation. A glut of activity often serves to hide the best material. The eye simply doesn't know where to look in the visual cacophony. So simplify. Unclog, clear away and remove the obstacles that distract from the clarity you seek. Less, perfectly served, is often just right.

Yet *Pseudopodia* is also dynamic and riveting. As critic Richard Christiansen put it: "When Jonathan Wolken moves effortlessly from a somersault to a slow, standing push-up in his solo, *Pseudopodia,* he actually appears able to break down his body into its components and put it back together again." The piece would become a lasting part of the repertoire, and a rite of passage for many of the Pilobolus dancers who would perform it.

Another unforgettable contribution came from Alison and Moses, who together created a nine-minute duet so luminously odd and weirdly beautiful that one almost doesn't want to describe it in words for fear of imposing limits on its evocativeness. Its title, *Alraune,* is both botanical and supernatural: it's the German word for the Mandrake root, which has a humanoid shape and in the Middle Ages was used in love potions. In German folklore it also had numerous creepy myths surrounding it, not least that when people tried to pick the mandrake it would scream like a person; that it was produced beneath the gallows by the blood or semen of hanged men; and that the root itself could be used to impregnate women or witches, resulting in an offspring with no soul. In some versions of the myth, it is the woman herself who is left without a soul. Most of these more macabre concepts are not suggested (at least not in any obvious way) by the duet that Alison and Moses made, but the concept of whispering as a kind of magical act, one perhaps followed by a "going crazy" or intoxication (as if by a love potion) is entwined throughout it. The word *alraune* is also an alternative name for a mythical creature more often called the *kobold,* a sprite with the power to assume the form of a small human, an animal, an object, or fire. That sprite-like shape-shifting is most definitely at the center of the piece, which begins with the two dancers configured as a single creature—or are they two? What follows is a series of images that have graceful, elegant tricks to them and that tell an unspecified story dependent on the transmission of nonverbal information, evading the literal. The soundtrack includes singing in an enigmatic language, one that seems made up or misunderstood, adding to the sense of mystery.

Within that playful mystery, with its impressive lifts, flips, and witty reconfigurations of the two bodies onstage, the theme of whispers—the confiding of secrets—and sharing of, perhaps, a secret madness, tenderly intoxicating, lends it an unmistakable erotic charge and suggests that the duet itself might be the product of a sweet but wild secret, a clandestine love affair. It is easy in retrospect to see it as, like *Untitled,* a document of what was happening during its making, and it embodies what people who were in and around Pilobolus at the time mean when they say of Alison and Moses that she brought him an essential ingredient, not in the trite sense of being "the yin to his yang" as a female balance to a male, but in the more nuanced sense of two distinct energies, each a vibrant source of skill and knowledge, fusing into something greater. Most of all, *Alraune* is a prime example of the Pilobolus signature, the merging of bodies into a single larger, usually fantastical creature, accomplished in this case as a duet. It marked an advance over the group's more obviously mime-related visuals (such as the joust in *Monkshood*) into a more sophisticated clever-ness that felt freer, and still feels perpetually fresh.

6

On March 5, 1976, Pilobolus opened at the Brooklyn Academy of Music and played a sold-out engagement. The program consisted of *Untitled, Pseudopodia, Alraune, Walklyndon,* Martha's solo *Pagliaccio, Ocellus,* and *Monkshood's Farewell.* On the day of the opening, the *New York Times* ran a laudatory profile by Anna Kisselgoff, with interview quotes from Moses (whom she called "still the driving force behind the group"), followed the next day by chief dance critic Clive Barnes's positive review. Among other things, Barnes noted with approval the troupe's humor, and saw in *Untitled* "a kind of Thurberlike view of the war between men and women."

A few weeks later, in her dance column for the April 5 issue of the *New Yorker,* Arlene Croce wrote about Pilobolus for the first time, declaring them a "brilliant acrobatic-mime troupe" that blurred the lines between gymnastics and dance with "its use of poetic imagery." In the first, long paragraph of her two-paragraph review of their appearance at the Brook-lyn Academy of Music, she moves swiftly and succinctly to the essence of early Pilobolus: "The company gives us something to look at besides prow-ess; it makes pictures, and its best pictures are of a very special trompe-l'oeil variety. Added to the sense of physical dislocation that clever contor-tionists can convey is a sense of visual paradox and allusion. We get to see two ways at once or to see correspondences between things." In her second paragraph, she tells her readers that the six performers have a stage pres-ence "more sexually realistic" than that of dancers and identifies the company's humor as a kind of "cultured ribaldry," its partnering as "more likely to show symbiosis than sentiment," and its world view as "compounded of imagination, physical daring, and humor."

It would be the first but not last example of Croce's eloquent articulation of the Pilobolus achievement. As an ardent ballet critic entering her forties, the founder of *Ballet Review* magazine, a worshipper of Balanchine, she may not have seemed the most likely candidate to become a fan of Pilobolus, but she would prove an extraordinarily astute champion of their early work. Perhaps she recognized, on some level, a collective kindred spirit in this company whose new art resembled a physicalizing of writerly virtues. The Pilobolus process involves observation, invention, distillation, and concentration—essentially a physical form of writing (with bodies) and editing. It isn't hard to spot the parallels between what Croce at her best does in her pieces and what Pilobolus at its best does onstage: the emphasis on precise perception and the artful remaking of it into a composition that will surprise a waiting audience with its power and wit. And her prior experience as a film critic, for *Film Culture* and other publications, may have fine-tuned her taste for crisply orchestrated visuals and clever tableaux. Pilobolus, already the beneficiary of so many positive reviews, had struck critical gold.

FIVE

Broadway

1

In Paris, Pilobolus performed for the designer Pierre Cardin. The renowned couturier, who decades earlier had designed costumes for the films of Jean Cocteau, had established his theater, the Espace Cardin, in 1970 with a presentation of the Félix Blaska Company that set a record for ballet (seven consecutive weeks); subsequently the Espace Cardin had hosted dance companies, theatre companies, and performers ranging from Marlene Dietrich to Ella Fitzgerald to Alice Cooper. Now Cardin was eager to expand to Broadway, and given his tastes as a gay man, fashion designer, and lover of theatre, along with his fascination with geometric shapes, this athletic company of handsome young men and two beautiful women that combined themselves into a witty array of images elicited his enthusiastic endorsement. What's more, they had debuted *Untitled* at his theatre, an extraordinary way to make a first impression, and were already on an unmistakable upward trajectory. He loved *Untitled,* loved Pilobolus, and decided to sponsor them.

In 1976, with six months' worth of underwriting from Cardin, the troupe—now temporarily a quintet while Martha worked on other theatre projects—spent several months developing a long but uneven Irish-themed piece, *The Eve of Samhain,* that they performed a few times but would decide to abandon, salvaging only a trio and Robby's solo (in which he grappled with a snake made of steel). Along with the monthly stipend that supported their studio efforts, Cardin subsidized a tour to South America and Japan, in return for which Pilobolus performed at some of his fashion shows. An old State Department employee with a bottle of bourbon stashed in his briefcase escorted them on the South American tour. More problematic, their new manager—an older man, well-known in the business of booking dance tours—had given the job of stage manager to an extremely nice but completely incompetent young man of whom he was enamored. When Pilobolus arrived in Rio de Janeiro for its big premiere at the Opera House, the stage manager had nothing ready and couldn't get anything together; after an hour of waiting, audience members began to leave. Pilobolus ended up not even performing, having disappointed a full opera house on opening night. Yet despite this debacle they still managed to have a good tour, and in Japan, after they performed in a Cardin fashion show with extremely tall German models, their benefactor gave them the gift of a day at a Japanese inn. Robby recalled it as "amazing": "We couldn't find it, it was just a door. Finally we figured this must be the door, so we knocked. It was like walking into this other world, everything was perfect. The little flower and the little sconce. They sewed the sheets on your futon every day. You were constantly being brought little things. Little fountains, and water running in bamboo troughs everywhere, the trickle of water . . . It was quite something."

By this time another addition to the offstage world of Pilobolus had arrived. A young woman who had worked at the local bookstore in Washington, Connecticut turned up in the Pilobolus office, having been hired by their in-house manager while the group was on tour. When Robby met her at the office he remembered her as "the girl from the bookstore" who had, like many people at the time, often confused him with Moses. She would do so no more. Susan Mandler would become company manager, and, a number of years later, Robby's wife.

Over the following year, as Pilobolus continued to tour, to create, and to promote itself with Cardin's help, its fame grew accordingly. On Wednesday, May 4, 1977, PBS aired an episode of its series *Great Performances: Dance in America* featuring Pilobolus. The one-hour program included *Monkshood's Farewell*, movements from *Ocellus* and *Ciona*, and the complete *Untitled*, as well as brief conversational segments recorded in the studio. The *New York Times* gave the show, which ran at 9 p.m. on Channel 13 in the New York area (and on PBS stations across the country), a positive advance notice—and proposed it as a pleasant alternative to its chief competition, *The Nixon Interviews with David Frost*, a chat with the nation's disgraced ex-president.

With the *Dance in America* episode, Pilobolus had achieved its highest profile yet. Six months later, on November 20, the *New York Times* ran a long feature by Anna Kisselgoff in advance of the company's Broadway run. The article, though positive, acknowledged that the collaborative process could be difficult, with Alison likening it to "six radios going at once" or "a six-headed monster." Four days later, on Thanksgiving night, Pilobolus made its Broadway debut in a limited engagement through December 11 at the St. James Theater, to great acclaim. Even though they had discarded most of the material from the studio time subsidized by Cardin, after six years of energetic existence Pilobolus no longer had a beginner's shortage of strong work. They filled two programs with a rich variety of well-polished favorites and a few new offerings, a cornucopia that ranged from the quartet *Ocellus* and the group pieces *Ciona, Monkshood's Farewell,* and *Untitled* to the two duets by Alison and Moses (*Alraune* and *Shizen*), and a handful of solos: Robby's solo *Bone* from *The Eve of Samhain,* two from Jonathan (*Pseudopodia* and *Renelaugh on the Randan*), and three by Martha (*Vagabond, Pagliaccio,* and the premiere of *Wakefield*).

The next day, Anna Kisselgoff, in her *New York Times* review, called the group "fabulously innovative" and "different and fresh," and declared (as if in response to the question raised by Arlene Croce's earlier description of Pilobolus as "an acrobatic-mime troupe"): "Yes, it is dance if the definition of dance is stretched." Kisselgoff praised Pilobolus as "zany enough to make any family's holidays merry" and "smart enough to appeal to the mind's eye . . . they have created their own wonderland." A few days later, on November 30, the *Times* announced the appointment of Kisselgoff as its new chief dance critic (Clive Barnes had resigned the previous week). She and the *New York Times* would continue to cover Pilobolus as a major force in dance.

Among the more recent pieces, the two duets that Alison had created with Moses—*Alraune* from 1975 and the new piece *Shizen*—attracted well-deserved critical acclaim. The latter, with music composed and performed by Riley Kelly Lee using the shakuhachi, the Japanese bamboo flute, drifted into Eastern sensibilities with serene grace yet remained unmistakably Pilobolus-like in its fresh, odd inventiveness, adding gravitas to the company's trademark wit. In the *New Yorker,* Arlene Croce reviewed the Broadway run with brilliant analytic descriptions of *Monkshood's Farewell, Untitled,* and *Shizen,* and declared that "The Chase-Pendleton duet in which their bodies merge . . . reaches a new peak of refinement in *Shizen* . . .

A pure object of contemplation, it marks a decisive advance in Pilobolus style; it's the movement from prose to poetry."

Arlene Croce knew of what she spoke. Her explication and celebration of Pilobolus remains, like much of her other writing from this era, a paragon of the art of criticism. Because the *New Yorker* in those years still strictly adhered to a design that interspersed cartoons throughout the articles but forbade photographs, Croce had to convey, entirely in words, not only the movement but the overall visual experience of any dance program she reviewed. Given this heightened need to paint the full picture herself, her descriptive powers were a distinguishing feature of her work, often functioning as simultaneous snapshot and commentary. Her deft verbal portraits of Pilobolus, accrued over the course of a decade's observation (she wrote about them several times), remain indelible: Moses and Jonathan, for example, are "the glinting satyr Pendleton and the wolfishly jovial Wolken" who "could be brothers brought up by different tribes" whereas Martha and Robby, often paired, have, as she would later write, "the same kind of sensitive, slightly battered clown face" and "appear to have been born for theatre in the same minute."

Given the rave reviews and corresponding ticket sales, Cardin wanted the group to extend its run, but the prevailing attitude within Pilobolus was *No, I want to go home for Christmas.* A Broadway triumph couldn't tempt them away from life's more traditional pleasures, though they did consent to an "encore engagement" spanning the last five days of December. Only a few weeks later, in January, perhaps because they had left the New York theatre world wanting more, the *New York Times* ran another feature profile, this time in its Connecticut section. It focused on Pilobolus "at home" in the town of Washington and noted that the members each did their own workouts independently, tailored to their own needs and preferences, and met in the town hall in the afternoon to rehearse or to develop new pieces. It also noted that Alison and Martha each had homes with their husbands, and the four men of Pilobolus had paired up into two sets of housemates, with Jonathan and Michael sharing "a home, parts of which are 200 years old," and Moses and Robby sharing a house that Moses described as resembling "an old country inn" that consisted of "three independent suites, even down to these old individual door-knockers . . . It's so private that Robby and I once went for three days, living under the same roof, without seeing one another."

Not that they would be home for long. As the article noted, the group's itinerary included two performances in Hartford followed by gigs in the Virgin Islands, and later a lengthy tour to include Iran, the Middle East, and Europe. In another sign of success, in this new year Random House would publish Tim Matson's book *Pilobolus,* a collection of his black and white photos of the group rehearsing and performing.

It seemed they had triumphed, and in fact they had. As Martha later said, "It was really Cardin who made all the difference." And yet as she also acknowledged, "It changed. The more Pilobolus became successful, the more everyone had at stake. It puts more pressure on everything."

2

While dining out with Pilobolus, Martha had an argument with Jonathan. They were seated at a table that had flowers on it, and at the height of the dispute (about some now-forgotten subject) Jonathan, growing nasty, removed the flowers from their bottle, then shoved the bottle of dirty flower water at Martha and told her to drink it. She would look back, from the vantage point of decades, and think that perhaps the dirty water started the feeling in her that she should leave the company, which happened six months later. Nonetheless, her reasons were multiple. Back in 1975, she had done, as a non-Pilobolus side project, a two-woman show with the actress Linda Hunt, *L'histoire du Soldat,* at the Long Wharf Theatre in New Haven. After that, she continued to do a little bit of theatre, separate from Pilobolus, along the way. "Once I had the experience of working in the theatre proper, I wanted to do my own stuff." She found that she enjoyed working with actors. As for Pilobolus, she "had had enough of being a human projectile." Her son David was getting older, and he didn't want to go on tours anymore. She had "nodes on my vocal chords from yelling during the making of *Untitled.*" Six-way collaboration had exhausted her: "I had enough of it, every idea out of my mouth being thrown around the room and looked at by five other people." She vividly recalls that she awoke one morning, saw a peacock on the balcony of her beautiful home, and thought, "I can't do this anymore."

As only Martha could, she had channeled her frustration into a grotesquely comic homicidal art piece. The title of her solo *Wakefield* (1977) refers to a type of cabbage. As she explained, the French "think babies come from cabbages" (rather like the legend that the stork brings them), a folk concept that had led Jean Cocteau to write a tale about a child who, infuriated by the birth of a sibling, uses a hatpin to attack cabbages in a garden. Martha had prop cabbages, with Styrofoam in their centers, placed all over the stage, and performed a "mad scene of stabbing cabbages" while secretly, as she later admitted with a hysterical laugh, she "pretended they were members of Pilobolus." It was, she would realize in retrospect, her "farewell piece."

That summer of 1978 the American Dance Festival moved from Connecticut to Durham, North Carolina. After Pilobolus performed, Martha came offstage and mimed lighting a match and burning her unitard. Charles and Stephanie Reinhart, the festival's directors, seeing her intense frustration, asked: Would she like to do her own work at the festival next summer? She certainly would. And with that commitment in place, she left Pilobolus.

Somewhere along the way her affair with Robby ended, too, with neither drama nor pain. Looking back, she would see it as a part of her youth and of the era: "We were creatures of a time capsule. It dissipated like a rainbow—not difficult on anyone's part." Her departure from Pilobolus would coincide, for her, with the end of a certain recklessness, that avidity for experience that both characterizes and propels youthful exploration. As for her and Robby, the mutual affection that had drawn them together would continue to inform a lifelong friendship.

3

Several months after she had left Pilobolus, Martha went into town to pick up her mail and found Robby and Moses standing on the stairs of the post office on the Washington green, with champagne, pink roses, and chocolate truffles. They had known she would have to come there to get her mail, and they were waiting. The replacement they had gotten to cover her roles wouldn't do the upcoming tour to Montreal and Los Angeles and they desperately needed Martha to come to the rescue one last time. They had chosen the correct way to ask. She agreed to do the shows, and Pilobolus played both Montreal and Los Angeles in February and March 1979.

She brought with her a new solo, *Nocturne* (1978), initially performed on that Pilobolus tour, but made entirely on her own. Built on the concept of "an old woman who couldn't remember why she was on stage" and "what it would feel like to remember having been a performer," Martha considers it "a statement of how I felt artistically, old and used up. I had no idea if I had a future." Yet what makes the piece remarkable is its profound mixture of decrepitude and grace, its echoes of genuine beauty buried under severe, hopeless limitation. When *Nocturne* premiered, in Montreal, some audience members laughed and others told them not to, because some saw it as dark comedy and others as tragedy. Either way, Martha could see the piece was "very successful right from the beginning." A poignant filmed performance of *Nocturne* was later included in a French television program featuring Pilobolus, and properly credited as a solo work by Martha. It was also included in the repertoire of her new company, Crowsnest, which premiered at the American Dance Festival that summer, on July 17, 1979, and would have its New York debut nearly two years after that.

When Martha had decided to form her own company, she had informed Robby nonchalantly "And of course you'll be in it." Their other collaborator would be Félix Blaska, one of the most acclaimed dancer-choreographers in France—the man whose company had enabled the Espace Cardin to set a record for ballet attendance when the theater had first opened. Martha had met him when Pilobolus was performing there, around 1976. While taking off her make-up, pulling the mascara off with cold cream, a man appeared behind her: "this beautiful young man whose reflection I saw in the mirror." His circle included internationally famous piano duo Katia Labèque, who had been his girlfriend, and her sister Marielle. The three had a château in the middle of Paris, a three-story structure from a bygone century, with a central court into which a car could be driven. When Pilobolus met them, by some accounts, Jonathan became smitten with Katia and courted her assiduously but unsuccessfully, seated cross-legged at her feet while she played the piano.

Martha invited Félix, whom she considered "a wonderful beautiful instinctive creator and performer," to come to the US where she eventually made a duet with him based on a Goya painting, *The Countess del Carpio, Marquesa de la Solana*. "Félix is a Polish Jew and they walked from Kiev to Paris during World War II. He had a very difficult childhood due to the war. He and I did wonderfully together. He had wonderful taste." Martha called Robby "the little arpeggio" because "he'd go off verbally and Félix and I would roll our eyes. Robby's head always came between instinct and action. He's very verbal and analytical, whereas Félix and I were very intuitive—which set up an interesting dynamic." According to Martha,

Robby always had "an intellectual detachment from the work." She and Félix would say "I *feel* this" whereas Robby said "I *think*." Whatever its contrasts and ratios, all that feeling and thinking would contribute to a genuinely interesting body of work.

Throughout most of the 1970s, Moses had continued to live with Robby, and by the last years of the decade Susan Mandler had moved in too. As Moses later explained, they called her "Sugar Butter Cream" and, because she and Robby both loved to cook, the two spent countless hours in the kitchen. They would feed Moses, but, by his account, the two lovebirds were soon so involved with each other that they would giggle over the making of desserts until late at night while he still awaited his salad.

If only every roommate in a "three's a crowd" situation could have the good fortune to resolve it as elegantly as Moses did. While searching for a new rehearsal space in Washington, Connecticut, he had been shown a small barn that seemed just right, and the realtor had told him that the old house across the road from it could be added for a bargain price. It had been built nearly a century earlier, in the 1890s, as a "summer cottage" though to some the word "mansion" would seem more accurate: it was a twenty-four-room Victorian house. Moses found the light, the wallpaper, and the offer irresistible, and bought the house, the barn, and the accompanying eight acres for $162,000. The house had a quality of fantasy, as if it existed outside of time: "No one seemed to have done anything to it for a hundred years—and that's just what I loved." The house and property, to which he would add a dazzling layout of magnificent flower gardens, would come to play a large role in his life and art.

In 1978, Moses had also made his first big break from Pilobolus, though unlike Martha he had not officially left the company. He took on a project for the Paris Opera, and Pilobolus brought in a new dancer, Jamey Hampton. Jamey, a native of Portland, Oregon, had taken Alison's class during her final year teaching at Dartmouth, and had graduated from Dartmouth in 1976 with a BFA in drama. He had watched Pilobolus from early on, knew them, revered them, and had desperately wanted to join, asking repeatedly. Now he had his chance, and for the next few years he would tour and perform with them.

Moses's project for the Paris Opera, for its celebration of Erik Satie (*Integrale Erik Satie*), gave him his first opportunity to do non-Pilobolus work. His research for it led him "into a kind of Dadaism—not even that, into instantaneism—on this mission to liberate the Paris Opera." The dancers of the Paris Opera Ballet, including Patrick Dupond and Isabelle Guerin, were treated to a new experience of playful improvisation, and next Moses assembled a European tour that mixed modern and ballet works on the same bill, performed by Dupond, Noella Pontois, and Carla Fracci, as well as Alison and himself. That project, once the ballet dancers departed, would in turn lead Moses and Alison to continue to tour as a team, with their solos and duets. For Alison, this sideline had evolved, in part, from the fact that she too needed to step away from that six-headed monster of collaboration, Pilobolus, in which she had become the only female voice, without Martha and the sisterly solidarity they had attained.

The branching out—Martha into Crowsnest, with Robby as part of it, and Moses and Alison as a separate duo—wasn't simply a matter of artistic growth. As the 1970s came to an end, Pilobolus had begun to crack, and the unpleasantness behind the scenes ran deeper than in the past. When Jamey had joined in 1978, the troupe seemed to him to still have a solid group dynamic, and though the members were extremely competitive with one another, that seemed merely a function of their sharp intelligence. It was one-upmanship, not so far removed from the creative one-upmanship of Alison's classes at Dartmouth a decade earlier, where it had all begun, and intense as the competitiveness might be, the humor and the conversation were also extraordinary and would evolve into a crescendo of laughter. Yet as the decade closed, Jamey felt a change. "Everybody was mad at everybody." Like Martha, they had grown tired of constantly fighting for their ideas, and the battle fatigue had led to acrimony. They had been "like a perfect six-sided crystal" but now that crystal seemed, at times, irretrievably broken.

A certain tension had always existed between the women and the men—or, as Jamey observed, "There was always tension between the sexes because the women knew more about dance. They were so fabulously trained—not a finer modern dancer than Alison or Martha ever lived—and the guys would say they *hated* dance, but they said that because they weren't good dancers. They weren't good 'dancers' but they were great movers." Now, with Martha's departure, Alison had been left as the only female founder, the only woman with a vote, in a company that she had inspired but in which, despite her greater training and knowledge, she felt that she had been largely relegated to a secondary role. Her alternate path, with Moses, depended on collaboration with a brilliant but complex man with whom she had a complicated and often contentious relationship—one that, if off-the-record tales are to be believed, led her at least once, in a restaurant in Brussels, to throw a glass of wine against a wall in anger. (That shattered glass is doubly startling given the gracious, nurturing Alison that so many love and admire.) Robby had essentially departed, in practical terms if not officially, with Crowsnest. The harshest change, however, was between Moses and Jonathan. The two men, though entirely different, had had a lot to talk about in the early years, when everybody needed each other, but with the onset of success that sense of mutual purpose had gradually evaporated. They had fought before—there were even tales of a fistfight between them in the mid-1970s—but now something had broken more deeply. It wasn't clear exactly what, but Jamey, who lived in an apartment upstairs in the house that contained the Pilobolus offices, once overheard the two of them, and the group, shouting and swearing at each other.

Before long, Jonathan and Moses were no longer speaking. Despite the group's supposedly egalitarian ideals, they considered themselves the founders, and now fame, ego, and a will to take greater control were all in play. Although some observers had seen Moses as the primary magic-maker, and he had seemed the ringleader from the start, Jonathan and the others had never deferred to his leadership; and Jonathan especially, who could still summon youthful enthusiasm but also had an aggressive outspokenness and perpetual readiness to fight, of course would not yield to any increased assertiveness on Moses's part. Others would now see the two men pass each other silently on their way in and out of the studio. For Jamey, who had long worshipped Pilobolus and finally become a part of it, "It was terrible and sad to watch Moses and Jonathan walk past each other. There was such animosity."

He wasn't the only one who felt that way. Steve Johnson—Moses and Jonathan's partner in the very first trio, *Pilobolus*—although not a first-hand observer of the dynamic at the end of the decade, would come to the same view. In the beginning, he recalled, "Jonathan was a ball of energy, a dynamo, completely positive. Moses was less organized but more creative. They were a great team. It was an entirely positive connection. Jonathan's energy and organizational skills were essential to Pilobolus's taking off. It was tough to see the rift between them years later."

4
———

Into this fraught atmosphere came the invitation to Pilobolus to make a new piece for the 1980 Winter Olympics. Officially known as the XIII Olympic Winter Games, the event would take place from February 13 to 24 in Lake Placid, New York, but the question of who within Pilobolus would accept the commission—as there was no longer any possibility of the entire group working together—led to a fiery dispute. In the end, the commission got split, with Pilobolus signing on to create and present two new works rather than one: a solo from Moses and a group piece without him.

Jonathan, Michael, and Jamey, along with Georgiana Holmes, one of a few female dancers with whom they worked after Martha's departure, would create and perform in the latter, entitled *The Empty Suitor*. The piece's most lasting legacy would be its solo, one of Michael Tracy's finest moments, in which he adeptly trips his way through a slippery obstacle course of PVC pipes, gets tangled in some furniture, and narrowly avoids all manner of personal injury, to the tune of "Sweet Georgia Brown." As Michael later explained, "It was a comedic solo that was in a way inspired by Charlie Chaplin and Buster Keaton. This is my idea of that kind of physical comedy which I saw as I was growing up. It's now kind of a long tradition, and it seems unusual on a modern dance repertoire, but it's a lot of fun to perform. You have a real instantaneous connection with the audience." The solo, later extracted from the larger piece and billed simply as *Solo from The Empty Suitor*, would be performed by Michael and subsequent Pilobolus dancers for many years, a perpetual delight.

As for the solo from Moses, it too would make a powerful comic impression and have a lasting effect. It would herald a new phase in Moses's artistic evolution, one that involved both Jamey Hampton and a new friend, Daniel Ezralow, a dancer with the Paul Taylor Dance Company who had previously worked with both 5 by 2 Plus and the Lar Lubovitch Dance Company. A couple of years earlier, Moses and Alison had been commissioned to create a piece for 5 by 2 Plus, in New York, and Danny had bonded deeply with Moses (the piece they created, named *Bond's Eye* after the fictional spy James Bond, would later become a Pilobolus piece called *Bonsai*). Danny, a West Coast native, had then gone to see Pilobolus when they performed at UCLA, had hung out with the group for a week, and later spent time with Martha and Moses in Paris. He was primarily connected to Moses and Alison, and would come to regard Moses as a key mentor: Paul Taylor taught him about strength and craft, he would say, and Moses taught him about creativity.

In the summer of 1979, Danny had come up from New York while on hiatus from the Paul Taylor company and had worked with Moses, Alison, and Jamey as a quartet, to create a piece based on music from the 1977 album *Exodus* by Bob Marley and the Wailers. (Bob Marley generously granted them permission to use the whole album, for free.) The song and album title *Exodus* resonated with the fact that Moses felt he was "exiting" Pilobolus, and the piece also included Moses in a white suit with cane (what would later become known as his *Momix* outfit) as he performed to the song "Waiting in Vain"—a selection that, for a few close friends, evoked Moses's hope that Alison might give up her husband Eric for him. The finished piece, entitled *Parson Nibs and the Rude Beggars,* a typically shameless Pendleton pun on *parsnip* and *rutabaga,* was in Danny's estimation "wonderful" but it was only performed six or ten times. It would be dismissed in the *Washington Post* that October as "an unsavory combo of sadomasochism, sex, and reggae" and quickly forgotten, but the appeal of the reggae music and the white-suited persona was not.

In the run-up to the creation of the two pieces for the Olympics, Jamey took home, as he sometimes did, another piece of music that had been lying around in the studio, to play in the house. It was "Rapper's Delight," the pioneering hip-hop track by the Sugarhill Gang, and this particular vinyl copy had a skip at the end of it. Jamey made a mix tape in which a reggae song transitioned into "Rapper's Delight," and gave the cassette to Moses as a gift.

"Here. It's for you," he told him. "It's a Momix."

"What a great name," Moses replied.

"Well," Jamey said, "It's a mix and I made it for you. So it's a Momix."

That mix, which included the skip in "Rapper's Delight" from the vinyl record that Jamey had used as a source, became the inspiration and soundtrack for Moses's solo, entitled *Momix.*

Legend has it that when it came time for his Olympics performance, Moses wouldn't tell anyone what he was going to do, right up until showtime, and some were furious that he wouldn't tell the lighting designers, the sound or tech people, or anyone else what he needed. The assumption was that he hadn't come up with anything, down to the last moment. When the time came, he had been smoking lots of pot backstage; he was totally stoned. Costumed in white suit and panama hat, he walked onto the bare stage with a chair and a boombox, turned on the boombox, playing the "momix," and proceeded to do what appeared to be a madcap improvisation, replete with instantly repeated movements that mimicked the skip in the record. The musician Paul Sullivan, who by then had become a Pilobolus friend and sometime collaborator, was among those present. "It was so homemade, so DIY," he recalls. "It absolutely took the roof off. He was so brilliant. It was a blockbuster. Sensational." It was, to Paul, a performance that epitomized Moses's stunning inventiveness, his wild free flow of ingenuity. "He could just *go*. He was to movement what Robin Williams was like to humor and free association. Stopping was the hard part." Despite its appearance of spontaneity, however, the solo had actually been developed in advance; Danny and Jamey had worked with Moses on it in the studio and had contributed moves—yet it had a freedom to it that perhaps Moses had to be stoned in order to capture.

Beyond the brilliance of the movement, the solo owed part of its impact to the unprecedented nature of the music. Most of the audience had likely heard reggae before, but the use of very early rap gave the piece a sound that was completely new. It would not be until nearly a year later that rap music as a genre would begin to be widely popularized, triggered in part by the success of the Blondie song "Rapture" as a number one single in January 1981. At the time of that first *Momix* solo in early 1980, the Sugarhill Gang's music added greatly to the sense that Moses was presenting the audience with something strange, delightful, and unlike anything they had ever known, underscored by the comic incongruity of a white man in a white suit responding to black music—which he was neither satirizing nor appropriating, but celebrating, albeit in a bizarre and whimsical way. Because it pushed so many different buttons in so many different ways, all at once, the solo had the multiple dimensions of postmodern art.

Moses would reprise the persona of "the man in the white suit" or "the man from Momix" in various future solos, mostly improvised, and *Momix* would subsequently turn up on Pilobolus performance programs as an improv slot, experimental and often audacious, with Moses solo or accompanied by guest performer Danny, who once pulled Moses across the stage on a sled. (Alison and Jamey chided Danny afterward, saying it was beneath him as a trained dancer from the Paul Taylor company, but Danny aligned with Moses on the idea of creativity as the breaking of the old, taking risks, and risking embarrassment; Alison came around to this view, having of course introduced Moses to a less extreme version of it as his teacher a decade earlier.)

"Moses was ready to stop lifting and start dancing," Danny recalled. "*Momix* was an improv moment on the Pilobolus program in which he could move. Very Dadaist. It was an opportunity to create something new. Sometimes together, sometimes solo, just searching for how to create something new."

Within a few months of that first dynamic *Momix* piece, Moses and Alison began to apply the name Momix to the project they had cofounded, their programs of solos and duets, and thereby declare themselves a company. They premiered as Momix at the Milan Festival on June 10, 1980, at Milan's Teatro Nacional. With that launch, and Robby now more fully focused on Crowsnest (Robby had stopped choreographing with Pilobolus by the late 70s, but had still performed with them until 1980), it seemed time, after a decade of enormously hard work, to officially disband Pilobolus. They informed their agent.

Their agent, Sheldon Soffer, became apoplectic. He begged them not to throw away what they had achieved. He explained to them that they could hire dancers, and that the Pilobolus name, now known and valued, could go on. As Robby recalled, "That seemed like a ridiculous idea. Because there was this kind of one-to-one relationship. We were Pilobolus. Pilobolus was us. It wasn't dances. We didn't really see how change could happen. But we said, 'what the hell'—and we did it." The group hired five dancers: Jamey Hampton, who had been working with Pilobolus since 1978, Rob Faust, Carol Parker, Peter Pucci, and Cynthia Quinn. Together with Michael Tracy, who still wanted to perform, and who could now provide a valuable voice of experience and direction on the road, they became the Pilobolus touring company of the early 1980s.

5

In the late 1970s, Alison had gotten in touch with Paul Sullivan, a talented young musician who graduated from Yale in 1977 and played jazz in New Haven and New York. Paul went out to Stony Creek and met with her, and they soon began what would become a long and fruitful collaborative relationship, not only between Paul and Alison, but between Paul and

Pilobolus generally. The usual method was simultaneous improvisation: as Alison, or Pilobolus, would improvise movement, Paul would improvise music. In the early days of their collaboration, he would go to Stony Creek and stay over with Alison and Eric, and that became the start of something else: a warm and cherished lifelong friendship between all three.

One night, Paul and Alison were rehearsing in Moses's barn—the one he had converted into a rehearsal space—when the lights went out suddenly due to a power failure. Moses came over from across the street, to bring them each a flashlight—and, being Moses, of course he promptly went into an improv. As Paul recalled, "He did this unbelievably brilliant improv with the flashlights, and afterwards we all just had a good laugh." After Moses left, Paul and Alison spent the rest of the rehearsal, and the next few, exploring the possibilities offered by the flashlights. Alison's resulting solo, *A Miniature* (1980), performed with two flashlights in hand, would be, in the words of Arlene Croce, "a composition in swirling lights and darks, as elegantly turned as a sonnet, as turbulent as a painting by Munch." As in so many of the best Pilobolus pieces, Alison had achieved the rare alchemy by which ordinary, even lusterless ingredients fuse and reignite as radiant art.

Martha, meanwhile, continued her work with Crowsnest, even as she navigated a profound change in her personal sphere. Her life with her husband Phil had appeared idyllic, the two artists, dancer-choreographer and sculptor, sharing life on a farm; but in 1980 Martha ended the marriage, or as she later put it, "I threw myself out of Eden." She would continue to consider her ex-husband "a lovely man" but, she explained, she had been "too young to get married." Crowsnest opened its New York debut season in late May 1981 at the Public/Newman Theater, and a one-hour film that depicts her work on it, *Martha Clarke Light and Dark*, was screened at the theater as well. The filmmaker Joyce Chopra had approached Martha with the project, intrigued by a new beginning for Martha at age thirty-two, and intrigued too by Martha's willingness to walk away from something so successful as Pilobolus had been. It was, as Martha later said with a laugh, like someone "walking off a successful sailboat onto a dinghy." Conceived as a meditative evocation of a year in the life of an artist, *Light and Dark* consists of a delicately constructed sequence of glimpses into Martha's creative process as she develops and rehearses Crowsnest pieces, with only a few telling traces of the life around it: early on, there is a brief, hilarious comic improv as Martha feeds her horse, and later a quiet, touching scene in which we observe her and her son David together in Paris. With only the most minimal narration or guidance for the viewer, in its restraint it captures a quiet sense of life unfolding, and succeeds as a work of art itself, an artful microcosm of the work it documents.

As for Crowsnest, it represented, in the words of Jamey Hampton, "the deepest integrity, flawlessly expressed." He considered Robby and Martha "a fantastic collaboration" and of Martha he says: "There is a bravery in her that is not based on trying to be outrageous." Jamey experienced the company from the inside when he filled in for Robby on a number of occasions, and once for Félix; and he would never forget the profound pleasure of dancing with Martha. "Her entire body emanated wavelengths of energy and power that I've never felt from anyone else. Every gesture had a meaning behind it."

6

In June 1981, Pilobolus returned to the studio to create a new piece for that summer's American Dance Festival, commissioned again by the ever-supportive Charlie Reinhart. The assignment had been given to Moses to oversee its making, with none of the other founders involved except Michael, who remained in the touring company and in this case participated as a dancer. The process was to take place at Moses's mansion, or rather his nearby studio.

On the first day of work—referred to, in terms of the rehearsal calendar, as "Day One"—Jamey Hampton brought into the studio *My Life in the Bush of Ghosts,* the album by Brian Eno and David Byrne that had been released in February. With its embrace of African and Middle Eastern rhythms, it appeared to be a follow-up to *Remain in Light,* the exciting Afrobeat-influenced album that Eno and Byrne had made with Talking Heads and released only a few months earlier, but in reality *My Life in the Bush of Ghosts* had been recorded first, and delayed due to the legal clearances necessitated by its prominent and at that time unconventional use of sampled vocals. In its sensibility and many of its experiments it had set the stage for the polyrhythmic compositions of *Remain in Light,* and the freshness of both albums inspired many musicians and artists at the time. On Day One, however, the Pilobolus dancers improvised to no real effect; despite their fervent efforts, the day yielded nothing useful. On Day Two, however, things would change.

A package had arrived in Washington Depot that contained a teddy bear, sent by a guitar builder in Portland, Oregon, Jamey's hometown. This was the second teddy bear he had sent, having also sent one a year earlier. Jamey had asked him to send this one because he knew that he and his colleagues were going into rehearsal. It wasn't that he felt stuffed toys were in themselves particularly good luck, but this teddy bear had a hole in its butt, and if you squeezed it you could get it to "poop out" its contraband contents: gelatin capsules filled with powdered psilocybin mushrooms.

The next day began early, in Moses's kitchen. Humbert Camerlo, a director with the Paris Opera whose *Integrale Erik Satie* Moses had choreographed two years earlier, made a mushroom tea that he, Moses, Danny Ezralow, and John Job, an assistant and collaborator of Moses's, all imbibed. A storm was coming, and not just a metaphorical or hallucinogenic one. Soon it would be 80 degrees and raining, with what Moses described as "a very violent and incredibly energetic thunderstorm." The thunder, lightning, and downpour—the storm directly overhead—and the extraordinarily intense tea, would all conspire. First, Danny ran naked into the hedged-in garden and started to improvise in the warm rain. He came back and as he sat with Moses, telling him that he should try it too, Jamey came over from the studio, looking for them—he and the other dancers were wondering where they were—and he drank the tea. Soon, Danny and Jamey ran across the street naked and looked in the window of the studio. One by one, starting with Rob Faust, they all came over, the numbers at the studio dwindling. Those who wished to do so imbibed the tea, but there were several who chose not to. Everyone got naked. By some accounts those who had taken the mushrooms jumped out a window—they were on the first floor—and those who hadn't done so followed by walking out the door. As Moses explained, "Some of us felt like taking off our clothes and going out into the rain . . . We went out and began to play in it, and that was contagious."

Moses went out and, legend has it, stood on one leg for an hour and upon his return declared that he had been struck by lightning. By another account, while he kneeled on the ground "a bolt of lightning hit so close . . . that his wild hair stood on end and he levitated for several seconds." Others improvised in the garden. Rob Faust and Jamey Hampton wrestled Greco-Roman style in the mud, which became an inviting proposition for others, and while the men were in the mud, the women, Carol and Cynthia, kicked water down from the roof onto them. Eventually the full company was, in Moses's phrase, "out running around in the rain and performing this kind of New Guinean mud-men and -women ritual" as a different kind of thunder emanated from the high-ceilinged mansion, the polyrhythmic thunder of Brian Eno, David Byrne, and Talking Heads, blasted into the atmosphere and the ever-morphing landscape. The rain, visions, and revelry cascaded onward for a few hours, as, in Jamey's words, "the boundaries of what you thought was possible were melting."

Jamey later recalled that while he and Rob were wrestling, with a pool of sweat beneath them, Rob knocked Jamey down and Jamey slid about four feet. They had an idea! They got water, then shampoo or dishwashing liquid—the then-popular brand name Prell arises here—and poured it on the hardwood floor in the studio and experimented with sliding. They didn't realize how much sand and grit their feet had accumulated from the dirt road that led to the studio, nor did they realize how much sand and grit they were sliding in. The next day their bodies were inflamed—but though the slides had painful consequences in the short term, they were destined for a joyful future.

The rain ended in the early afternoon and, as Danny recalled with pleasure, "We sat like lions in the sun, this outrageous day until the sun went down. An explosion of a ritual of life." The vibe continued for weeks. The group began to refer to itself as The Tribe, and Danny, Jamey, and Moses even had a "tribal greeting" in a secret language of their own that meant "get honest" about being "physically grounded" (a sensibility tied to the use of mushrooms). They and the other dancers worked to re-create the best images and ideas generated during the storm, improvising, revising, and adding others, such as a kneeling-bowing sequence invented on a subsequent evening. Danny recalls developing the "slides" with Jamey on the last weekend of June, using soap and sliding with Jamey in the studio with Moses watching. The image of the women on the roof, kicking water down onto the men, had an effect on the finished piece, too, as Jamey explained: "That's why the women were angelic, exalted, and the men were animal, menial." The piece's working title, *Day Two*, eventually became its official title, its private reference to the second day of rehearsal wrapped within a public reference to the second day of Creation. (In this, Pilobolus took some artistic license. As those familiar with the Book of Genesis know, the Biblical "Day Two" saw the creation of the sky and heavens, not of creatures—the latter occurred on days five and six. Still, the piece does begin and end with the roar of thunder, the sky as it pours forth, and so evokes both the creation myth and the contemporary thunderstorm caught up together in the work.)

First: the sound of a thunderstorm, with the stage in darkness. Six dancers, near-naked, leap into view as the song "Houses in Motion" by Talking Heads bursts into our consciousness: the dancers hop, arms spread like wings, suggesting some kind of nonhuman creatures, a full Pilobolus sextet walking and hopping in various ways through an opening sequence mostly about motion itself. The song fades, the two women exit, and the four men align in a row, seated on the stage with their legs tucked under them, a seated kneeling posture. They begin a series of bowing, rising, falling, praying movements with outstretched arms and almost spasmodic motions that suggests, as does the music, a cross between devotees in a Middle Eastern setting and a surreal vision of mystical fervor, not as parody, travesty, or blasphemy, but rather a tapping into this energy. The men tilt far backward, they make faster and faster up-and-down motions that verge on frenzy; when the music segues into the next sequence, the women return, their arms in the angular pose of Egyptian hieroglyphics; the men watch the two women dance in what seems to be a tribal rite. Eventually, four dancers exit and the two remaining dancers, one male and one female, become a single entity, the female perched around the male's shoulders and head, her back blocking the audience's view of his face; they are a new kind of creature. A second such creature walks onstage, a third cartwheels past in the background. This is a major moment, not only in the piece, but in Pilobolus: from the group's original combination of bodies for effects of leverages and weight-sharing, through its combination of bodies for visual evocations consistent with the dynamics of mime (the joust in *Monkshood,* for example, or the giantesses of *Untitled*), to the Chase-Pendleton lovers duets (*Alraune* and *Shizen*) in which the combinations represent a physical and spiritual merging, a path can be seen that now leads to this logical artistic culmination. In *Day Two,* the Pilobolus art of combined-bodies-for-effect blossoms into an entire population of creatures, the definitive signature to the troupe's aesthetic.

As soon as these creatures are onstage, a panorama of unconventional partnering ensues as the three pairs of dancers change shapes, but each pair of partners remains intensely connected, their bodies linked in ways that suggest various movements or metamorphoses of an evolving creature. At one point each of two standing male dancers, with one arm raised, holds his female partner aloft by the base of the spine in a nearly vertical position as if the partner is standing in midair; the two women move from this position onto their partners' shoulders and now we see these two "creatures" of double height (each made of two persons) dancing while a pair of men in the background perform in other linked combinations and variations as a third two-person creature.

Throughout subsequent changes of music and mood, the full sextet at times separate to stand as individuals, at times work with horizontal poles on which some are lifted in various ways, and at times again become three pairs of partners in various combinations. Eventually one male dancer faces us, as he stands balanced on the soles of another male dancer's feet (the supporting dancer is flat on his back with his legs extended straight up). The standing, balanced dancer slowly lifts and lowers his arms like a creature discovering wings. This is followed by a sequence of leapfrogging motions in darker lighting that suggests night.

The figures have vanished. The "ground" begins to heave; a sense created by the tremors of the marley on which the dancers had been performing, and out from under which they arise, in an image of dramatic rebirth. The sextet emerges from almost total darkness, all six standing, their arms raised above them and crossed, slowly moving—then they disperse in slow motion and segue yet again into more of the unconventional partnering, strange poses, inversions—and walk into the distance as three winged creatures, their arms slowly rising and lowering. Darkness. Applause, sustained applause, as the audience responds to the piece's epic, transcendent energies—and then, suddenly, explosively, joyously, the most unexpected of encores: the sliding across the stage of the dancers, over a slippery thin layer of water, to exuberantly rhythmic music. These are their "bows" and they clown, spin, splash, and explode the evening's program into a final effusion of gleeful vitality.

Those closing slides were, as Anna Kisselgoff observed, "the curtain call to end all curtain calls" and they would become an audience favorite and a lasting company tradition. Over the years "the slides" (as they are known in Pilobolus) acquired added layers of meaning for insiders: the arrival of a new baby in the life of a dancer or veteran dancer could occasion a joyful slide, with baby in lap; and in later decades, the closing night of a summer season in New York would always end with *Day Two* and a raucous round of slides that all members of the Pilobolus team, including nondancers, were welcome to join, to celebrate the successful run.

Day Two in retrospect is the bookend to the company's first decade of existence, the era in which Pilobolus created and defined itself, and earned a place in the history of modern dance and theatre. A logical outgrowth of earlier Pilobolus works, it connects back, on a deep level, to Moses's earlier experiences in San Francisco and his embrace of the counterculture ideals of that time. It conveys the sense of nudity as freedom, of sexual energy as the life force, and of physical naturalness as the vital birthright of the human body. Yet its wild spirit is channeled into segments that flow together into a perfect sequence guided by a compositional aesthetic that seemed to move Pilobolus a step forward. The highly original music—drawn not only from Talking Heads' *Remain in Light* and Byrne and Eno's *My Life in the Bush of Ghosts*, but also from Eno's critically acclaimed *Another Green World*, released a few years earlier—is integral to *Day Two*'s energy and dynamism (and, in a fitting reciprocity, the success of *Day Two* as a lasting repertory piece has served as an ongoing reminder of the music's durability through the decades, and a magnificent showcase for it).

In an interview taped at the American Dance Festival at the time of *Day Two*'s premiere, Moses stated that the piece was "built around the physical and mental capabilities" of the new dancers, "new people who can do different things and beautiful things." It benefited too from David M. Chapman's subtle and evocative lighting, and from a certain serendipity that seemed to bless it from the beginning. At its American Dance Festival premiere on July 23, 1981, the sound of the thunderstorm at the end of the piece was so strong that everyone thought the theater's sound system was extraordinary. Afterward, when the stage doors were opened, it became apparent that the audience had been hearing something far more powerful than a good sound system: a heavy rainstorm, an absolute downpour, outside the theater. A case of Creation applauding creation.

7

Moses Pendleton Presents Moses Pendleton, a 1982 film by Robert Elfstrom and Lucy Hilmer, features Moses contemplating life on his thirty-third birthday, in late March. The breathtaking artistic high point comes thirty-seven minutes in, with a powerful performance by Moses and Alison of their Pilobolus duet *Shizen*. Impeccably filmed, it's a gift to posterity, a performance for the ages.

But the one-hour film is mostly a self-portrait in which Moses explicates his own identity in various ways: he talks about himself in the third person as a character, and in the first person in moments of sometimes painful, sometimes playful candor. We are told that "rehearsing a major motion picture was his fantasy" for his birthday. To "explain" what Pilobolus is, he turns on an old television and we see a very brief black and white clip of *Monkshood's Farewell*. To the subsequent question "And who is Moses Pendleton?" Moses answers: "In 1978 he was holding up 300 pounds and screaming like crazy that it was hurting his neck." He then adds that in 1980, he is Momix, which is the name of "that man in the white suit" who is "not just a dancer, he is a performer." (We see a photo of him in character, from his solo *Momix,* then a performance clip.)

Just as we begin to wonder if we're watching a portrait of someone a little too easily amused by his own thoughts, a bit self-obsessed, we see Moses wander upstairs to look at old clippings in an empty room, as his voiceover—now speaking in the first person and without affectation—delivers an unforced, unfussy, and heartbreaking brief monologue. "My father you see he was the romantic you might say," he begins, telling us that his father was a ladies' man but his life took a tragic turn, and he somehow ended up "badly burned on seventy-five percent of his body which disfigured this man." His father was nursed by the woman who would become his wife, and he went to northern Vermont where he created a farm and lived a "fantastic" life with his wife and six kids—until one summer day "during the middle of haying season" he committed suicide with no warning. Of his mother he says, "I witnessed her disintegration into madness and [she] died four or five years after that with cancer."

As the film continues, we again and again see the mind of the artist-showman in, for example, his view of the mansion around him as a tool for both self-exploration and storytelling ("This house is the ultimate costume for me, it's one of my best costumes I think"), the shrewdness mingled into his eccentricities ("It's good business for me to remain somewhat a kind of a crazy man"), the slightly unsettling obsession with relentlessly tape-recording his own words, which begs the question: Where are the demarcations between the artistic, narcissistic, and therapeutic? Yet his warmth, his sense of humor and of "making fun" (even if often simply goofy), his quirky but quietly valiant project of working through the tragedies of his parents' lives and his tragic early loss of them, the desperate need for "balance" (the mental version of which he seems able to achieve through constant physical movement), his psychological imperative to make sense of life by making sense of the past: all of these lead us to admire the complex "character" placed before us, and to take him at his word when, late in the film, he tells us, "These things that I've kind of run away from, they no longer scare me." With a last-minute surprise and the delirious "birthday dance" finale set to Soft Cell's "Tainted Love" (with Moses again joined by Alison, alongside Danny Ezralow), we realize that he has concocted a brilliant, life-affirming film.

The recovery that led to that life-affirmation was earned. As Danny recalled, in the early 1980s "Moses was working out the trauma of his childhood with therapy. I felt a great deal of compassion for him. This [the making of the film] was going on at the same time. *Moses Pendleton Presents Moses Pendleton* became a kind of dialogue of the self."

That same winter of 1982, a year that would see a number of productions of Richard Wagner's *Parsifal* timed to the opera's centennial, Rolf Liebermann, who had run the Paris Opéra for seven years, staged a futuristic production for the Grand Théâtre de Genève. Jane Kramer, writing in the *New Yorker*, called it "lavish and improbable" but also "important" and "a mirror of its own moment" and noted that in one portion of this unconventional staging, Parsifal "stumbles into" a nuclear reactor "discovering the naked Moses Pendleton and Alison Chase, two dancers of astonishing talent and ingenuity who are stamen and pistil in a ritual dance that, alas, has nothing to do with the opera."

Whatever the critical assessment of Moses and Alison's contribution to *Parsifal,* their sojourn in Geneva would become their final act. In private, they had reached a crisis point, and Alison, still deeply committed to her husband Eric, made a choice. Her relationship with Moses, and their artistic partnership with it, was over.

SIX

Reinventions

1

Winter 1983. The phone rang in Martha Clarke's home, a house that had earlier belonged to the surrealist painter Arshile Gorky. The caller, Lyn Austin, of the Music Theater Group, needed an idea for an NEA application; Martha told her to give her ten minutes, then turned to her large personal library, where, for her, the history of art is a playground, her bookshelves a combination divining rod and muse. "I kind of skimmed down my books," she later explained. She spotted Hieronymus Bosch, called Lyn back, and proposed *The Garden of Earthly Delights*. They didn't get the grant but did proceed with a production, thanks to Pierre Cardin and the Lenox Arts Center/Music Theater Group (for many years to come, as long as she lived, Lyn would remain Martha's most unfailing patron, saint, and patron saint). Soon the room that had been Gorky's studio, with its high ceilings and history, would become the workspace in which Bosch's angels and demons would be teased into a new existence by Martha and the nine other performers she assembled—six dancers, including her Crowsnest comrades, and three musicians—and composer Richard Peaslee.

Her spontaneous choice of subject matter may have seemed purely intuitive, but Bosch's famous triptych, its panels devoted to the Creation, earthly pleasures, and the torments of eternal damnation, encompassed a diverse yet unified range of material (lyrical, sensual, beautiful, bizarre, grotesque) filled with possibilities ripe for adaptation to Martha's tastes. Wrapped in ambiguity for more than half a millennium, its maker's intentions a matter of perpetual speculation, the triptych offered both a cornucopia of image-driven ideas and *carte blanche* as to what to do with them. What's more, Bosch and other medieval influences had been at the heart of *Monkshood's Farewell* nearly a decade earlier, one of the greatest successes of Martha's years with Pilobolus. Robby, for whom *Monkshood* had been one of the happiest of collaborative experiences, would be among her collaborators on this piece as well. And with phantasmagorical creatures among the *dramatis personae,* Martha could realize a longtime dream: "I wanted to be Chagall's bride, flying in the air with a load of lilacs. And when I decided to do the Bosch, I thought, 'Oh my God, I've always wanted to fly; this is the perfect show,' because they're angels, they're demons, they're devils." Despite her troublesome back, she and some of the others in the cast would indeed fly out over the audience, with the aid of wires and harnesses.

She set about interweaving the erotic and the crude, the nightmarish and the comic, the divine and the infernal, into what would become one of her signature works. Amid the triptych's three sections she inserted a fourth, the Seven Deadly Sins. She worked on the logistics of flight, and the role of musicians as performers integrated into the action onstage. For her own role, she chose to play, with both droll wit and seething silent fury, the serpent, carried onstage by Robby to confront Adam and Eve and pull an apple from her crotch.

Unveiled off-Broadway in the spring of 1984 at St. Clement's Church, *The Garden of Earthly Delights* stunned and delighted audiences with its intensity, as well as its successful blend of disparate elements of dance, theatre, and visual tableaux, combined with disparate moods and effects. Crowsnest had enabled Martha's artistic growth through an experimental variation on the kind of work she had done with Pilobolus, but *Earthly Delights* represented a greater blossoming of all that she had nurtured for years: her knowledge as an art lover and avid reader, as a dancer, choreographer, director, and conceiver of comic and dramatic performance art. The cumulative effect, as fresh as if a new art form had been discovered, elicited raves.

"The evening becomes a flight of fancy," wrote *New York Times* critic Mel Gussow, "as actor-dancers are borne aloft, swirling in seraphic patterns. With the agility of aerialists, they appear to levitate, performing cartwheels in space." For those who cherished Martha's own gifts as a performer, not least among the show's virtues was her electrifying personification of evil, on a knife-edge between play and profundity: to watch her in the show's final moments is to know that anger, hatred, and contempt are the seeds of true evil, as they boil over into their—and the serpent's—impalement by a cello.

In private, the show's darker elements, including her own performance, had derived from a tortuous wellspring: "I was having a desperately hard love affair at the time," she would later explain. The "turmoil" had seeped into her work, making it, in her view, "quite autobiographical." That unhappy love affair had been with the artist Robert Parker, seventeen years her senior, and had lasted through the three years leading up to *Garden of Earthly Delights;* they had lived together, in what Parker later called "a very cataclysmic, tense relationship," yet however painful it had been, Martha had felt she needed to go through it, to experience it.

2

Summer 1983. A young woman from Missouri, who had seen Pilobolus on PBS's *Dance in America* and signed up for a workshop with them, arrived at Club Hall and saw the five artistic directors (Moses, Robby, Alison, Michael, and Jonathan) seated in a row on folded chairs, in dark sunglasses, their faces impassive. She found the vision so intimidating and downright "creepy looking" that she hesitated, considered leaving, and almost turned around and left. She had traveled a thousand miles, with the incentive that comes from a powerful dream and the intuition that she must gravitate toward the energies that drew her, so she overcame her fear and decided to stay—to later discover that those initially daunting figures had put on their sunglasses and stoicism for a simple, un-creepy reason: blindingly bright sunlight streaming into Club Hall from the direction they had been facing. In her four-week workshop with the five directors, she had the opportunity to work with each and found it to be a great experience, even if she was a little taken aback that Moses, still blithely unconcerned by social norms even in the Reagan 80s, always wanted everyone, regardless of gender, to take their tops off ("Well, let's all take our shirts off," he would declare with nutty nonchalance, an instruction she chose not to follow). She was already twenty-seven, but she had delayed her college education and had another year left. Robby liked her, and told her to stay in touch. Her name was Jude Woodcock Sante—that last name, her married name, was pronounced like the French word for health, *santé*—and after she had completed her final year of college she returned, the following summer, to take the workshop again.

Right after her second workshop a sudden and unexpected chance to audition came up. Cynthia Quinn, who had joined Pilobolus in 1980, had decided to leave Pilobolus to be exclusively with Moses full time, both personally and professionally. An audition to replace her was held at Moses's barn. It was still the summer of 1984; the second workshop had just finished, but Jude had sprained her ankle. She auditioned anyway. The ankle was not as bad as she had first thought. Carol Parker had rounded up a few others to audition, but there were only eight total. Jude got the job very fast—that night—and has always suspected that they invited a few others to audition so they could say they'd had an audition, but that they had known they wanted to hire her. She took over Cynthia's roles, with Cynthia's help, and Carol Parker and Peter Pucci mentored her on how to be a professional dancer, how to carry herself on the road, and, in her words, "how to represent the company as it should be represented."

The company she joined had undergone a profound realignment. The transition to a second generation of Pilobolus dancers had been bumpy, especially once the stage contained more new dancers than founding members. Just as the replacement of original members of rock bands often met with resistance from longtime fans, to some observers this was no longer the "real" Pilobolus. There had been, too, a few fumbles along the way, among them a 1982 television special produced by CBS Cable, *Pilobolus on Broadway*, which, contrary to its title, was filmed in a television studio with no audience. Rife with bad choices, the show committed its worst sins in its second half, with a disastrous remake of *Day Two* in which the music of Talking Heads and Brian Eno had been replaced by a lifeless alternative score—one that started with feeble, ersatz disco (in place of the spectacular "Houses in Motion") and only grew worse as the elevator music descended to lower levels. At its end, the beloved closing sequence of slides across the stage lost all joy as well, accompanied not by music but instead subjected to "zany" sound effects. The fortunate thing about forgettable shows, however, is that by definition they tend to get forgotten, as this one did.

Pilobolus had weathered bad reviews and pressed onward. It also had to weather another conundrum common to rock bands: the questions of crediting, ownership, and work for hire. When new dancers joined Pilobolus, unlike in most other dance companies, they participated in the choreographic process. They were not hired merely to perform but to contribute ideas, to improvise new material from which the directors would select as the group built new pieces, and in some instances the contributions of the dancers could grow larger than that of the directors. Yet the new dancers, while credited as collaborators, did not share ownership of the work and were not "Pilobolus" in the same way the founding members had been. All of this was initially approached, on all sides, with a casualness and naivety characteristic of the time, a recipe for conflicts that would eventually awaken the company to the need to clarify its agreements with dancers.

As for the directors, Robby had returned to active involvement with Pilobolus after six years; he had performed in *The Garden of Earthly Delights* in New York in 1984, the year after his and Susan's son Isaac was born, but he had soon answered the call of family and stopped touring. He and Alison had then made an elaborate new piece for Pilobolus, *Return to Maria La Baja,* in collaboration with Rob Faust and Lisa Giobbi. Paul Sullivan, who had moved to New York in 1981, had composed the music, and continued to work with Pilobolus. He would go up to Connecticut and jam with them; he would play, they would move.

Moses had come back to the company as well, but was in and out, more interested in his other projects. He and Alison no longer spoke to each other much, though according to Jude and other observers, Jonathan was "always the one with whom people had the most difficulty getting along." But, as Jude also noted, "In those days, the artistic directors could still talk to one another," even if somewhat selectively.

Michael was still dancing—he liked to travel, and wasn't eager to get married yet—and Jude got to partner with him quite a lot. When they toured he could be, as she put it, a bit "elusive" as he would often stay in a different hotel than the other dancers, but he "really listened when there were problems. He was very diplomatic about trying to make everyone happy." And the company was still making money. Between what Robby had earned from Crowsnest and what he and Susan made from Pilobolus, they were able to buy a house. Life, and life in Pilobolus, proceeded.

Jude had performed *Monkshood's Farewell,* first in Alison's role, then Martha's. She found Martha's role difficult, especially as it was obvious that Robby could never be satisfied with anyone in it but Martha; but she loved *Monkshood* and found it great fun to perform, even if it didn't stay in the repertory for long. She also loved *Molly's Not Dead,* a 1978 piece that had been created by the original troupe minus Martha, which had introduced what Pilobolus calls "fat gnomes": comic creatures made of two dancers, one in a kind of hunched waddle and another hanging upside-down and backward wrapped around the torso of the first dancer. The chin of the forward-facing dancer rests on the upside-down dancer's butt, while the upside-down dancer's head, bent at the neck, stays tucked out of sight (except, perhaps, for some hair hanging down suggestively between the gnome's legs). The fat gnome thus makes its way forward with the burden of a doubly thick "middle" made of both dancers' torsos. (Pilobolus had appeared on Johnny Carson's *Tonight Show* on October 29, 1981 to perform a portion of *Molly's Not Dead,* and with a brief demonstration even taught Johnny how to be a fat gnome himself.)

When it came to performing *Day Two,* of course, Jude now had to do what she had refused as a workshop participant: she had to take off her shirt. In regard to the piece's sexual sensibility, however, Cynthia told her that in the dancers' performances everything had to be understated, and that she should allow the choreography to speak for itself, as it was so sexually charged already. More challenging was the pole dance segment, which Jude found exhausting—far more strenuous than it looked. She recalled that when she had auditioned, Michael was concerned that all of the auditioning dancers try the move known as "The Big Sit" with him lifting them, because he would have to be able to do this move with them on stage. She was now learning how every move worked, and which were the most demanding.

Michael, who continued to tour with the various new dancers throughout most of the decade, would later observe that "part of what happened in the 80s was figuring out how to actually add the unique talents new dancers had into our choreography." Through their annual appearances at the American Dance Festival, their longtime advocate Charles Reinhart had an ongoing view of the difficulties of Pilobolus's transition. He knew from experience that it was nothing out of the ordinary, that it happened to all dance companies, even though each company always imagines that its struggle is unprecedented, unique to its own choreographic idiosyncrasies. Every choreographer initially creates based on that choreographer's own strengths and physical realities and those of the original dancers in any piece; therefore adjusting the work to a second generation of dancers is always a challenge, a labyrinth of problems, refinements, and puzzles to be solved.

In the studio, there was new work. In those days the dancers had big blocks of time off, three or four weeks at a time, so Jude continued to live in Missouri and Pilobolus would fly her in for studio work and tours. In 1985, Alison and Robby again partnered with Lisa Giobbi, this time to choreograph a duet, *Televisitation,* which they then set on Jude and another Pilobolus dancer, Josh Perl. Jude and Josh were the first to perform the piece and, in Alison's phrase, "put the fairy dust on it." Or perhaps an even stronger magic: the "visitation" in *Televisitation* is that of an aggressive, succubus-like female wraith who teases and torments a hapless pajama-clad male after he dozes off in front of a television. Jude's eerily comic and wondrously athletic performance enabled her to combine stylish grace and badass toughness—and it not only earned critical raves but made her something of a legend to subsequent female Pilobolus dancers. The piece was, for her, "total fun" and decades later it still resonated in both her consciousness and in her unconscious mind: "I have dreams about *Televisitation,* can I still stand on his back and still do all that. It was hair-raising. Tricky balance."

3

In the fall of 1985, Lyn Austin asked Martha to team again with composer Richard Peaslee, this time to create a piece for the fortieth anniversary of John Hersey's classic novella-length work of reportage *Hiroshima,* regarded by many as one of the finest works of American journalism, which had originally appeared in the *New Yorker* of August 31, 1946. As Martha recalled, Peaslee found the assignment daunting: "Dick came up to the house in the country and we were sitting in beautiful golden light, I'll never forget it, and he dropped his head in his hands and he said 'I don't know what the sounds of Hiroshima are.'" Not terribly committed to the subject herself, she knew to turn to her bookshelf once again, from which she pulled a volume on fin de siècle Vienna, having been entranced by an exhibition on the subject during a visit to Venice not long before. The art of Egon Schiele had been, for her, a particular revelation; having been married to a sculptor and in a relationship with a painter, she had been an artist's model, and "Schiele's nudes felt very much like my own body. I identified with the physicality, the twistedness, the angularity." She proposed the subject matter be changed to Vienna at the turn of the century, and both composer and producer readily agreed. Some weeks later, when Martha had lunch with the playwright and historian Charles Mee (to discuss a different possible project), she found him "wildly charming" and knew that together they had the kind of dynamic surprise-filled chemistry she sought in any collaboration. When she told him about her Vienna project, he declared, without being asked, that he would write it. What he wrote for her—abandoning sequence, clear characters, and conventional dialogue—were fragmentary literary texts that served as muse or mystery, invocation or evocation, to be interpreted by Martha and her actors and dancers. Martha enjoyed the process immensely and continued to use it in future collaborations with him, but in early 1986 she would also endure weeks of artistic paralysis and feelings of fraudulence, alongside a sinking sense of unease on the part of her collaborators, on the path to the show's April unveiling. By then she had chosen to omit the show's most literal historical ingredients ("The waltzes stuck out like a maraschino cherry on a steak") to focus on surreal dream imagery. In a final, severe reckoning she cut twenty minutes and consolidated the rest into the distilled, re-sequenced, and perfectly flowing essence of its own id.

Nameless figures inhabit a skewed reality of angled walls and shadows, in which monologues overlap and music becomes incrementally more ag-gressive as a culture edges toward war—and in the unspecified logic of the surreal, a naked man becomes a horse, pure whiteness becomes unnerving, soldiers continue to march even after falling onto their backs, impeccable fin-de-siècle costumes and nudity and secrets and fragments of Freud's letters and evocations of sex and death and art and militarism drift and disturb; one man recollects a vision of the Danube at its most glorious ("It rained on only one half of the river, leaving the other half and its bank in brilliant sunlight"); another performs an initially hilarious one-man mime of copulating partners, with shoes on his hands, that edges from the erotic to the sadistic; naked women confer, complicit with each other; a seated man, bare-chested, wide-eyed, obsessive-compulsive, undoes, with dis-comfiting intensity, the top of his red britches, exposing a glimpse of bright white underwear; and in a final death-scene-as-love-scene-as-death-scene (with a dying soldier) the question "What colors does a body pass through after death?" elicits a clinical "Light pink, red, light blue, dark blue, purple red" amid a soft snowfall; and the falling snow a final ingredient, final mo-tion, seems to complete, or seal away, the montage, with the elusive power of visual art.

The day before the show's opening, in an anxiety dream, Martha rode a white horse that tried to leap over a river but instead floated up like a bal-loon and burst; she stood beside its crumpled form; she awoke knowing the horse was her show—but the vision proved the opposite of prescient.

Vienna: Lusthaus inspired raves from critics and audiences; Frank Rich declared in the *New York Times* that Martha had "succeeded beyond one's wildest dreams—perhaps because she has tapped into everyone's wildest dreams." An off-Broadway hit (first at St. Clement's, then at the Public), the show then traveled to Washington, DC's Kennedy Center and onward to Houston, Los Angeles, and venues in Europe. Its impressive run solidified Martha's reputation for brilliance, further enhanced when the show won an Obie for best off-Broadway play.

In addition to its resonant historical references, "It's also about my life," Martha told the *New York Times,* and to the *Washington Post* she later added, "A lot of it is about disappointment in love." She avowed that for her, the "tenderness and complicity" of close friendships with women was "sacred" as opposed to male–female relationships wherein "there's always the struggle for dominance."

Her affair with Robert Parker had not endured, but she, and her work, would. She would weather devastating reviews of her next efforts and, later, a slow climb back to high critical esteem (and, later still, major struggles to find the financing to continue to bring her visions to the stage), but at the end of the 1980s, in the midst of the worst year of her career, Martha would win a MacArthur Foundation grant—the award colloquially known as a "Genius" grant—and through the years, now as a director and no longer a performer, there would remain for her the other, less tangible but perhaps more profound incentives for carrying on, not least to be around a certain rare breed of human: "I love their intuition, sweetness, their way of living, way of moving, way of seeing," she told *Dance* magazine years later. "Dancers have the uncanny intelligence of animals."

4

After *Day Two,* almost none of the pieces Pilobolus created in the 1980s and early 90s stayed in the long-term repertoire. It wasn't that none were good, but none were sufficiently extraordinary to eclipse the best, most revelatory, most enduring pieces from the group's first decade. Even by the mid-80s, Arlene Croce sounded wistful. In the *New Yorker* of March 18, 1985, as she reviewed Pilobolus's season at the Joyce, she praised Pilobolus at its best: "The metaphors sparkled, the acrobatics delighted, and when the metaphors were produced by the acrobatics—by the extreme extension of physical wit—Pilobolus was at a peak of expression." But, she added, "When Pilobolus loses its humor, it loses its grip on style, too." Largely dissatisfied with the newer (and darker) pieces, she recalled their "wonderful satyr plays" of the 1970s and called *Day Two* "the last of the epics of Priapean joy." Tellingly, she treated *Day Two*—at this point barely four years old—as an established classic.

All told, in its first decade Pilobolus had created more than thirty works, of which only a handful would continue to be performed through subsequent decades. What is forgotten is that approximately half of the 1970s pieces were solos; and when one also subtracts the first trio, the early quartets, and the duets, one is left with only *two* pieces that were actually made together by all six members of the famous Pilobolus of Moses, Jonathan, Robby, Alison, Martha, and Michael: *Monkshood's Farewell* and *Untitled*. The legend of Pilobolus as a troupe that did everything together—lived together, created entirely through collaboration, and functioned as a single unit—rests on its origins and the early four-man version of the group, but applied to any later configuration it contains a trace of mythmaking. Pilobolus was for the most part, to use a word Alison has used, a *collective*: six artists who worked, together and sometimes in smaller units or separately, on works that sailed into the world under a common banner. They didn't bother to define Pilobolus as any particular sort of entity until, at the end of their prolific and successful first decade, they decided to go their separate ways but then, at their manager's urging, chose to reverse course and turn Pilobolus into a dance company.

By the late 1980s they had added another dozen or more pieces to their list of creations, but the essence of what "Pilobolus" meant to critics and audiences would continue to be based on the most important earlier works, and a sensibility that had coalesced sufficiently to define the company's place in the theatrical landscape. Deborah Jowitt, another of the finest dance critics of the era, had observed Pilobolus closely from the beginning and identified its male founders as "athletic guys with Ivy League educations and brains to match, lively senses of fantasy, and lusty wits." She drew a direct line from the group's counterculture origins to its revolutionary energies, noting that the sexual candor and taboo-breaking appreciation of the human body so significant to the counterculture were "crucial" to their works; the audience, in considering the inventive configurations of the bodies onstage, inevitably considers the bodies themselves quite closely.

"With Pilobolus," she observed, "the erotic or suggestive is never far away. The shapes—beautiful or grotesque or whimsical or enigmatic—may be achieved by intimate contact; the heads against crotches, the bodies sliding together can emit fleeting images of idyllic group sex. . . . And always you get the dual image of a bunch of personable athletes *and* the fantasies that their physical skills engender . . . the visible interaction between illusion and reality."

Jude Woodcock had found her calling. She would remain in Pilobolus for ten years, from 1984 to 1994. Of her many colleagues among the dancers, some became disillusioned and dissatisfied with Pilobolus and some cherished the experience but passed through faster than she did. Jude stayed for a decade, no matter what the chaos, conflicts, or comedy around her, because she loved it and she knew that it was, for her, the achievement of a lifetime. "For me Pilobolus was something I dreamed about when I saw it on TV, and I *actually did it.* It was a monumental thing to me."

It also involved continuous growth and the overcoming of fears and insecurities. Alison, who Robby called "Queenie"—from an old joke that Alison and Martha were queen bees and the men were the drones—had, in Jude's words, "a way of pursing her lips and rolling her eyebrows and eyes up" that could unwittingly unnerve some of the dancers ("You think she hates you, or what you're doing, but she doesn't. She's a queen"). Jude came to cherish Alison, who helped shape her professional development, as did Robby. "Robby made me feel I was a *valued person,* like I was smart and I could do this." She had come from humble beginnings, with little sense of her own worth. "It took Alison and Robby saying 'You could do this!'"

Life in the studio, while perhaps not as surreal as the pieces made, had its own colorful qualities. All the directors had their little quirks. Jonathan would pull his hair. Everyone knew Robby's drug of choice was coffee; he liked the buzz of alertness, the crystal clarity. Moses would expound almost absentmindedly, his freeform imagination astonishing, while largely oblivious to social decorum; but even he was moving a step closer to life's conventions. A few days before Christmas 1985, he and Cynthia had welcomed their baby daughter into the world.

As time went on and the directors continued to ease into middle age, marriage, and parenthood, the presence of children, especially Robby's, sometimes added to the madhouse atmosphere. "Sometimes," Jude recalled, "we would have three kids in the studio at the same time, running around. [Robby's son] Isaac nearly killed his sister with a hanger. Once he tied Robby to a chair with some rope." She laughed. "It was a family affair."

If the Pilobolus "family" appeared, to outsiders, as slightly wacky and fractured, its members were smart and kind-hearted nonetheless. In 1988, the directors helped Jude deal with the break-up of her marriage, which was traumatic; they got her into therapy and were good to her. The crisis in her personal life took her out of the company for several weeks, but Pilobolus helped her through it, and in 1989, five years into her time with the company, she reached a new level of involvement. She moved to Connecticut, focused on the art, and evolved. By now she had become the senior member among the dancers. Michael, who had toured with Pilobolus for fourteen years, including eight years in the 1980s as the only director still touring, had decided to stop, so Jude ran rehearsals on the road. Directors and dancers were all still inventing their roles as they went along.

Each director had certain strengths: Alison, a feminine energy with a sense of subtlety and timing, a necessary slowing down (which, in her years of direct collaboration with Moses, had been the ideal balance to his intensity); Jonathan had an artful craziness and determination; Robby had, from Jude's point of view, "pure athleticism"; and Michael had a "very musical" or lyrical power. Their cumulative attributes were extraordinary, but they were rarely aligned; the company had become one in which the dancers received conflicting notes from the different directors, all highly opinionated. As a result, the dancers would play the pieces differently depending on which director was watching, a symptom of company dysfunction that would continue through the years. Yet even in this, Jude found a silver lining: "It did give you a kind of versatility," she recalled with a laugh.

She would forever remember with affection the directors, dancers, and friends who populated that era in her life, but the thing that would shine brightest would be the work itself: "What sticks in my head the most are the pieces I got to perform. Whenever I hear the music, my muscles start twitching. The athleticism and then the theatre on top of it. It always made sense to me. The work, the pieces. I *loved it!*"

"I was totally insecure with who I was as a dancer, but once you got out on that stage . . ."

5

In 1988, Moses created for Pilobolus a full-company piece that in retrospect seems to point the way toward his later works under the Momix name. In it, the dancers appeared behind a scrim onto which could be projected slides of various images, enhancing the range of visual possibilities open to Moses and lighting designer Neil Peter Jampolis (whose expertise, beginning with *Untitled,* had already long since become one of Pilobolus's best and most long-running secret weapons). The piece's title, *Debut C,* is a pun on the name of Claude Debussy, whose symphonic poem for orchestra *Prélude à l'après-midi d'un faune* (*Prelude to the Afternoon of a Faun*) is used in the piece, along with conspicuous references to its famous counterpart, Nijinsky's ballet *L'Après-midi d'un faune.* Watching the piece, one wonders: Epic or camp? Poem or joke? The first eight or ten minutes, the male-quartet opening section, seems like a celebration of the male physique with grandiose music and dramatic lighting, in many ways beautiful but also not far removed from the sort of masculine gay fantasy that involves near-naked muscular men flexing and posing. After a quick blackout the erotic equation flips, so to speak, to a scene centered on two females, topless and tender. Throughout the half-hour piece it remains impossible to sort parody from purposefulness, but the celebration of sensuality, and the sumptuousness of the presentation, are unmistakable. In the *New York Times,* Jennifer Dunning criticized its sophomoric elements but recognized its success at reveling in visual poetry for its own sake. Calling it "a lush light show" and "an extravaganza of a different sort for Pilobolus," she noted that *Debut C* "wavers between kitsch and dance of a straightforward, even heroic mold." She praised the subtle painterly beauty of certain segments, such as when, in one crystalline moment, "the dancers are simply splashes of white moving through a field of blue haze," and she discussed the piece's intertwining of eroticism, tenderness, and inventive humor. One year later, she would profile Moses for a feature story timed to a New York run of the newly resurgent Momix, and describe him, at forty, with "his trim haircut, scholarly eyeglasses, and intent stare" as resembling "one of Chekhov's impoverished young intellectuals." By now he had choreographed music videos for Prince ("Batdance") and Julian Lennon ("Too Late for Goodbyes"), hung out with Mick Jagger, and, more importantly, zeroed in on the difference between Pilobolus and Momix, in a formulation he would repeat to more than one interviewer: "Pilobolus uses bodies as props and Momix uses props as extra bodies."

Momix had gone through several transformations in its first decade. After using the name for his memorable 1980 solo and then reapplying it to his and Alison's touring program of solos and duets, Momix had become, after his split from Alison, a name that resided with Moses—and he had a booking as Momix that he didn't know how to fill. Seeing an opportunity, Jamey Hampton, Danny Ezralow, and two other dancers—Ashley Roland and Morleigh Steinberg—offered to go out on tour as Momix to fulfill Moses's obligations. He agreed, and the quartet began working with him in all-night sessions that would remain among Danny's most cherished memories. From the days when Danny would ride up from New York on his motorcycle and stay "at Mo's house" it soon evolved to a life in Connecticut, as he and his three colleagues abandoned their jobs and moved to the area, shared a house in the country, and worked in Moses's barn studio to become Momix.

"We would start at about eight o'clock at night working in the studio," Danny recalled. "And we all worked for about a year in that studio in the middle of the night. We'd eat dinner about three in the morning, we'd sleep 'til noon, we'd read books until three or four, we'd start warming up and go back to the studio. It was this extraordinary incubation process of creativity in movement."

Along the way, the Momix name, the word, kept getting redefined—it meant "Moses's mix" or "the mix of the moment"; it was also said to be the name of a brand of cattle feed. Moses, of course, loved to play with words, and Danny would recall Moses's friend Phil Holland sometimes being present as well, talking about the name.

For Danny it was like jazz in the instant—endless nights of improvisation in the studio.

Jamey saw Moses as "a master of his own body" who could bring something out of another person—even the greatest of dancers—that the person could never have brought out on their own. "He would be so encouraging of you to do things that were so outside your wheelhouse. He could encourage you to do something so positive. Moses was always about squeezing the most you could get out of the molecules in the air."

The group would have small showings for local friends, neighbors, and invited guests, some famous, some not, as they honed their work and identity. The four dancers, with their impressive prior training, were in some ways more confident, more polished, than many new Pilobolus dancers, but they also benefited from the example of the early Pilobolus collaborative process. The quartet aspired to, and did, make pieces that expressed a group mind, and they had Moses as a brilliant collaborator and facilitator. Danny, especially, would feel forever indebted to Moses for their deep personal connection and the abundance of what he learned from him about creativity. Soon the four friends were roaming the world, on tour as Momix, while Moses stayed in Connecticut; the quartet went everywhere for five years, in a triumphant building-up of the Momix name. On November 5, 1985, they appeared at Fashion Aid, at the Royal Albert Hall, performing for their friend and sometime sponsor, the designer Issey Miyake, with whom they had already been working prior to that appearance; he had told the *Washington Post* a year earlier, "They are like a laughing body, so happy and so free." Interestingly, in the mid-1980s—as in the November 1984 *Washington Post* article in which that quote appeared, and more strikingly in a *Los Angeles Times* profile ("Momix Finds Creativity Amid Chaos" by Donna Perlmutter) on May 8, 1986—press coverage of Momix sometimes did not mention Moses at all, as the quartet seemed to shape their own public identity and Moses appeared content to let them take over the world on his behalf. Then, suddenly, in 1987, in Torino, Italy, Moses's name appeared on the theater at a Momix show as the artistic director. It took the dancers by surprise. Jamey had been frustrated when, years earlier, *Day Two* had been credited as "directed by" Moses, the first hierarchical split between directors and dancers; now he discovered, to his dismay, that this new directorial credit signified exactly what he thought it did. Moses owned Momix, the name and every bit of the choreography, and he had determined that he needed to assert that fact, unambiguously and nonnegotiably. He was taking control.

Danny, Jamey, Ashley, and Morleigh didn't want to continue as work-for-hire employees, now that they realized that this is what, in fact, they had been for the past few years. They had, like so many other young performers, blithely enjoyed a heady run of success, and, in a free-spirited way, had not anticipated that the realities of business would intrude. With the realization that ownership of Momix was not theirs to share in, even if they felt they had co-created it, they decided to leave and form their own company, ISO. (All four would have long careers as choreographers: Jamey Hampton and Ashley Roland eventually formed BodyVox, which celebrated its twenty-fifth season in 2022; Morleigh Steinberg appeared in U2's music video for the song "With or Without You," worked with the band as a choreographer and dancer, and married guitarist Dave Evans, better known as The Edge, before cofounding the company Arcane Collective; and Danny achieved great success with his own Daniel Ezralow company and an eclectic mix of projects in film, theatre, music, and live spectacles, with such high-profile collaborators as Julie Taymor, Hal Prince, Francis Ford Coppola, and Cirque du Soleil. Because he had the deepest bond with Moses, he perceived that Moses felt devastated and abandoned, when the four friends left, and he has remained on good terms with him.)

Moses reconfigured and relaunched Momix with a greater emphasis on his own vision, circa *Debut C,* and on spectacle. On Wednesday, December 27, 1989, Momix opened a brief limited run, through the first week of January, at the Joyce Theater in Chelsea, and received a positive review from Anna Kisselgoff in the *New York Times,* who declared that it now offered "polished entertainment" with "a fresh ingenuity" and had achieved a "haunting theatricality." Its identity would continue to be increasingly sharply focused. As Moses explained decades later, "The word 'Momix' implies a certain kind of controlled nonsense and visual poetry with amazing bodies doing amazing things . . . We use props and imagery and take the human body to make connections to the nonhuman." And while it draws deep inspiration from nature, "Momix is also about escaping the so-called 'real world' to experience the surreal."

6

At the beginning of 1990, as the economic boom of the 1980s crashed into a recession, Susan Mandler, in her role as company manager, informed the directors that Pilobolus no longer had enough money to continue. With what little money they had, they continued to pay Susan and the dancers and paid for their office space, but the directors went without paychecks, and went on unemployment. During the several months in which they had to regularly stand in line at the unemployment office in Danbury, Connecticut, to collect their checks, their unwelcome, humbling new reality prompted them to question their choices, their futures, and the prospects for the survival of Pilobolus. They had all, independently, engaged in various side projects, teaching and choreographing for other organizations. They decided that perhaps if they stopped freelancing as individuals and instead allowed themselves to be hired for special projects only through Pilobolus as an organization, they could boost, or at least stabilize, the company's fortunes. In essence, the idea was to go "all for one" and, if it worked, as employees of Pilobolus they would each get a paycheck, perhaps modest but sufficient to live on. In order for it to work, however, everyone had to be either "all in" or completely out, and Moses, for whom Momix had become a profitable business, had already long since rebuffed any suggestion of bringing Momix under the Pilobolus name. It was his, it made money, and he couldn't reasonably be expected to incorporate it, and its profits, into the Pilobolus group venture. The new plan for Pilobolus was therefore, in effect, a future without Moses.

The split proved to be not too bitter, with Moses taking with him most of the works he had made in the 1980s but leaving the more thoroughly Pilobolus-branded pieces—the collaborative works of the 1970s, his duets with Alison, and, most importantly, *Day Two*—in the Pilobolus repertoire. He would still come by the studio and work on his Pilobolus pieces, especially *Day Two*, when they were being rehearsed. But now Pilobolus was officially down to four directors.

In another part of their effort to save the company, the foursome divvied up the administrative duties in ways that made sense: Alison, still the inspiring teacher, handled the educational programs; Robby, ever-logical (and married to the company manager) handled the touring; Jonathan, still the energetic entrepreneur, initiated new efforts at fundraising; and Michael handled commercial and corporate-sponsored projects—but he would later say of all their efforts in this phase, "It didn't work. We were just reshuffling the same cards." It's true; Pilobolus had fundamental difficulties that were yet to be resolved. Still, their new efforts helped for a while, and got them through the short-term crisis. And while most of the new works Pilobolus created in the 1980s and early 90s did not stay in the active repertoire, it did in those years accomplish something as miraculous as it had in its first decade, though less conspicuous. Despite the departure of two of its most inventive original members, it had turned itself from a collective of a half-dozen remarkable performing artists into a dance-theatre company that continued to employ dancers, create new work, keep earlier works alive, and tour the world—a company that could perpetuate its identity; a company that had endured for nearly a quarter-century and had made its way into the dance history books. It was a company that young performers dreamed of joining.

PART TWO

SEVEN

Among the Gnomen

1

A night in early fall, 1996. New York's Upper West Side. On a bench a man sleeps: a young man, twenty-four, compact but with a well-developed, muscular build; long, curly black hair; an earring in one ear. The night is not particularly cold, but it's a little chilly for a Georgia boy, which he is, having traveled to the city on his way to his new job. He had arranged to stay overnight with New York acquaintances and then ride up to rural Connecticut the next day with two of the other dancers (how strange to think that he was now a dancer), but the people he was supposed to stay with weren't there when he had arrived, and with no place to stay, and no way to reach anyone, he had opted for a bench. It didn't really seem that dangerous. After all, he knew martial arts; he had a third-degree black belt. And, too, he had a knife in his pocket.

His defiance of danger had started in the womb. A black widow spider had bitten his mother when she was thirteen weeks pregnant; doctors had thought it unsafe for her to continue to term, but she had insisted. As she lay in a hospital bed after the delivery, she had overheard medical personnel speaking in astonishment about one of the newborns in the nursery (this was the early 1970s, when mothers and their infants were not always immediately placed together). She wasn't sure what they were saying. What was it, she asked, and someone explained: one of the newborns, a boy, had flipped himself over in the incubator, a feat that babies aren't normally able to accomplish so soon. It of course turned out it was *her* baby. His name was John Matheson Kent, but he would always be called Matt, and his ability to astonish onlookers would be an ongoing trait.

He grew up in the suburbs of Atlanta, in the kind of suburbs that have a greener, more rural feel than some, a "preacher's kid"—his father was a Methodist minister—but Matt wasn't really conscious of it at the time. He was a hyperactive child and naturally interested in physical activities, like soccer. His parents divorced when he was in second grade, and he felt they explained it to him well, it made sense; he never found it traumatic. For what some people used to call "a broken home," their home never felt particularly broken to him. Still, at around twelve he went into therapy, simply because he "thought" a lot; that is, he was seen as pensive and perhaps "too sensitive." The therapist, licensed in hypnotherapy, mostly listened; Matt did try hypnosis several times and enjoyed the trance-like state, but even as a kid he saw it as something he could do on his own, a state of relaxed concentration like meditation. What mattered more was the talking and listening. He ended up having a very good long-term relationship with the therapist. It gave him the tools to deal with things.

He could also sit at the piano and invent. He clearly had musical ability, and during these middle school years he started playing bass. He had had an extremely creative fourth grade teacher who played the bass and was a huge influence; Matt would stay after school to help him. When Matt chose the bass as his own instrument he did not think about the fact that he had picked an instrument that was kinetic and large, the size of a body. Only in retrospect would that fit, like a puzzle-piece, into a larger story.

At fourteen he discovered another art. His mom ran a small business making signs, and one of her employees, Greg, had a book of poetry by someone named Stephen K. Hayes. Hayes had been an actor, and had based the poetry on his experience of going to Japan and discovering the martial art Ninjutsu. The book and its subject intrigued Matt and his mom, and when they found out that Greg not only had the book but was also a member of a local dojo devoted to Ninjutsu, mother and son went there to check it out. Matt was immediately taken with the experience, seeing how much fun everyone was having: "It was like boys wrestling, but being instructed how to do it better. It was the only thing I'd met in my life that made me feel like 'Yeah, I'm doing this!'"

The master of the dojo was Bud Malmstrom, a man then in his late thirties and, to Matt, "good-looking in a biker way." He wore jeans and a t-shirt, but not a leather jacket; he was short but had "that air about his posture that you wouldn't mess with him," very fit with broad shoulders, a former Marine. Dark hair and a moustache. Perhaps because his wife was there as well, to Matt and his mom "It felt like family right from the beginning." With martial arts, Matt now felt he had a way "to connect what's going on in my head with what's going on in my body."

He had always loved school but in middle school that had reversed, and he hated high school. He would say blunt or "provocative" things that challenged others' egos and assumptions, even if they were adults. Sometimes sarcastic but not belligerent, he would point out that someone was wrong, and he got into fights based on social injustices: "If a kid insulted a girl . . . I didn't walk away from situations that I probably should have walked away from."

"I thought that high school was a scam. I hated the system of it. I didn't go to the graduation. I was a really smart kid who occasionally got in fights."

Matt's younger brother Scott went to a military high school and Matt considered switching to it, but his own school had an unusually good young drama teacher, and the quality of the theatre program kept him from dropping out. He did a lot of acting and got a private teacher for the bass. Between martial arts, acting, and playing the bass, he was collecting his talents.

At the University of Georgia he chose music therapy as his major, because he liked psychology and had been in therapy to good benefit. Still, he didn't want to be too focused. He would study lots of different things, on the theory that "then you're going to get lucky and find something that works." His mom continued to be his sounding board, their bond "intimate and deep and honest, an authentic connection. She was very supportive of everything I was doing. It was like the term 'we grew up together.' She loved all of the new age and martial arts stuff." Having identified and gathered his talents in high school, in college he was asking himself how to put them to good use. Now clearly an arts person, he was ready to make something.

One of his high school theatre friends, a girl named Ashley Sowell, was also at University of Georgia, though it being such a large school they didn't see each other much at first. By the time they were sophomores, however, Ashley—a tall brunette with brown eyes, full lips, perfect posture, and "great arches"—was taking a modern dance class and told Matt to come see it. When he did he felt an immediate connection, particularly to the idiosyncratic instructor, a woman who had renamed herself Bala Sarasvati and who found Matt's background in martial arts intriguing.

Bala, then in her forties, very petite, was not foreign but had taken on the name and had a look that seemed Indian or, by the standards of the time and place, "exotic." Teeny but a bundle of energy, her mind always seemed to be racing. She had lived and danced in New York in the 1980s, in the downtown CBGB-influenced scene where a punk approach to art-making prevailed, but she was also the classic new age crystal-oriented person who calls a spiritual advisor and had read all the Shirley MacLaine books. Bala had an instant kinship with Matt and asked him to collaborate on a dance piece based on martial arts. It would be the beginning of a weird but loving (though nonamorous) relationship: Bala liked to introduce Matt to others as her son from a previous lifetime.

As Matt got involved in dance he gradually became the unofficial star of the dance department without ever joining it or making dance his major. It seemed everyone, including faculty, wanted him in their productions. For example, in Bala's later avant-garde creation *Journey to the Hindbrain,* one of her most popular pieces at the time, Matt stood out dramatically, with a long ponytail and wearing black biker shorts, and with much use made of his physicality.

One day Ashley told him to go to the college library and look up, on videotape, an old episode of the PBS television series *Dance in America* featuring a troupe called Pilobolus. He did, and the following year, when Pilobolus came to Atlanta, Matt saw them perform live. The program consisted of an intense male quartet, *The Particle Zoo,* the women's duet entitled *Duet 92,* the solo from *The Empty Suitor,* and, for the second half, a long piece inspired by James Joyce, entitled *Rejoyce.* Matt was already happily familiar with Joyce, which gave the piece an added appeal; but while he responded to the physicality and humor of Pilobolus—and it suggested to him that he could make similar kinds of work—the thought that he might ever be in the company, or particularly want to be, did not occur to him. Something else, however, did. That sophomore year, seated in a dining hall surrounded by dancers, Matt realized while talking to Ashley that he liked her, that they could become boyfriend and girlfriend, that *this could work;* a deeply pleasing realization; a glowing moment; and they did.

Despite having no conscious ambitions to become a dancer, the appeal of Pilobolus was sufficient that in the summer of 1995, after his junior year, Matt, Ashley, and two other girls (one of whom would later marry Matt's brother) drove a van from Athens, Georgia to Maine to take a Pilobolus summer workshop taught by Jonathan Wolken.

"I met Jonathan and instantly had a connection." Matt listened but also argued with him in a way that others would not have dared. Right from the beginning there were "elements of antagonism that we both enjoyed. We would sort of spar, but it was all positive." During the workshop week, one morning as Jonathan was having breakfast in a diner, he spotted Matt walking by and waved him in, and asked him if he might ever consider "doing this for a living." The idea had never occurred to Matt, and he let the moment, which in any case wasn't a concrete offer, pass by.

Back in college, months later—in the late spring of 1996—an audition announcement from Pilobolus arrived in the mail to the dance department. It was promptly thrown away. One of the dancers, however, found it in the trash, and put it on the bulletin board, thinking that perhaps Matt might be interested. Matt saw it and took it off the board, saying he thought it would be cool to audition but that he couldn't afford the ticket to New York.

The next day, Ashley approached him. By this time their lengthy college romance had ended, with the two of them remaining dear and enduring friends, so it was in a characteristically matter-of-fact way that she presented him with the surprise gift she had bought. She placed the ticket in his hand: *Here, you're going to New York.*

2

What am I doing here? he thought as he looked around, surrounded by over a hundred male dancers putting on tights and dance gear. Yet here he was, at the Joyce Theater in Chelsea, where the auditions, which were for male dancers only, would take place over the course of three days. New York was early-summer hot, but it wasn't bad: moderate summer weather. By networking through his martial arts connections, Matt had been able to find a place to stay, at the apartment of a woman who belonged to a dojo in New York. He went to the auditions by day and trained at the dojo in the evenings.

At the audition it turned out that despite his relative lack of dance experience he had a few things going for him: "When you're a martial artist you're used to someone trying to stop you rather than help you! I remember partnering being very intuitive. I knew how to help maneuver someone's body. And I remember being way better at the improvs than everybody else." Trained dancers are often masters of imitation, not invention, so Matt's instinctual theatre sense gave him an advantage, along with the fact that he had gone "just to see what it would be like," the opposite of the typically desperate hopefuls at an audition. It was fun.

All six of the then-current dancers of Pilobolus were present, and Matt found them "charmingly eccentric" as well as talented: Kent Lindemer ("He had the partnering expertise"), Becky Jung (lovely, beloved, and with several years' experience and the ability to mentor any newcomers), Darryl Thomas, John-Mario Sevilla, Mark Santillano ("He was super fun, lots of energy, laughing"), and the company's most recent addition, Rebecca Anderson ("stunning and charming, but quiet"). Rebecca had joined Pilobolus in 1994 at age twenty-three, having studied dance at UCLA, where she first saw Pilobolus perform, and then danced in New York for Alwin Nikolais and Murray Louis prior to Nik's death in 1993. In Pilobolus she succeeded Jude Woodcock, who, at thirty-eight, had bowed out after her memorable ten-year run; Jude, along with Becky Jung, had trained and mentored Rebecca, and all three would remain close friends. In addition to her extraordinary grace and elegance as a dancer, Rebecca would quickly become identified as the platinum blond Pilobolus "poster girl" of the 1990s. (In her past she had experimented with different colors, but she had auditioned for Pilobolus with platinum hair, which "kind of happened by accident but then I realized it worked. I realized I needed to keep it up. It becomes your persona in a way.") As for how the dancers perceived Matt, he says: "I had really long hair. They thought I was a hippie."

The new auditions had been called because Kent Lindemer and Darryl Thomas were leaving, but during the auditions John-Mario Sevilla announced that he too had decided to leave, which meant that Pilobolus would need not two new dancers but three—half the company. Becky Jung, Mark Santillano, and Rebecca Anderson would remain.

On his way to the audition Matt had stopped in a small grocery store and had run into another young man on his way to the same destination. Gaspard Louis, born and raised in Haiti, had moved to the US with his family at the age of twelve; they had settled in Newark, New Jersey, where in high school he had played soccer and done martial arts. In college at Montclair State University he had been part of a martial arts club and had been asked to participate in a dance piece because of it; with a growing sense of discovery he had gradually switched the focus of his ambitions from business to dance. Gaspard knew of Pilobolus through books but had never seen them perform; nonetheless, when he had heard they were having an audition he decided to go, thinking he might make a fool of himself but *Why not try anyway?* In the little grocery shop, as he and the long-haired, energetic Southern boy on his way to the same audition chatted, they bonded over their shared interest in martial arts and then, together, they headed off to confront the sea of close to 125 men who they imagined had better chances than themselves of being chosen. When the number came down to ten men left, Gaspard and Matt were still in the running. After the callbacks, the new dancers chosen were Trebien Pollard, Gaspard, and Matt. (One of the aspirants not chosen, Otis Cook, would make it into the company on the next audition.)

The male artistic directors saw in Matt something of their younger selves, unschooled in dance but full of a dynamic male energy. Alison, however, objected. He was raw, untested; with no dance training whatsoever, he had never undergone the disciplines that prepare a dancer to tour. He might be a fascinating wild card, but could he be relied upon to deliver on his promise, to adapt? They offered to hire him on a trial basis, for one year. Gaspard and Trebien each received a two-year contract, the Pilobolus standard at the time.

Although Matt had been at University of Georgia for five years, his wandering exploration of multiple subjects hadn't led to a clear goal, and he had planned to embark on yet another year of college, still unsure of whether even that would earn him a degree. Instead, he left to join Pilobolus. He was already twenty-four, and it made sense to move on. Still, there was one other aspect of leaving college that had to be considered. He had recently begun a new romantic relationship, with a student in the dance department named Emily Milam.

3

They had met when Matt was midway through college. He had seen Emily around the dance department and they had had a couple of years of knowing each other and being friends. They hadn't started dating until recently and had only just realized they would be a couple, right before Matt got the job with Pilobolus.

Although three and a half years younger than him, Emily, a brilliant student, was only one year behind him in college, and had one year left of school. That would mean one year of Matt on tour and Emily still at University of Georgia.

She had grown up forty miles north of Atlanta, in a rural-turned-suburban landscape where her heavily religious, Southern Baptist family had lived for three generations. Until she was about thirteen, Emily's grandfather, a minister, was a pastor at the church she attended. Her conservative upbringing included church three times a week as well as vacation Bible school. Her mother raised her with most of the same rules she herself had been taught: no alcohol, no cursing, no sex before marriage, and so on. On one subject, however, her mother had become less strict: though she herself, as a child, had not been allowed to dance, as an adult she felt no need to continue that prohibition, and she would allow her children to dance if they wished.

As a child, Emily had so much energy that if her mom wanted to reward her for something, such as a correct answer when doing homework, she would let her do a cartwheel or jump off the couch or climb up on top of the refrigerator. "I was always moving. My mom always jokes that probably if I had been born later they would have put me on some kind of drugs, you know, ADHD drugs or something. But I was always flipping and jumping . . . so when I was about five she was like 'OK, my living room's not big enough to hold you in anymore.' So I started doing gymnastics."

At age twelve she switched to dance. She joined some friends in a jazz dance class and the next year she added ballet. From the very beginning she had the good fortune to have well-trained teachers, and this continued to be the case throughout high school, where she learned traditional ballet but also modern dance, something to which many students didn't gain access until college. By the time she was fifteen she had begun teaching dance to little kids. She would also babysit her dance teacher's kid, and would stay at the dance studio until nine o'clock at night. The summer after her junior year of high school she took a six-week dance course at a state college in Georgia and soon knew that she wanted to major in dance in college. She chose the University of Georgia.

She had never been particularly rebellious toward her conservative upbringing. She had always participated in the church activities and liked some of them. She didn't feel desperate to get away from that world, but when it came time to go to college she thought *OK, now I have a choice.*

Like many college students, she found her first year difficult: "I struggled. The university was so big it was like you'd get lost if you didn't have a group to connect with." Because her training had been ballet-based she joined the ballet company, but after spending her freshman year doing mostly ballet, by her sophomore year she knew she wanted modern. For her, as for others, modern dance professor Bala Sarasvati was a major influence ("I had never seen movement like she had done movement until I got to the University of Georgia"). She had seen abstract dance before, but this was "more nonlinear." When she saw Matt in Bala's *Journey to the Hindbrain,* with its postmodern aesthetic of dancers in skimpy clothing, not dancing in unison, with a spoken poem on top of the music, Emily thought: *This is nothing like anything I've ever seen before.* She found it all "wacky and out there but really cool."

Matt and some others encouraged Emily to come try out for Bala's company. When she didn't show up for the audition, Matt went looking for her down the hall and found her; she had gone to the wrong classroom. They barely knew each other, and Emily thought it was nice of him; however, no romance suggested itself. She had a high school boyfriend she was still dating for the first couple of years of college, and Matt had Ashley.

4
———

"Matt had a piece-of-junk car, he always had pieces-of-junk cars," Emily recalls. Time had passed; and, in the spring of 1996, they were making a show with the music department, attending a lot of rehearsals. They had gotten to know each other a little better. One night his car broke down and the next morning he had to retrieve it; Emily went and met him with her car so they could remove the cargo from his: odds and ends that they were donating to the dance department to furnish a lounge that the department was setting up. To thank her, Matt invited her to breakfast at the Bluebird Café, a cute little breakfast and lunch place, a local favorite. She said yes, and as he drove there, via the tree-lined streets of Athens, Georgia, under blue skies, he began to tell her about a friend.

Emily listened with curiosity. "And all along he's telling me, 'You know, there's this guy I think you might like, he's into music, he's a really good mover . . .'" As Matt went on listing attributes, Emily thought: *Oh, I get it. This 'friend' of his, it's himself.* Neither she nor Matt were dating anyone at this point, and by the time they arrived at the restaurant, she felt flattered, confident, and pleased—until Matt said, "Oh my gosh, don't look now, but there's the guy I was talking about!"

He *hadn't* been talking about himself, building up to ask her out. Emily was crushed. She somehow extricated herself from the painfully awkward introduction that followed—but it had all led her to an important realization. She wanted to date Matt.

They continued to see each other informally, with other friends, and within weeks they were dating. And then, suddenly, Matt had to heed the call from Pilobolus.

"I was so blown away that he got the job," Emily recalls. "I thought he would be great at it, but it was such a long shot. It seemed like I couldn't let myself be too upset about it. We had only been together a couple of months. I was twenty, and he was twenty-four, which seemed much older, so I thought *All we can do is just see what happens.*"

5

The day after his night sleeping on a bench on the Upper West Side, Matt had been picked up, as planned, by John-Mario and Becky, who lived in New York and had a car. They met him at the appointed time and they all drove up to Connecticut together.

In his first couple of weeks in the area, before he found a place to stay, Matt would sometimes break into Club Hall and sleep there. It wasn't that he wanted to be a squatter; there was a cultural disconnect. As "a good Southern boy" he didn't think it would be polite to ask anyone to help him find a place to stay. He thought he was supposed to wait for someone to offer. He hadn't yet learned the directness of Northerners.

As for the work, "You show up. You start learning the rep you're going to be performing. We just dove in—you're too busy to worry about it."

But, he adds, "I was lonely. I got along with everybody but I didn't feel particularly close to my fellow dancers." He was focused on Pilobolus as a job, not as a family; he imagined he would only be there for a year or two. He wasn't ambitious in terms of a future with the company.

Regarding Emily, "Without really talking about it, I think we didn't really have much of an expectation. I would call her. I would walk to a pay phone in town and call Emily at her apartment and we would chat one or two times per week."

Emily's senior year was so busy that in a way it helped her to not be constantly seeing someone at school. ("I think it was way worse for him," she says, "because he went to this new job where he didn't have any friends.") Yet they still saw each other quite a bit, because Matt's tour his first year with Pilobolus kept going to places that were only a few hours away from her.

Earlier that year, prior to Matt's arrival, the four artistic directors had created a lighthearted new piece, *Aeros,* to celebrate the group's twenty-fifth anniversary, one of the very few pieces since the 1970s on which all four had collaborated. As Alison explained at the time of its world premiere, "We decided to go back to our early roots and do something that was fun, had a sense of fantasy." Michael Tracy added that the directors had likened the piece to *Le Petit Prince,* "a story about a man who falls onto the surface of a planet." The main character, whose outfit suggests he is a pilot, encounters a "very foreign culture where all the other creatures seem to move in odd ways. They have locomotion and psychological connections that he can't quite figure out."

With a premise that allowed plenty of Pilobolian play and creature-comedy, and a sweet showcase for Rebecca Anderson's star quality, *Aeros* earned positive reviews as a crowd-pleasing throwback to sillier days and enjoyed a good run as an anniversary treat. In retrospect, it has acquired a less welcome distinction: it would be the last piece that all four artistic directors would ever create together. Behind the scenes, the tensions within Pilobolus had grown only more severe.

"We were told 'It's supposed to be light, airy, and fun like a birthday cake.' It might have been Jonathan who said that," Rebecca recalled. "But there was a lot of infighting in the studio between the directors. I knew it was happening but I didn't realize it was so deeply rooted." Some of the *Aeros* disputes, such as, for example, whether to put in coarse humor, sound like a caricature of the college-jocks-meet-fine-arts origins of Pilobolus ("Alison wanted to keep it more elegant"), but the underlying animosity was real.

It didn't take long for Matt and most of the other dancers to perceive the group dynamics between the directors, which had resulted in what many saw as an even split, Jonathan and Robby in one camp and Alison and Michael in another. (Robby has always objected to this diagrammatic interpretation, having never felt completely allied with Jonathan; and Gaspard says he was naively unaware of the behind-the-scenes conflicts, having come from "a society where you do what your elders tell you.") Whatever the wound, the pain throbbed perceptibly. "Everyone's stance was defensive," Matt recalls. "It was clear that they didn't get along. The dancers could feel it even though nobody ever talked to us about it." Like kids whose parents had a dysfunctional marriage, the dancers quietly carried on.

6

Matt spent countless hours studying videos of vintage Pilobolus performances. He would borrow the videotapes from the company's collection, with a particular interest in the pieces from the 1970s—such as *Untitled, Monkshood's Farewell, Alraune, Shizen*—as originally performed. Other dancers watched videos, too, but none to the degree that Matt did. He not only studied the nuances of the performances for his own use as a dancer learning the rep; he also questioned the ways in which the presentation of the pieces had changed through the years and whether certain changes had been for the better or the worse. It didn't occur to him that this mindset went beyond that of a dancer, edging into the directorial sifting and analysis that befit a future choreographer.

As a dancer, his experience creating new work with Pilobolus did not begin auspiciously. The first new piece made after his arrival, *Olympic Dances* (later retitled *Elysian Fields*), choreographed by Alison and Michael, put classical imagery in the service of what turned out to be an unintentionally campy ancient-statues-brought-to-life conceit. Much of the problem seems to have stemmed from the initial concept: both Alison and Michael taught at Yale part time, and Yale had commissioned them to create a piece to a new composition by the American composer John Harbison. The music had a comparatively grand, classical feel, markedly different from, and even antithetical to, the troupe's sensibility; what's more, the music arrived finished and immutable, whereas Pilobolus usually choreographed first and added music later, tailoring it as needed.

To Matt, "It felt very much that people couldn't get it together. I think it was the style of it. Its aesthetic didn't work for me." It didn't help that he, Gaspard, and Trebien were all rookies. "We had a lot of images but it seemed kind of random. I felt like I wasn't giving them good material." Nor did the music, which Matt disliked, offer any inspiration. In fact, Matt disliked pretty much everything about the piece, and his instincts were sound. *Elysian Fields* would have a relatively short public life before being consigned to the Pilobolus dustbin and forgotten.

Matt's next experience making a piece, however, would be radically different. It would be choreographed by Jonathan and Robby, whose approach represented a startling shift. "It was so fast—the Jonathan erratic attention, and Robby the calm energy, like a lion with a little mouse behind him." A brilliant, wise mouse whose insights the lion recognized.

They began with the simple premise that the time had come to create a men's quartet, as Pilobolus hadn't made one in several years, but an understated poignancy dwelt in the background as a subtle influence. According to Matt, "Jonathan and Robby stated at the beginning that it would be for the memory of Jim Blanc." Jim Blanc, a dancer with Pilobolus from 1987 to 1989, had died of AIDS in May 1996, at the age of thirty-six. Matt had not known him, but Jim had been a beloved colleague of the dancers of that earlier era, including Becky Jung, who was still with the company. To Jude Woodcock, "He was just a wonderful person. A good Southern boy."

To the best of Matt's recollection, the intention to honor Jim wasn't stated again, or at least not emphasized again, during the process of making the piece; but even without its participants being overly conscious of the influence, the piece would partake of the spirit of elegy, and of honoring a fallen comrade.

Made in the spring of 1997, after the first several months of Gaspard, Mark, Matt, and Trebien working together and, according to Gaspard, "everyone getting under each other's skin" due to the variety of personal temperaments, Jonathan and Robby "saw the different personalities, and the piece came out of the contrasts." Those contrasts led to a dynamic in which the four men, one by one, are each set apart from the others, and tested, or even tormented, before being re-absorbed into the foursome. Gaspard felt that "the 'odd man out' theme was the directors' way of creating a connective tissue" between the four personalities. Matt later realized that "Pilobolus loves the odd-man-out theme because they're outsiders themselves." The last male quartet the company had made, *The Particle Zoo,* had dealt with the same idea, but with a speed and frantic energy that hadn't allowed it to take on the gravitas of this new piece, which would be given a title as inventive as the physical vocabulary it utilized: *Gnomen.*

The neologism "gnomen" derives from the word "gnomon"—which most commonly refers to the pin of a sundial but can also mean any object whose shadow indicates the hour of the day. By changing "gnomon" to incorporate the word "men," "gnomen" suggests that the four-man tribe on stage are somehow men of time, themselves indicators of the hour, and by extension tied to time's ominous, implacable force, as evoked too by the somber tolling of a bell, as if from a tower, that the audience hears at the opening and close of the piece. The etymology of *gno-* (from *gnō-*) also ties the word to the concept "to perceive, to know" and to the idea that these men are embodying or acquiring knowledge, or that they represent the process of obtaining knowledge, while the sound of "gnomen" evokes the phrase "no men" with its subliminal suggestiveness: men who deal in rejection? negative forces? absence? loss? limitation? the fearful space of a "no man's land"? The old adage "no man is an island"? Never has Pilobolus wordplay been used so wisely and powerfully as in this single word, or nonword.

From its opening moments, when the men roll onto a dimly lit stage linked together, and one is separated only to reach out to the others longingly, to be brought back into the group, the theme of *Gnomen* begins to gently assert itself. The first several minutes, which are largely built around this image of Trebien reaching out, establish the group interactions. When the focus shifts to Matt, who becomes the next "odd man out," there is humor: the other three men hit him, rather like a gong, and he shudders as a clanging sound reverberates, and he then seems to lose control, repeatedly leaping forward dangerously as the others catch him. Perhaps to rein him in, they turn him upside-down and seem to try to screw him into the ground. Next they gang up on him again and seem to do something terrible—the audience can't see exactly what, until the three men step away to reveal Matt, twisted into a pretzel-like dwarf, a human knot left to try to walk, as best he can, on one hand and one foot, with the result that he keeps tipping over and smacking his head on the floor. It is funny but also poignant, at once a comic delight and a disturbing metaphor for bullying, disability, and human struggle. The other men take pity on him and restore him to normal by "clanging" him like a gong once more. A change of lighting lends a more moonlit ambience, as the men lean on one another, and link together to produce a kind of human wheel, tumbling together as the piece enters a mellower mood, to what sounds like the delicate chiming of a wind-up toy in a child's nursery. The theme of gentleness and cooperation seems to advance, as, at one point, Matt appears to listen to Gaspard's heart. Gaspard, now the focal point, creeps around, hunched over, as if trying to sneak away, and is manipulated by the others in various ways, eventually left standing on one leg. Throughout *Gnomen,* each time three of the men begin to walk away from whichever one is left out, the three stop, pause, turn back, and relent; they retrieve the fourth rather than abandon him. So it is with Gaspard as well, and he is restored to standing position, as part of the group.

As the focus shifts a final time, to Mark, the music again shifts, and underscores the graceful back and forth lifts and postures in the air that characterize what will be the concluding section. Throughout, Mark is mostly aloft, frequently horizontal, sometimes supine, like a swimmer afloat in the air. At one point he is positioned at a forty-five degree angle off the side of one of the other dancers, in a breathtaking, gravity-defying pose known within Pilobolus as "the flag"; at another moment he lies on the stage as if asleep and the other three dancers slide their feet beneath him and together lift and rock him gently, like a baby in a cradle; at yet another point, in what amounts to a pageant of compassion, the sleeper is lifted and held overhead, his arms outstretched, as if being honored as the music grows more moving and gently swells; he is rocked again and lifted and repeatedly turned in various ways, and in a final crescendo—the music has become magisterial without ever losing its subtlety, now heartbreakingly tender and powerful at once—he is lifted and carried and returned to stand. The others stand behind him, as all stare straight ahead (whether into the void, or life, or time itself). He kneels and the others follow. Slowly they lower to a seated position, still staring ahead, and slowly bow their heads, with dignity and humility, as if in homage to a force larger than themselves, as the bells toll again and the lights dim.

This ritual of brotherhood and male bonding, with its poignant culmination mingling notes of celebration, valediction, and elegy alongside its sensuousness, humor, and physical inventiveness, seems to encapsulate a universe in just seventeen or eighteen minutes. As to its creation, "We all worked on all the different parts," Matt said. "It happened very organically in a way that's kind of rare. We were in the flow." They had worked, in part, to a Van Morrison song called "Full Force Gale" as performed by Elvis Costello and a male chorus, which had been played at Jim Blanc's funeral. Although not used in the finished piece, it had influenced the lifting theme that eventually turned into the last section.

Matt was cognizant of being able to bring his own influence to the piece, through movement alone. For example, he contributed that pretzel-like human knot he gets twisted into by the others, a comic creation known within the company as "Igor," and while "Igor" has been taught to subsequent generations of male Pilobolus dancers, it would never have been created if not for the consequences of a minor injury. Matt had broken his toe and had a shoe on that foot during rehearsal, and he had been trying to find a way to move around without putting weight on the toe. Because the shoe enabled him to hold the foot more easily, in his experiments he discovered the one-footed, twisted-pretzel Igor identity. But there was a downside, quite literally: during a rehearsal he accidentally smacked his head on the floor while in this contorted position; he managed to get back up and continue on, but the directors were laughing; they loved the fall, and after the run-through they asked him if he could do that each time. To Matt's reply of "It hurt!" they responded "How *bad* did it hurt?" and Matt said "I'll only do it if the audience laughs." He agreed to try it once, and if the audience laughed it would become part of the piece. As it turned out, he had set himself up for self-inflicted suffering night after night: the audience loved that moment, and he would have to smack his head against the stage in every performance. (In revivals of *Gnomen* through the years, the "Igor" sequence would remain a key component, but with the tipping over and crashing omitted—not in the interest of a kinder, more compassionate vision, but simply because it is generally accepted that only Matt Kent could smack his face against a stage every night with his leg behind his head and not break his nose.)

The other new dancers, Trebien and Gaspard, also each brought their own distinct gifts to *Gnomen.* Trebien, a "deep thinker" in Matt's opinion, brought a noble self-possession, while Gaspard brought a sense of mystery, restraint, and a willingness to play the part of someone getting pushed around, with a quiet dignity. Both were key ingredients. Mark Santillano, the one experienced Pilobolus dancer in the quartet, brought a playful nature that could find a vocabulary of movement that supported the piece when he wasn't in the spotlight. As Matt recalls, "It wouldn't have turned out the same without Mark. He knew how to help define the character of the whole thing."

Like such Pilobolus classics as *Untitled* and *Day Two, Gnomen* exists in a postmodern space between the literal and the abstract, between narrative and ritual. While open to interpretation, it can be seen as the story of four men testing each other and eventually fusing as a unit—and then, perhaps, being further bonded by the loss of one among them. The brotherhood theme was likely enhanced by the fact that three of the four young men making the piece were new to Pilobolus and were not yet a group (which, Matt felt, was part of the problem with the one piece they had made prior to this). With *Gnomen* they became a group by making a piece about becoming a group. The three "new guys" projected their outsider feelings, at this vulnerable moment in their lives, and brought their selves to the task of creating art.

Given Matt's background in music, he was excited to meet the composer Paul Sullivan. In the process of speaking with him, and "just to show off," Matt demonstrated one of his idiosyncratic secret talents, his throat singing, and Paul was impressed. (Throat singing, also known as overtone singing, produces a kind of guttural chant.) When Matt remarked that it "would be cool if I could be part of the music someday," he received a surprising reply from Paul: "Well, if ever there was a piece to do this in, this is it."

Matt went to see his fellow dancer Mark, who had an apartment in a little house behind the post office and café that were a stone's throw from Club Hall. He knew Mark was "a gadget guy," and Mark obligingly recorded Matt on a cassette tape doing his throat singing. Matt mailed it to Paul. When Paul listened to it he realized it would fit into the piece exactly as is. "It's sort of a funny little miracle," Matt says, "that I randomly happened to sing it in the key he was working in." The throat singing would add another quirky but strikingly effective dimension to the sequence in which Matt suffers his various comic indignities.

Paul Sullivan, who by now had been working with Pilobolus for nearly two decades, outdid himself with the score, which builds and delineates the emotional arc of *Gnomen* flawlessly, and contributes immeasurably to its sense of the sacred, the tribal, and the profound. The thing that stood out for Matt was how unexpected it was—it wasn't what had been playing in his head. "It has such a nice range, it goes all over the place, soaring melodies, weird percussion, it creates atmospheres of different kinds."

Everything else about the piece seemed to be fitting together too. Jonathan and Robby were concerned, however, that they didn't have an ending.

"And then they realized, 'What if they just sit down and bow?' We tried it and it was one of those moments when you immediately know 'OK, that's it.'"

Gnomen had instant success with audiences, and it had, among its many virtues, one that is particularly rare in theatre: it didn't need to change. Matt, Gaspard, and Trebien, on only their second try, had, with their colleague Mark, helped Jonathan and Robby make a Pilobolus classic.

EIGHT

Pools of Light

1

Emily, having kept her academic focus throughout her senior year, graduated magna cum laude from the University of Georgia, with a degree in dance education. Once she had received it she went directly to the American Dance Festival to see Pilobolus perform, and from there she went with Matt straight to New York. She had gotten a scholarship to take classes at Peridance, and Matt would be living in the city while he performed as part of Pilobolus's annual summer season at the Joyce Theater, so she moved in with him. To her way of thinking, "It was kind of like the relationship version of the summer dance camp: I can try it for six weeks and if I don't like it I can come home."

Their accommodations were on 35th Street between Park and Madison, where the Unitarian Universalist Church owned two small apartment buildings, only a few stories tall, which were run like a bed and breakfast. Most of the Pilobolus dancers, other than the ones who already lived in New York, would stay there during the Joyce run each year, which had by now become as firmly established on the company's calendar as its high-profile premieres at the American Dance Festival. Emily and Matt had a little apartment on the third floor.

In moving in with Matt, however, Emily risked estrangement from her religiously conservative family. Her brother, the first to react, told her that she was living in sin and would be going to hell. Her parents had the same reaction. Their beautiful daughter had run away with an intense, long-haired artistic guy, with a dark macho look and an earring, who danced in a bizarre modern dance troupe. It was a Southern Baptist parent's nightmare.

"My dad thought it was a rock and roll lifestyle, with drugs. He didn't understand that when you're using your body in your work every day, that's impossible. Matt could never have had that kind of life and still done his job."

On occasion, Emily's father would angrily quote Bible verses at Matt, who would surprise him with his ability to quote Bible verses in response. (Matt had, of course, a minister for a father.) No amount of debate could bridge the divide, however, and Emily and Matt's relationship with her parents would remain difficult for the next several years.

Yet Emily, never a rebel but always her own person, had made her choice. That September, she moved in with Matt in Connecticut, where they occupied the small second-floor apartment in the little house behind the post office and café near Club Hall, previously rented to Mark Santillano. The space consisted of one big room with their futon, bed, and television; they also had their own bathroom, and shared a kitchenette with the man who rented the house's other one-room, second-floor apartment.

Through her interest in José Limón and the Limón technique, Emily learned of a remarkable woman named Ernestine Stodelle, who had danced in Limón's first company and had also danced with Limón's mentor Doris Humphrey. Stodelle, then in her mid-eighties, lived in the town of Cheshire, Connecticut, and maintained a beautiful studio in her home, in the space a living room might occupy. There she continued to teach old-fashioned classes, using a vinyl record that had been made specifically for her purposes, with musical selections placed in a sequence of her choosing. Gorgeous photos by the distinguished photographer Barbara Morgan, renowned for her images of modern dancers and for having cofounded *Aperture* magazine, appeared throughout the house, and Stodelle spoke nonchalantly of the legendary people she had known, from Martha Graham to Joseph Campbell. Emily, incredulous at her good fortune, began taking classes with this new mentor, feeling that she was touching dance history.

Her job prospects were decidedly less rarefied. She worked as a nanny for six months, taught yoga classes, filled in as a substitute teacher in the local schools, took assignments as a life model for artists, and babysat Moses Pendleton and Cynthia Quinn's daughter, in that enormous house that had been featured years earlier in the film *Moses Pendleton Presents Moses Pendleton*. (The house was much the same, but now crammed full of stuff.)

She joined a gym to meet people her own age, and acquired a number of girlfriends to create for herself a social life. Still, an obvious concern hung in the air: she was thrilled for Matt's success, but she hadn't devoted herself to dance simply to become a dancer's wife. In her quiet, un-egoistic but independent way, she knew she would have to find her own path forward.

2

As if in a mute stand-up comedy routine, a dark-haired young man appears onstage, picks up a rubber mask of an ape head, and holds it before him like Hamlet about to address a skull. With his hand inside it, he puts fingers through the mouth opening to form a pantomime tongue, then suddenly, compulsively, engages in a frantic, hilarious "tongue kiss" with it, as if to furtively answer an erotic obsession. Clearly this boy has some unaddressed needs, ones that make him unpredictable, and allow an element of comic suspense: we, the audience, wonder what he will do next. He puts the ape mask on, clowns a bit, and suddenly, as a woman enters, the first strains of music are heard. The man, played by Matt Kent, dons his sombrero and tilts it so far down as to hide under it, as if embarrassed by his ape identity—so now there are two levels of concealment. The sombrero complements his suit, which suggests a gaucho; yet we sense that no matter what else he may be, he is fundamentally an imposter. Likewise the young woman, played by Rebecca Anderson, poised and starlet-stunning in a red dress, though far more assured, is not predictable. She haughtily stubs out a cigarette that he has offered, and promptly endeavors to teach him how to tango.

So begins *Orangotango* (1998), with its narrative arc of fumbling, teaching, discovery, taming, exposure, and amorous assertion, all rolled into ten or eleven minutes of stage time. The ape-man's awkward attempts at the tango, his beautiful partner's discovery of his ape-face, a beauty-and-the-beast tenderness that opens into some delightfully Pilobolus-inflected anti-gravitational romance and lyrical partnering, and the back-and-forth of a sexually charged power struggle with abrupt reversals, all fuse into a duet as gorgeous and disarmingly comic as its protagonists. Rebecca's ever-changing responses to her bizarre, insecure suitor are measured and registered with comic precision even while both dancers rise to the challenges of the choreography and display the remarkable onstage chemistry with which, as a pair, they became emblematic of Pilobolus in the 1990s.

On one level pure tomfoolery, on another level witty and knowing, *Orangotango* culminates with Rebecca pulling off Matt's mask, a stunned moment of uncertainty, and, suddenly, a final decisive move as Matt, now with his human head exposed, nonetheless dares to follow his ape nature: he seizes Rebecca and carries her off, over his shoulder, as he lopes off-stage. It's a psychologically astute moment that brings closure, laughter, and applause, but early versions of the piece did not include it. Originally, the mask remained in place throughout—but at some point the realization was made that the unmasking, with its significant difference in psychology, turned the key to a more satisfying ending.

Alison had created the duet by working with two pairs of dancers (in the studio, in addition to Rebecca and Matt there was another Rebecca—Rebecca Stenn—and Adam Battelstein, a veteran Pilobolus dancer). Rebecca Anderson and Matt were still getting to know each other, and still getting to know Alison; Rebecca would recall it as the period during which she developed a close connection to both of them. As for Matt, Alison's hesitations about him and an initial misperception of him as macho (due to his husky voice, martial arts background, and overall look) had yet to fade. It would take a while for the two of them to become close.

Alison had entered a new phase in her life and art. The year before, she and Eric had moved to Maine, to an area on Penobscot Bay where his family had lived for generations. She would come to Connecticut to work with the dancers, but she no longer worked in collaboration with the other artistic directors. Her collaborators now were the dancers and the creators of costumes, lighting, sets, and music; but she made the final choices herself. In other ways, however, the Pilobolus process of invention remained intact. For *Orangotango,* as Rebecca recalled, "Alison came in and played tango music and we improvised a lot, and didn't know there would be a monkey mask."

Sly and a touch surreal, surprising, endearing, physically impressive, *Orangotango* encapsulates much of what is most beloved about Pilobolus. With its seamless interweaving of lyrical grace into its shenanigans, it makes use of sharp contrasts between the romantic and the satirical, in the way that a novel that poses as a parody of romance can cause readers to let down their emotional guard and be touched by an unexpected element of the genuinely romantic. (The literary critic William Empson referred to this concept as "pseudo-parody to disarm criticism" and Edmund White later used it to explain how Vladimir Nabokov achieved an effect "beyond parody.") *Orangotango* mixes the idea of the dancing gorilla—an old comic trope used in American humor for decades or longer (on greeting cards, in comedy sketches, and once, long ago, in an extraordinarily obscure one-act play called *This Is Not a Play!*)—with the tango, a beloved form that it redeploys. Fittingly, the music is by the late Argentine composer Astor Piazzolla, who revolutionized the tango with the addition of jazz and classical elements. Just as White saw Nabokov achieving an effect "beyond parody," *Orangotango* achieves an effect beyond travesty, or slapstick, or mockery. As White and others have suggested, parody, in the postmodern age, may be the only way, or at least the most effective, to revive romance.

Alas, not everyone saw it that way. The piece met with enthusiastic responses from most audiences, and critics generally greeted it as an amusing comic offering; but a year and a half after its debut, a performance at Mexico City's renowned Teatro Metropólitan provoked a scathing editorial in the newspaper *Processo* under the headline "El fracaso de Pilobolus" ("The Failure of Pilobolus"). Signed only by "The Editor," the piece panned the entire program, and Pilobolus itself, as "antiquated" before getting to its real point: *Orangotango*, "a duet that showed a ridiculous Mexican charro with the head of an orangutan who danced with a 'Mexican Miss' dressed as an Andalusian. . . . In addition to highlighting the serious problems of geographical and cultural confusion that many Americans suffer, the piece turned out to be a real affront to the public because of its racist and discriminatory content." The editorial went on to note that the audience responded with "everything from boos to shouting" in the face of this "fraud." Although Matt had only noticed one person shouting amid the applause, he was horrified that *Orangotango* had been so painfully misunderstood and misrepresented. He spoke to a reporter to try to make a public statement clarifying that his role was not a caricature of a Mexican, that the piece did not ridicule the tango as an art form, and that Pilobolus, on the contrary, held Mexico and its culture in high esteem. He was never able to determine whether his comments were published, and no record of such a publication has been found, but through the years Pilobolus has continued to perform in Mexico to the cheers of appreciative audiences.

For any artist, there is always the danger that one's intentions will be misperceived. *Orangotango* has not been performed for many years and it isn't easy to revive, as it requires performers with an unusual combination of comic theatre and athletic dance skills, and exactly the right sensibility; even many Pilobolus dancers, though extraordinary, would be miscast in it.

What's more, who knows whether it would be further misconstrued now, given the complicated history between the US and Mexican immigrants—and how, too, would its playful view of male and female relations resonate today? Still, it might be wondrous to behold. The ingenious *Orangotango* deserves a place alongside *Walklyndon* as a Pilobolus comedy pearl.

3

By the late 1990s the real story of the directors' conflicts had begun to become clear to many of the dancers. Those conflicts, according to nearly everyone who had a window into Pilobolus over the years, went largely as follows: Jonathan hated Michael; Robby was often the peacemaker, avoiding conflict; Michael was the one being abused; and Alison, annoyed by it all, and with an attitude of "That's not the way it's done," was like an increasingly exhausted nanny among bickering boys. Many felt that the animosity between Jonathan and Michael dated to the origins of Pilobolus, when Michael had been asked to replace Lee Harris. Michael, as the last to join, was not seen by some (read: Jonathan) to be as completely a "founding member." As Matt observed, "Jonathan being a bully just kept rubbing it in his face. They just didn't respect each other."

Matt's own connection to Jonathan, however, was magical: "I would have dinner with him. I only realized later that the other dancers didn't."

"He shared Zappa albums with me. I wasn't a Zappa fan until I met Jonathan." The occasion for listening to Zappa had been while driving to a shooting range. Matt had taken Jonathan to the gun range to shoot revolvers, something Matt is fairly certain Jonathan had never done. Although Matt's family had not had an interest in guns, he had met people through martial arts who did, and while he had never been deeply into guns, he had some interest; in fact, on his first date with Emily they had gone to a gun range (a choice that Matt explains with a simple "It *is* Georgia, after all"). With Jonathan's love of intensity in all its forms, the idea of shooting high-velocity bullets excited the same element in him that liked driving cars fast, whether racing his Alfa Romeo at Lime Rock Park or, more inappropriately, alienating old friends who might find themselves in the passenger seat as he drove dangerously through treacherous rural terrain. Matt recalls an image of Jonathan at the shooting range with a giant grin on his face and wearing ear protection. Jonathan apparently enjoyed the experience too much for his wife Joanne's comfort, because afterward she told Matt—whose idea it had been—never to do this again. Matt obeyed, but he and Jonathan would recall the experience happily and refer back to it many times: "I drove around with him and we listened to *Apostrophe* and he was totally into it and laughing and bubbling with enthusiasm, like reliving the time in his life when he was first into it, rediscovering it. I felt like I was his college buddy."

The positive relationship would last for years. And, having effortlessly bonded with Jonathan, it wasn't long before Matt was having dinner with Robby and Susan. Matt found Robby smart and thoughtful, and he could tell that Robby not only liked him, but liked him even more once Emily showed up, her own smart thoughtfulness immediately appreciated.

Robby and Jonathan were together a lot, and whenever they would go to a studio in New York to work on sound recordings to accompany performances, Matt would beg to go with them, to observe and to learn. He quickly discovered that they hated going into the city and, in true Pilobolus fashion, they would argue about which way to drive there. He sat back quietly and took it all in, as he continued to piece together the interpersonal dynamics around him.

Of Michael, Matt says, "I have so much respect for what he did and for what he contributed. Very charismatic and good-looking onstage. Beautiful, committed as a dancer, so graceful." As a director, Michael particularly impressed Matt "when he was using his body to demonstrate what he was talking about" because Matt and the other dancers could see, and be inspired by, the gift that Michael had always had onstage. "He brought a kind of physical intelligence and performance 'relatability' that the others didn't have."

That the four artistic directors couldn't get along struck Matt as a terrible loss. "I used to always say to Emily that if only Jonathan and Alison would work together they would make something so amazing."

Much of his life as a dancer, however, was spent away from the directors and the studio, devoted instead to tours, travel, and the endless need to be mobile. In those years, the dancers toured with a lighting supervisor and a stage manager, without the artistic directors. It would start with, as Matt put it, "piling into a car or taxi and sleeping against each other like a bunch of puppies," then, on the airplane, attracting attention, with other flyers under the impression that these good-looking young people must be a pop band. Then hotel life, which "can be lonely but sometimes luxurious." Airline flights and rental cars, and "the shifting of worlds": "One moment you're drinking champagne and the next it's like you're the help. You're on a different schedule than the rest of the world. Being disoriented by different locales. In hotels you realize you're the only one who uses the gym. The hardest part is finding good food."

During this period Rebecca Anderson, known as Becca to her colleagues, served as dance captain. She and Matt became closer, both as dance partners and as friends, through touring, as he recognized that she was "professional, with such grace and presence, a beauty and captivating" and "very open, very personable."

4

In the late 1990s Pilobolus invited Maurice Sendak, author of the classic children's book *Where the Wild Things Are,* and his directorial partner, Arthur Yorinks, with whom he had developed an ongoing theatre project, to collaborate. The process would span from November 1998 to June 1999 and result in a Pilobolus piece entitled *A Selection,* as well as a feature film documentary by Mirra Bank entitled *Last Dance,* released in 2002.

In the film, Sendak, at the age of seventy, speaks of his "fiery passion and devotion to Judaism" and to remembrance of the Holocaust, a "loyalty to all the dead" and "especially to the children who would have been my age now." Central to the project he brings Pilobolus is the horrific historical reality of Theresienstadt, the deliberately deceptive camp located in the town of Terezin, in Czech lands occupied by Germany, that served as both an intermediate stop for unsuspecting prisoners being sent to Auschwitz and a fake "settlement" that, for propaganda purposes, perpetuated the idea that Jews were merely being relocated. Here small children performed in what appeared to be happy theatre productions, in which they sang the Hans Krása-Adolf Hoffmeister children's opera *Brundibár* before being sent off to die. With this history in mind, Sendak and Yorinks had conceived a new production of *Brundibár* that paired Krása's music with an English libretto by Tony Kushner. With Pilobolus they wanted to create a complementary work about the Holocaust.

Although the thematic base of their work-in-progress is heartbreakingly dark, the film *Last Dance* is not. A time capsule and beautiful illustration of the late 90s Pilobolus, it prizes among its ingredients the humor, invention, and breathtaking athleticism—the *light*—of the company itself. We see the "free play" phase as the directors begin work in the studio with the dancers; arts critic Terry Teachout, an on-screen observer, aptly compares their method to that of a jazz ensemble, and never could an ensemble contain a more winning sextet of performers than these. In addition to Rebecca, Matt, and Gaspard, it includes three new members of the troupe, who, though it is never stated in the film, had begun their tenure only the past August: Josie Coyoc, an elegant, petite dancer who had made the wrenching decision to leave Bill T. Jones's company after five years, partly in quest of more financially stable employment; Otis Cook, a shaved-headed, intriguingly emotive young man who had first auditioned alongside Matt and later returned to try again, this time with success; and Benjamin Pring, sometimes referred to as "Bendable Ben," an Asian American boy next door with an unusual combination of incredible flexibility and extreme strength, his contortionist qualities seen to jaw-dropping effect. (To Matt Kent he would remain, even twenty years later, "physically one of the most amazingly supple and strong people I've ever worked with.")

The hiring of these newcomers had been detailed by Teachout in a *New York Times* article about Pilobolus auditions, in which he had reported that the pool of candidates, once winnowed to a half-dozen male and a half-dozen female dancers, were advised by the directors as to the less glamorous and potentially off-putting realities of life with Pilobolus: the strains of touring, the absence of understudies, the consequent need to perform even when injured, the nonnegotiable participation in pieces that contain nudity. In this serious, thoughtful instant, Matt had interjected "You're going to be lonely, hurt, poor, and naked," getting a laugh from everyone in the room—and leading Teachout to label him, accurately, as "Pilobolus's class clown."

In *Last Dance*'s footage of improvisations, Matt clowns with Otis, "Bendable Ben" dazzles everyone with his exceptional contortionist abilities, and Otis displays such strong theatrical gifts that he becomes the center of the piece (despite the conspicuous skepticism on his face at certain moments in the directorial process). In the tradition of early Pilobolus, the women—Rebecca and Josie—bring, with Gaspard, a more graceful dance component while matching the phenomenal athleticism of their colleagues. Throughout the film we get to know the troupe through successive glimpses and brief comments: Gaspard, on the improvisational process ("Everybody gets to contribute something"), Josie on Maurice Sendak ("I love his mind"), Rebecca on her frequent stage partner's intense nature

("Sometimes we have to just say, 'Matt, chill out'"). But in the piece being made, the greatest intensity will emanate from Otis, whose ability to pivot from the soft to the demonic makes his character a riveting symbol of evil.

The film's focus, however, is the directors. Robby, Michael, and Jonathan (Alison is not a part of the project and is not in the film) work alongside Maurice and Arthur, happily at first, and show themselves to be extremely articulate. Soon Jonathan, true to form, challenges the assumptions of those around him, especially Maurice. An exterior shot of falling snow registers a change of season, and of tone, as tension creeps in. When Jonathan advocates for "movement that speaks for itself," Maurice replies "But you could do that yourself," that is, without himself and Arthur. Things soon get worse. When, one morning, Robby and Michael gently ask Jonathan to be more diplomatic in his dealings with Maurice, Jonathan replies with a highly undiplomatic refusal. Robby, though Jonathan tends to accuse him of not "speaking up," has no trouble speaking up here: "You can't necessarily employ the scorched earth policy with the same impunity with Maurice that you do with us. I'm used to it. I know you can't build your new city until you've razed ours, but Maurice doesn't know that."

Given Jonathan's double standard—a refusal to rein in his own insensitivity and impatience, paired with zero tolerance for accepting the same bluntness he regularly inflicts on others—the argument quickly degenerates into his pointed "*Fuck the directors*" as he walks away in anger. A separate comment from Robby, intercut into the sequence, adds perspective: "We all at some point feel like fighters who've bloodied each other's noses, and you sort of collapse on each other. Finally you don't have the energy, because your arms are too tired to fight anymore."

Yet neither Jonathan nor Maurice *ever* seems "too tired to fight." Jonathan refers to Maurice as an old friend, and though their prior interactions are not specified (Jonathan had served as choreographer for the Glyndebourne Festival Opera Company's 1985 production of Sendak's *Where the Wild Things Are*), their history seems only to have further emboldened Jonathan. As for Maurice, he comes across as alternately crabby and charming, an angry troll who turns into an enchanter and back again, while harboring the conscience of a sensitive child, wise and tormented by his knowledge of the world's evil.

Their conflict, much of it related to questions of where and to what degree to be explicit or ambiguous in various aspects of the piece, rever-

berated throughout those around them and threatened to derail their entire project, and the film with it. One person who desperately wanted the
group to find its way forward was Mirra Bank, the documentarian, who
had been given no warning of the interpersonal tensions that awaited. Her
prior works—*Anonymous Was a Woman,* a documentary about women
who made folk art, which she had also turned into a successful book, and
Nobody's Girls, a film about minority women in the American West—had
established her as a serious, thoughtful filmmaker but hadn't primed her
for the instability of Pilobolus. While making *Nobody's Girls,* a grateful student intern from Smith College had offered to take Mirra to see her uncle's
dance company; her uncle, Mirra discovered, was Michael Tracy. Mirra
had seen Pilobolus long before, but not in recent years; she went backstage
afterward to thank Michael, and while speaking with him she asked what
he and Pilobolus were doing next. He told her that their next project would
be a collaboration with Maurice Sendak, on a dark, Grimm-fairy-tale-like
piece (which quickly, upon further description, turned out to include the
element of children and the Holocaust). Immediately interested, Mirra met
with the Pilobolus directors and with Maurice; she got them all to sign a
release; then she set about raising money for a year or so, with her collaborator Vic Losick.

Mirra worked with a very small crew, in among the dancers, immersed
in what they were doing (Rebecca recalls "maybe three people, or a few,
filming" and consequently no real self-consciousness), and with digital
"run and gun" filmmaking becoming more prevalent, Mirra could watch
a monitor while shooting. In the performance venues she used three cameras; in other locations just one or two; there were also situations where a
camera could be set up for a wide shot if absolutely needed—but she didn't
want anything pre-arranged. The only rule was that she needed to be present whenever the collaborative work was being done. Beyond that, as she
put it, "Whatever happened, happened. That was the deal."

When the contentiousness between the directors arose, Mirra recalls,
"I was completely blindsided by it. It was all happening as you see it in the
film. That is what Direct Cinema is. People said what they said, and they
felt what they felt. I went back, at the end, after the dance had premiered,
and filmed their reflections, looking back on the experience."

"I had many sleepless nights worried that the whole thing would fall
apart. I wanted the dance to be made. I was a huge advocate of continuing

to work. I think the fact that we were filming was a big incentive for not giving up."

Off-camera things were, if anything, even worse. With Jonathan's aggressiveness, a kind of Oedipal tug-of-war between him and Maurice, his longstanding abusiveness toward Michael, and, further in the background, the ongoing deterioration of Alison's relationship with the other directors, seismic tremors continued. Yet for the dancers it was an exciting, often joyful time, as Rebecca planned her wedding and the troupe knew they were in a film, and collaborating with Maurice Sendak, whom they revered. In *Last Dance*, we see the magic when he unfurls for them his magnificent designs for their costumes, and later draws on a bodysuit that Otis models in order for Maurice to decorate it. His visual artistry entrances all who see it, and especially the dancers, who will have the unique privilege to wear and inhabit it.

And the show goes on. As Maurice and Pilobolus haggled over the story they would tell, and whether it should even *be* a "story," an onstage drama that hovered between narrative and abstraction took shape. Finally titled *A Selection* (after more haggling), it would portray a theatrical troupe stranded after missing a train, "their village's last train out of Nazi Germany" as a Pilobolus press release would call it, and their confrontation with a bizarre stranger—Otis, as an incarnation of evil.

One of the most telling sequences in *Last Dance* takes place in an otherwise empty theater in the hours prior to *A Selection* being performed in front of an audience for the first time, at a preview. Matt and Otis have recently run through a final rehearsal of the scene in which Matt is stripped naked. Still feeling uncomfortable with it, Matt is seated on a bench onstage. Jonathan, standing, commiserates and offers advice, but says, "Frankly I still think it sucks." A moment later Robby walks onto the stage, not having heard Jonathan, and congratulates Matt. "That was excellent," Robby says. "I think we're really in good shape." Matt politely but rather glumly acknowledges the praise. The irony of the contrast between the two directorial comments is comic and revealing. The viewer empathizes with Matt, and, by extension, with any performer caught between the differing visions of multiple collaborators.

One of Matt's favorite memories of the project, however, would involve a moment that isn't in the film. Regarding the nude scene, at some point Maurice Sendak had said to him, "Matt, you're completely naked—but you're *still not naked enough.*" Matt understood immediately. The emotional nakedness had to *exceed* the physical nakedness. He considers it one of the best pieces of direction he ever received.

In the end, he and Otis and the rest of the cast, in keeping with their extraordinary abilities, would deliver; but despite that, and the impressive set and costumes by Sendak, and the technical accomplishments of all those around them, the piece's uncertain sensibility would remain awkward and diffuse some of its potential. Yet if *A Selection* lacks the crisp, fully solidified strength of great art, it has power nonetheless. Caught between story, dream, and tragic reality, filled with interesting ingredients and admirable performances, it resonates as an evocative vision. The stronger work of art, however, is the documentary of its creation. The identity, clarity, and relevance of *Last Dance* are never in doubt. Filled with priceless footage of the dancers, vivid reminders of the grim theme at the core of their work-in-progress, and intelligent, articulate conversation, it never needs to point out the contrasts that abound throughout: the privileges of a life of free expression, the horrors of history that demand to be perpetually addressed and re-addressed, and the beauty and conflict that coexist in the arts and in all of life.

Among other things, the film, like Pilobolus itself, begs the question: *Must* collaboration come out of conflict? Can't it simply come out of *dialogue?* In both its triumph and its dysfunction, Pilobolus crystalizes one of the key issues that animate and frustrate the arts. Its history makes one ask, again and again: *Did it really need to be so hard?* And yet the squabbles and clashes of artistic collaboration are also put in perspective by *Last Dance* in another way. Near the end of the film, just before we are shown scenes from the finished performance of *A Selection,* we see a few more archival clips of smiling, laughing children who did not know they were soon to be murdered. Their heartbreaking faces provide the precisely correct context as Sendak passionately reiterates his lifelong commitment, that he will never stop talking about the Holocaust.

5

In 1999, during the making of *Last Dance,* while she and Matt were still living in the apartment behind the post office, Emily reached an impasse. She had taken a workshop with Jonathan in Maine the previous year and had then auditioned for Pilobolus—and had not been chosen. (Matt's concise theory: "She wasn't weird enough.") Since then, a year or more had passed, and she felt her options were depleted. "I was literally ready to move back to Georgia," she later recalled. "It would be better than sitting up here doing nothing." She reasoned that at least she had friends in Georgia with whom she could dance, and with whom she could try to start something, anything; and, too, moving back to Georgia wouldn't mean leaving Matt— but at this pivotal moment she achieved a breakthrough. Pilobolus hired her as a dancer in a spinoff project called Pilobolus Too. Initially developed three years earlier to provide an option for small venues that couldn't afford the full company, Pilobolus Too offered a shorter show that featured only two dancers—originally Adam Battelstein and Rebecca Stenn—doing solos and duets, reminiscent of the early Momix that Moses and Alison had toured. As Pilobolus Too evolved, however, it became geared more toward schools. When Rebecca Stenn decided to leave, Emily was asked to take over for her. The forty-five-minute show in which she and Adam would tour to schools around the country began with a duet, followed by a kind of mini-*Walklyndon* scaled down for just the two of them, a section on improvisation, and a final piece that consisted of the first half of the mid-1970s Chase-Pendleton duet *Alraune.* The show came as part of a package that included two classes afterward, so Emily began learning how to teach the Pilobolus approach to movement. She had not only taken Jonathan's workshop but had taught dance in various ways for years, so she could easily acclimate to being a teacher as well as a performer.

The work wasn't full time, but sporadic—yet for Emily, who had so often felt that she hadn't found a place for herself, it meant a lot. Matt had neither campaigned for her nor pulled any strings to make the job happen, so they both felt a genuine pride in her achievement. She was a working dancer at last, and now, together, they could settle into their adult careers.

The following year, when Matt bought a string bass, it almost felt as if another person were living with them, so he and Emily moved to a larger apartment in a two-unit house in Bantam. That same year, Emily participated in a special project, *Garden of the Heart,* commissioned for the American Craft Museum in New York City. Tommy Simpson, an artist who worked in wood, had received the commission and decided to involve Pilobolus: Emily and three other dancers worked with Jonathan and Robby to create a quartet with a Garden of Eden story, to perform inside his commissioned work in the museum. Emily would go on to perform in varied Pilobolus projects through the years, including classic rep pieces presented at special events, photo shoots for calendars and books, and assignments for film and television, but she did not yet realize that her most fulfilling work in Pilobolus still awaited her, many years in the future.

6

Against a black background, with slanted shafts of smoky light above, three dancers in kimonos (two women, one man) stand upright on the hunched backs of three other dancers (all male). The three crouching figures slowly move forward with their partners balanced atop them, a sense of mystery, expectation, in the air. As the dancers slowly segue into other positions and partnering, the piece builds toward more dramatic and rapid movement and sound. After a flurry of motion, there is one male alone on stage, on the ground, on his back, rocking back and forth, pulsing with the percussive rhythms, reaching, as if possessed by energy and a yearning, then—a leap; rolls and leaps continue until the other five dancers return and, in an instant, the six converge into a single creature, multiple bodies, and especially multiple legs, extended from one standing male figure at center, as if to suggest the multiarmed gods of the Hindu triumvirate. (Within Pilobolus, this position is called "the tree," and in fact there are two male figures standing, one behind the other, but the effect on the viewer is a sense of a single multilimbed entity.) The remarkable, deft suddenness with which the powerful image arrives is a showstopper. So begins *Tsu-Ku-Tsu*, a nearly half-hour work, its tone and texture established brilliantly in its first five or six minutes.

Alison had decided to collaborate with an acclaimed Japanese musician, Leonard Eto, a master Taiko drummer. In his late thirties at the time, Eto, the son of koto player Kimio Eto, had made an impressive career for himself, first in the 1980s as the principal figure in Kodo, an innovative, influential Japanese taiko drum group that had travelled to dozens of countries, and then, in the 1990s, as a solo artist.

Taiko drums vary in size, with the average the size of a wine barrel, and some as large as a car; for this job, Eto had to bring drums that could fit through the entrance to Washington Club Hall, where he joined Alison and the dancers to create the piece. His music, all analog, all composed and performed solely by him, would be the new work's primary inspiration and energy source: one guy with gigantic drums and some very tiny cymbals, whose intense drumming, with virtuosic flare and a little bit of a groove, could conjure ancient times, thunder, the pulses of life, to awaken the forces dormant beneath the present moment.

Rugged and fit, athletic and slim, with jet-black hair, and unkempt in a handsome rock star way, Leonard Eto was friendly but quiet, and Matt recalls him always going to his drum, "not wanting to talk about it, wanting to do it," an approach perfectly attuned to the way of Pilobolus. He would work the dancers hard with his drumming, his rock star ruggedness well matched to this most energetic of dance companies, and he and Alison would talk about *ten chi jin,* a Japanese philosophical concept that involves the relationship between *ten* (heaven or sky), *chi* (earth or ground), and *jin* (man). In essence, there's heaven and earth, and man in between the two—it is this in-between space we occupy, with a stretching up to heaven and a "grounding" to earth. This concept provided a lens through which to view the various improvisations and ideas that occurred in the studio, and to develop them.

Matt was excited from the beginning. To work with live musicians always excited him, and his martial arts background had prepared him well to draw on Eastern sensibility and thought. Otis, who could speak a little Japanese, also approached the project with obvious interest, and at one point had everyone over to his place for sushi. Gaspard saw Leonard Eto as "a very cool dude" whose drumming reminded him of the tradition of African drumming: "The drum reminds you of the sound of life." Throughout the creative process, all the dancers would ask their new collaborator lots of questions—and Matt, to his delight, got to play Eto's drum.

The music would eventually provide a name for the piece—*tsu-ku-tsu* is a specific rhythm in Taiko drumming—but first, and more fundamentally, the rise and fall of the music, with its thunderclaps and suggestions of the tribal and totemic, would help each component sequence become its own little world, each with its own arc to it. On one level a study of partnering, on three parallel tracks that allow the six dancers to pair up, *Tsu-Ku-Tsu* places multiple duets within a larger landscape, alongside other elements.

The fantastic male solo early on, created by Ben Pring, arose from the uncanny flexibility of his back. When his successor, Ras Mikey C, had to adapt it for himself (because neither he nor anyone else had the same insane level of flexibility as Ben) the solo gained other emotional wrinkles, with a more pronounced emphasis on a religious trance-rapture implied in the convulsions. Later, another dancer, Manelich Minniefee, would do his own dynamic take on it.

In the "mirror men" sequence, a quirky duet with Otis and Gaspard that played off of their two bald heads, one white and one black, and the "music" of breathing sounds made by Leonard Eto, the two dancers in their near-nudity suggest statues; but as their positions alter—one lifted straight above the other, now one in front of the other, and now the one in front moving to reveal the other's head—it begins to resemble a game that evokes totems, control, or manipulation (with echoes of Alison's unforgettable duets with Moses in the mid-1970s). Soon the full company is on stage again; there will be, among other things, a duet between the two females, and a collapse of four dancers into a pile left onstage as the backdrop to a second male duet (known in-house as "the rodeo boys"), that takes place between the other two, less naked males, whose interweaving and tumbling of bodies elicits another moment of audience applause.

The original rodeo boys were Ben and Matt, who together had begged Alison to let them continue developing a duet that they wanted to do, even though it didn't seem to be working, and she had let them. "Ben and I," Matt explained, "had a balancing duet that included moves that we knew we couldn't do, and we were going to practice until we got it." In the end, it became, in his words, "a super cool duet," which is no exaggeration: it employed leverage to great effect, and a remarkable move Matt and Ben invented called "body floss" in which, with their two bodies connected by their hands, one man dives through the space created by the arms and legs of the other. This is done repetitively (like floss) with only one of the two men having his legs on the floor at any given time. The finished duet, placed in the latter part of the overall composition, builds tension ("like winding a spring") as the piece moves toward its finale.

Alison approached the piece with an interest in "washes," her term for a sweep or a wave, of motion, energy, or people moving across the stage (for example, like tumbleweeds). In this case, if six dancers rolled across the stage, two might be left behind and the others would roll back and absorb them.

Matt found much of the movement "super fun to work on" but for any new performer coming to it, *Tsu-Ku-Tsu* ranks high on the difficulty scale, not in terms of stamina but of skill. It's hard to learn due to what Matt calls "a lot of weird technique. If you're experienced in Pilobolus it's not that hard, but any other kind of experience won't help." That's part of what makes it so strong. It has elements that are very much its own, not often seen repeated, and despite its intense energy, and the absence of a storyline or melody, *Tsu-Ku-Tsu* has within it a constant variation of tempo and mood.

The Japanese aesthetic of simplicity also informed the piece, including its lighting and costumes. Lighting designer Stephen Strawbridge's art here is exactly right: those aforementioned dramatic shafts of slanted smoky light provide atmosphere, but the dancers themselves are primarily lit by expertly judged brighter light, crisp but never obtrusive. Likewise the costumes by Angelina Avallone, in an earth-tone palette, contributed to both mood and clarity while never upstaging their wearers, barefoot and with bodies largely exposed. Once the opening-scene kimonos are shed, two of the men are bare chested, in knee-length olive-green khakis; the two women wear two-piece costumes in yellow, orange, pink; the other two men appear, after the initial scene, nude except for dance belts. Evocative of, but not overly concerned with, Japanese ritual, the piece sidesteps Western clichés of Asian "exoticism" and none of its ingredients feel like mere borrowings.

Tsu-Ku-Tsu premiered in Boston in May 2000, and ran throughout Pilobolus's New York season at the Joyce that summer, during which Leonard Eto performed onstage with the dancers ("His back glistening, he thunders on the giant drum, walks among the dancers with a smaller drum strapped on, or chimes finger cymbals," wrote Deborah Jowitt in the *Village Voice,* where she also praised "the stunning opening" and the piece overall). It subsequently toured in many Pilobolus programs over the next few years. It seemed then, and still seems, both a culmination and an opening, a portal to new discoveries, in Alison's art: an arrival and a departure, both, in the best sense.

Although one can find in it the suggestion of representational images, such as the already-mentioned Shiva-like figure created by all six dancers combined—or, as a reviewer for the *Washington Post* felt, tumbling autumn leaves, a snake, a mountain—the piece does not depend on any such one-to-one visual equivalences, nor does a viewer need to look for particular East–West cultural correspondences or contrasts; *Tsu-Ku-Tsu* only gestures toward such things as it swirls past; and the onlooker can simply revel in the cascade of glorious motion, as six extraordinary dancers interact in a constantly shifting series of mostly abstract tableaux, with fleeting suggestions of emotional exchanges, brief sparks between individuals, quickly dismissed or abandoned amid the physical motion. It is nonnarrative, yet there is, sprinkled throughout, the awareness that these creatures are humans, not symbols. The result is an abstract tapestry of human experience transmuted into a larger, unquantifiable work of art. Or, as another of its originators, Rebecca Anderson Darling, neatly summed it up twenty years later, while expressing her love for the piece and its "elegant subtle power": "It's like a moving rock garden, kind of Zen, strength and subtlety, like ink blots."

The time: within a year or two after the making of *Tsu-Ku-Tsu*. Traveling Highway 1 up the West Coast, taking the scenic route, four dancers in a car, on tour: Matt, behind the wheel, and three of his newer colleagues (Renée, Jennifer, Mark). Mid to late morning, the sun at mid-height. Driving through a redwood forest, perhaps in a national park, Matt pulled over, stopped the car, and they all got out. Multiple shafts of sunlight at a forty-five-degree angle, breaking through the forest, warmed the ground. A rising mist accentuated the sun-shafts, gave structure to the morning glow—the same effect that, in theatre, a lighting designer accomplishes with an artificial haze that makes streams of light visible to the audience. Matt thought of *Tsu-Ku-Tsu*, and how, while he performed it, "In my head I was always in a Japanese forest in which ninjas were about to drop down, and here it was." With his colleagues nearby but separate, perhaps two dozen feet apart from one another, yet together in the silence, he stood still among the redwoods and took in the vision, the balance of life and art in equilibrium, amid spears of radiance.

NINE

Combinations

1

Life, especially to a child, can feel like a puzzle, and often the components don't entirely interlock or coalesce until later. Suburban Long Island, in the 1970s and 80s. A series of houses, apartments, and condos in four different towns, all within approximately a half-hour of one another. Frequent shifts of location indicative of a deeper instability. A young couple that had married at age eighteen and, like many couples who marry too soon, hadn't been ready. Their split, when the younger of their two daughters was three. Their reunion, their next split, their next reunion, and so on, a pattern that replayed. Their divorce, when that daughter was eight. The mother's personal struggles. For the daughters, a particularly hard year after the divorce, when they live with their dad, mostly left to their own devices. Moving back with their mom the following year. An improvement: "When I was with my mom I didn't feel like I was alone. It kind of felt like we were tackling life together." From then on, mostly raised by mom, who had at that point a regimented, strict manner that could even seem cold at times, but it was, as her daughter understood, "because she had to be. She was doing the best she could."

That younger daughter felt different from others around her, and her life never felt stable, but she read a lot, partly to disappear into other worlds. Always a good student, she played the flute and she danced. The dancing had begun at age three. Even as a small child she had been so athletic that her mother couldn't keep her sitting still—clearly a common phenomenon among future members of Pilobolus—and as she was a bit pigeon-toed a

doctor had recommended that her mother put her in dance to cure the tendency. It worked, and also provided an outlet for her physical energy. She had the same teachers from age three to seventeen, and they set her on a dance career track early on. They pushed her to take workshops; they took her to New York City to explore the dance world; and dance became the one stable thing in Renée Jaworski's life.

In high school, even though she had never had a cheerleader personality, she became captain of the cheerleading squad. She took to the movement and to the dynamics of how to urge a crowd onward. She also liked writing and, in particular, finding arguments in writing, so she toyed with the idea of being a lawyer, but when she tried to express this interest to others she wasn't taken seriously. She told her high school guidance counselor she wanted to study dance and the arts, and, after much investigation of various schools, received a scholarship to University of the Arts in Philadelphia, where she studied theatre as well as dance, the first person in her family to go to college.

Her goal in high school had been to get into a college, but in the midst of her college career, ambitious but still trying to find her way, she realized that she had no further plan. In a bit of an "existential crisis" she began taking a number of different courses—in business, in education—not sure what she would do. A wise advisor, Susan Glazer, the head of the dance department, saw a great deal of talent in her and didn't want her to ignore it; she pushed her to audition, and to realize the broader scope of what she could do, the possibilities of piecing together a career from teaching, dancing, and other components.

Renée had studied Pilobolus in her dance history books. When she learned that Moses Pendleton had once done a solo on one leg—and then learned that this inventive choice had come about because he had needed to stay off the other foot due to a broken toe—Renée thought it brilliant; she loved the idea of working with one's limitations to create something innovative. She learned a lot about Pilobolus and Moses and savored "how renegade they were." She learned too that Moses had gone on to create another company, Momix.

In February of 1994, in the final semester of Renée's senior year, three hundred people, men and women, auditioned for Momix at City Center in New York. Only five were hired, Renée among them. She started with Momix in March, before she even graduated college. She would finish classes on Friday and drive up to Connecticut for rehearsals over the weekend, then back to school on Monday. This went on for a couple of months, until she graduated and could plunge in completely.

And the plunge felt wonderful, as the world of Momix provided a long-deferred liberation to the young woman who had always felt misunderstood. She admits even today there is a part of her that is simply that way, always feeling a bit misunderstood, but with Momix, for the first time, she discovered she could feel understood, heard, her idiosyncrasies valued in a way they had never been before. "I felt so comfortable," she recalls, and in those days she thought: *Of course this is where I am, where else would I be? These are the people I should have grown up with my entire life*—"because I could be quirky and they encouraged it and appreciated it, and they let me play. It felt comfortable and exciting and I was grateful."

Momix worked in Moses's tiny converted barn. The dancers took ballet every morning with a teacher and would later work on improvs on their own. In the afternoon, Moses would come by to see what had developed. Absent much of the time, he often left the dancers to their own creative strategies. At times they would "play outside" or do photo shoots in the giant, magnificent sunflower garden on Moses's property, or elsewhere.

Apart from the use of ballet training—which in Pilobolus would have been considered irrelevant, if not antithetical, to the troupe's aesthetic—the Momix approach had remained similar to the Pilobolus method, but with a subtle but telling difference in the nature of the improvs: Momix tended to start with a prop, whereas Pilobolus liked to start with a human connection and add the prop later. In general, Momix asked of its dancers "What can you do and how cool can you make it?" Or, as Renée put it, "The processes were largely the same but the feeling was different and therefore the end product was different." She started touring with Momix that summer, with three evening-length shows: *Momix Classics* (which included short pieces from the Momix repertory, such as *Table Talk, White Widow, Medusa, Spider,* and others), a separate show called *Passion,* and a new show, *Baseball.*

Renée got along well with Moses, they talked quite a bit, he liked her work as a dancer, she felt respected by him, and she admired the fact that, as she says, "He has made a choice to bring beauty to this world." She felt even more connected to Cynthia, who pushed her more ("in a good way") and served as an inspiration of another kind. "In terms of life experience, there were a few women I looked up to and really admired," Renée later explained, "one of whom was Cynthia. When I met her, she was turning forty and was still performing and had a child." Renée also admired a Momix dancer, Solveig Olsen, who later married veteran Pilobolus dancer Mark Santillano. "To see these women dancing way beyond what I had thought possible changed my mindset, to see Cynthia running a company, to watch these women making a career beyond what I had been taught possible." (Years later, in her mid-forties, Renée would feel she could still "jump on-stage and do it, because Cynthia did it.")

One day while on tour with Momix in Italy, perhaps a year or a year and a half into her time with the company, Renée heard that the Italian crew hired to move lighting equipment for Momix would be driving to another town afterward to do a similar job for Pilobolus. She got very excited and begged them to let her hitch a ride, and offered to help them, in exchange, with loading and unloading the truck. The reply: "We'll give you a ride but we won't let you help us lift things, because we're Italian and you're a woman." She said OK, and that she would go get their coffee. She rode with them, got a hotel room, and went to see Pilobolus. Like Matt Kent, she would remember every piece on the program from her first time seeing the company perform live, in her case particularly struck by how the imagery, the morphing of organisms, allowed her to see feelings and connectedness in the world. The show opened with *The Particle Zoo* ("It stood out because I had never seen a piece where men could be sensuous together and still be athletic—tough and rugged and masculine and sensuous and caring at the same time"), then continued with *Pseudopodia, Walklyndon,* and, after intermission, *Day Two.* The latter had lost none of its revelatory power. "*Day Two* transformed me," Renée recalled. "It made me see how human bodies can transform and create another world, around the dancers and around me."

In 1990s America, as the country experienced a new economic boom, possibilities seemed abundant, and Renée's thoughts would now and then turn to larger dreams. She wanted to go off on her own, to choreograph, to perhaps start a company. Then, in 1996, she and her husband Mark Melvin, whom she had met midway through her college years and had begun dating shortly before she had gotten the job in Momix, decided to have a baby. Others told her that as a female dancer, having a baby would mark the end of her career—it was "over"—an idea to which Renée rather happily gave the finger, thanks to the role models she had seen. She chose to leave Momix, though she performed through her fifth month of pregnancy. After the birth of her daughter, only a few weeks went by before Cynthia called to ask if she would come back and tour, and she did, occasionally, for another year or two, while living in Philadelphia. In 1999 she and Mark moved back to New York, where he had a full-time job, and they lived in Brooklyn for about a year. Renée, ready to go back to work full time, began to search for the right choice. She did a couple of tours with Momix; and she worked with Carolyn Dorfman, a choreographer and dance educator with an impressive troupe based in New Jersey. In 2000, Momix offered to take her back part time; but then, suddenly, Pilobolus was auditioning.

Rebecca was leaving the company after a long and successful run. Her skillful stage presence had benefited from a seemingly effortless cross between ingénue and bombshell, a prospect that might have daunted any number of auditioning dancers—but not Renée, who situated herself within the larger history of Pilobolus: "I knew exactly what they were looking for. Rebecca had replaced Jude, and I was more like Jude." Renée recognized both women as two of the best Pilobolus dancers ever, with contrasting gifts, Jude being "funny, gritty, quirky, athletic, tough" (and worthy of the supreme compliment: "When I think of Pilobolus, I think of her"), and Rebecca a dancer who "stands out, a beauty, so elegant to watch. She brought an elegance that Alison had." Renée saw clearly that she had more in common with Jude or Martha, "funny and athletic."

At the time, Renée's hair was already blonde, like Rebecca's, but she didn't feel pressure to be like Rebecca but rather to emphasize versatility. Renée felt "more like an actress than a dancer" so, when in doubt, she *played* a dancer. And it worked. Mirra Bank, still filming a range of activities in and around Pilobolus while making *Last Dance,* filmed the audition. She recalls, "We all knew she was hands down the most stunning of all the people auditioning." As Matt says, it was immediately obvious that Renée "had the goods." Still, the artistic directors of Pilobolus were hesitant to give her a job, because she had a small child. Renée told them she was going to dance anyway, if not with Pilobolus than somewhere else, and they decided to hire her.

Day Two, the piece that had so captivated her the first time she had seen Pilobolus, was among the first that she learned, along with *Aeros, A Selection, Femme Noire* (a solo that Alison had created with Rebecca, which Renée would reinterpret), *Tsu-Ku-Tsu, Pseudopodia,* and a few others. The first new piece she helped make was Robby and Jonathan's *Davenen,* in collaboration with the New York based klezmer band the Klezmatics. She found that she loved working with live musicians, but also discovered that a Pilobolus opening night did not end the developmental process, especially if, as in this case, the resulting piece proved a bit underwhelming. Pilobolus would still work on pieces, including this one, after they were already up on stage.

Of the artistic directors, Renée had been immediately drawn to Robby because of his easy, quiet nature, but Jonathan she initially found "totally intimidating." Fortunately she had exactly the right attitude to cope with his intensity: "Jonathan had a way of pushing people that got something out of you that you didn't know existed in you. Sometimes it hurt, but I appreciated that someone cared that much to find it." She would eventually become close to Jonathan, especially through teaching, and by gradually getting to understand him over time. He would become for her a person whose bark was worse than his bite, to whom she learned how to speak her mind, and to whom, in their mutual understanding, she could say "no" and he would hear her.

As for Michael, Renée found him "very sweet." She would soon help him make one of his most memorable works.

2

A flash of lightning amid pitch black—and then we see Renée on the ground, face up, leaning near or against Otis Cook; she is pulsing, liquid; they connect and rise, moving together in various configurations, with almost continuous physical contact; they appear to be nearly one creature, certainly two parts of a single phenomenon. Hence the title, *Symbiosis,* a word that had been used in reviews of pieces made in the earlier years of Pilobolus (and a concept central to the company's identity). Otis's shaved head is matched by the severity with which Renée's hair is pulled back; and, near naked, they roll, rise, fall, rolling up and down, lifted, tipping back and forth—Renée seems to live on Otis's body; he is more the host, more often standing, upright, the support, carrying himself like a living statue of a troubled anti-hero, a statue that Renée seems to effortlessly climb by rolling up him with anti-gravitational ease. Tumbling and linking, connecting again and again—eventually she squats on his shoulders and he walks, they move as one creature, in a classic Pilobolus combination—they, and the piece itself, are fluid, seamless, dynamic, flowing, emotive. As the lights fade, we realize that they will continue as symbiotic partners or as one entity, and we are left with a sense of human pairing and biological evolution as one concept.

At the time of the piece's gestation, Renée had been reading *Women Who Run with the Wolves: Myths and Stories of the Wild Woman Archetype* by Clarissa Pinkola Estés, a Jungian analyst; the book, published nearly a decade earlier, had been a particularly long-running *New York Times* best-seller, and now it fascinated Renée as it had fascinated others. She and Otis talked about a story from it, the Baba Yaga story, a tale of feminine initiation into one's own powers, and it became a strong influence on the images they would conjure to show Michael for the new duet the three were making. Another influence for Renée was *Titus,* the 1999 film adaptation of Shakespeare's *Titus Andronicus,* which marked the directorial debut of future Tony winner Julie Taymor. Its horrific image of a woman as tree—Titus's daughter Lavinia, whose tongue is cut out and her hands cut off by her rapists, shown with her hands replaced with twigs—stayed with Renée, and she and Otis connected on this image too, this "woman who was a tree," and improvised with it and others in mind.

"Otis was strong enough," Renée later explained, "that I felt safe letting him throw me around." And yet while she trusted him physically, part of the dynamic of *Symbiosis* reflects a fluctuation of trust and nontrust toward a partner. It wasn't simply that she had to calibrate her intuitions in regard to a new colleague; she also had to contend with stresses in her life outside the studio: being new in Pilobolus, many adjustments were needed—in her living situation, her personal relationships—and for a time those stresses found their way into her home life. She would navigate all of this successfully, but first the intensity of that time would find its way into the piece she was making.

"I never thought of myself as human in *Symbiosis.* I always thought of myself as some sort of creature, primordial ooze; I don't have eyes yet, I have to rely on scent and the touch of skin. When I approached the movement—I wouldn't say I was an animal yet; it was all instinct and biology. Whereas when I performed *Day Two,* although I didn't create it, I always felt I was a primitive human; I could see everything." Renée's concept of the piece thus places *Symbiosis* before *Day Two* if one were to create a timeline of these imagined worlds: "*Symbiosis* is immediately after the Big Bang."

Yet Renée didn't have *Day Two* in mind at the time. She did, however, approach the piece through a lens of Pilobolus and having worked with Moses, and a subconscious awareness of the sensibility of earlier "symbiotic" Pilobolus duets, including those that Alison and Moses had made a quarter-century earlier. Equally important, her instincts as an actress met an extraordinary match in the partner with whom she'd been paired: "Otis brought a ton of intelligent artistry. Every role he ever made had multiple layers," she says. "An incredible artist, dark and funny."

In response to what the two of them presented from their improvisations, Michael shaped a stunning fourteen minutes. From its opening lightning strike, which he saw as the stroke of creation, and its bizarre image of the female "reverse-birthed" into the male, a kind of mystical magician who forms her into a suitably magical companion, Michael assessed and assembled the visual possibilities. He saw the male draw the female like an archer's bow; he saw an evolving range of natural images (a rock, a tree, a bird) and mythological figures, including Hermes; he saw children at play, and a rocking horse; and he recognized that an audience would not need a narrative for it all to cohere into a vision of human experience that seems to spin through a timeless, eternal loop. *Symbiosis* was a breakthrough for him, and it would endure through the years ahead.

Audiences and critics quickly saw its virtues, not least the performances that resonated so strongly: "Ms. Jaworski is to the backbend born," quipped Anna Kisselgoff in the *New York Times*, where she also praised Otis as "amazing in his serpentine fluidity." A few years later, in 2005, Pilobolus performed *Symbiosis* at a TEDx conference in Monterey, California, and a video of that version, posted online, brought the piece to a vast additional audience: the clip has now been viewed several million times, and counting. Renée missed out on being the performer in it due to a schedule conflict—she was on tour at the time—but Otis, no longer in the touring company, re-created his role opposite Jennifer Macavinta, and they both turned in excellent performances. The strange blue lighting of this staging, quite different from the chiaroscuro original, alters the piece: the cold, science-fiction pale blueness makes Otis look like an alien or a variation on the Silver Surfer, but also, along with the proximity of the camera, allows us to see the dancers more clearly, and to see Otis's face, which has the emotive qualities of a born actor. Some, including Renée, find the change of lighting detrimental. "I think the lighting is integral to it," she says, and points out that even when *Symbiosis* is presented in its usual theater setting there are questions of precision: "The lightning strike at the beginning sets up the piece. It has to be just right in terms of the quality of the light." To Renée, the TED Talk's bluish lighting throughout "flattens it and makes it a bit of a caricature of itself," yet she praises the performers and recognizes that the video thrilled many viewers who had never before seen, or even heard of, Pilobolus. Many who discovered the piece online wanted to see it live—which, along with its considerable virtues, has helped keep *Symbiosis* in the active repertory as a favorite work.

3

When she joined Pilobolus, Renée had been "intrigued and inspired by Matt," somewhat to the surprise of some of the other dancers, who felt that as dance captain Matt had become too controlling. Renée, however, didn't find his leadership difficult; and to Matt's way of thinking, he was simply conscientious of details to a degree that others, including the artistic directors themselves, weren't. He made sure things happened, and he prevented crises that no one else would have bothered to avert. That Pilobolus was dysfunctional was by this time beyond dispute, and he knew it; in an environment of ever-tipping elements in danger of crashing, it was in his nature to run around rebalancing what he could, even if it meant coming across as a maniac.

Alison, although she had retreated to Maine, would come down to Connecticut and see the pieces that were being worked on. She hadn't been involved in the collaboration with Maurice Sendak and therefore wasn't in the film *Last Dance,* but she had been around for periods of time during its filming and had observed Mirra Bank at work. Between 1999 and 2001, Mirra had also filmed a number of additional Pilobolus pieces, including rehearsals of new works, to enable herself to better illustrate the full range of the company and its dancers; among the works she filmed were Alison's four most recent: the duet *Orangotango;* a trio, *Uno, Dos, Tray;* a solo, *Femme Noire;* and the full-company piece *Tsu-Ku-Tsu.* In the studio, away from the other directors, Alison was on a roll, making some of the best work of her career, and now, with a commission from the Wolf Trap Foundation for a new piece, she decided to enlist Mirra to make a thirty-minute documentary of its creation. Made after most of *Last Dance* had been filmed—though Mirra would return to do more filming for *Last Dance* prior to its release—this second, shorter look into the world of Pilobolus would be, in Mirra's apt phrase, "fundamentally different in terms of its DNA. In the studio it was Alison on her own, she had been commissioned, she had an idea in mind, working with dancers with whom she had a history."

The idea Alison had in mind rested on a solid narrative, one that not only already existed but dated back to the sixteenth century. She and the dancers would tell an ancient Chinese tale, inspired by a colorful gift that had entered her family years earlier: *Monkey and the White Bone Demon,* a children's book published in the 1980s, based on an episode from the classic Ming Dynasty novel *Journey to the West.* From the time the children's book had been given to her kids, Alison had thought the material had rich possibilities; now, years later, she obtained used copies of the book to give to the dancers, then traced the story back to the full novel, *Journey to the West,* and gave them each that as well. Together, she and the dancers would reset the fable in contemporary times but retain its magical premise. Three travelers and a monkey have their courage and resourcefulness tested during their search for Buddhist Scriptures, when they encounter a demon who disguises herself, appears in various forms, and engages them in mortal combat.

The story's vivid characters lent themselves to a delightful set of casting choices. Compact, cheerful, and flexible beyond belief, Ben Pring had all the right qualities to take the lead role of Monkey, who swings, pole vaults, and leaps his way to heroism. Renée, cast as a male character named Pigsy, began, as she would note in the film, "studying things that little boys study, like G.I. Joe things" because the piece is "like these little boys playing this fantasy game where we're warriors." She realized she had to toughen up her performance and "get on the guy bandwagon." In contrast, Gaspard brought a balanced presence to the role of Sandy, another of the three naive travelers, while Otis, who had played the incarnation of evil in *A Selection,* reversed polarity and played the monk, giving a subtle, almost tender performance as a holy man whose removal from earthly ways has made him foolish. As for the outrageous, androgenous, shape-shifting she-demon—a role that would be performed much of the time on stilts—Alison summed up her casting decision neatly: "Matt had the madness and the risk, and he was just totally game and never held back." Matt's performance would wrap camp, drag, and a dash of glam-rock—helped spectacularly by Angelina Avallone's costumes—into a fearless athleticism capped by an extended fight sequence on stilts.

The piece, staged in a minimal design that capitalized on the Pilobolus knack for conjuring entire landscapes with little more than the human body, premiered at Wolf Trap Park, in Vienna, Virginia, on June 13, 2001, and met with great and much-deserved success. Behind the scenes, how-ever, there had been a last-minute drama centered on the original score for the piece. Alison had given longtime friend and collaborator Paul Sullivan a video to work from as he composed the music, and when he had finished she came over to his home, a few days before the show's premiere, to hear the result. They watched the video together, with the music, and afterward she told him she couldn't use what he had composed. It was an anguished situation, not about their friendship but rather the work and her feeling about the music. Alison told him he would have to write an entirely dif-ferent score, even though they had only a few days left until the show. Paul worked intensely, all day every day for those next few days, and sent her the new score. After the premiere, Eric Chase called Paul from Wolf Trap to tell him the premiere had been a big success. "I don't know how to tell you this," Eric added, awkwardly. "She used your first score." And that became the score of the piece. Alison had reversed her opinion and felt so badly about what she had put Paul through that she had been afraid to tell him herself, so she'd had Eric call, knowing Paul would be angry. He was—but not enough to ruin a cherished friendship. (He recounted this incident with a laugh eighteen years later, having had dinner with Alison and Eric, his lifelong friends and longtime neighbors in Maine, the night before.)

Monkey and the White Bone Demon next went to New York as part of the Pilobolus summer run at the Joyce Theater, where it garnered a rave review in the *New York Times* from Anna Kisselgoff, who called it "a terse little comedy full of updated street smarts" and highly praised its cast, es-pecially Matt, who, she noted, "strides admirably through a performance of some physical risk." (Several days later, in a second review of Pilobolus, she would observe, in reference to Matt, Renée, Josie, Gaspard, Ben, and Otis, "This is one of the best groups of dancers Pilobolus has had." She was right.)

Years later, asked how he managed to remain balanced on the stilts dur-ing the extended fight sequence, Matt admitted "It wasn't easy" and that he had, of course, at times fallen during a live performance. "The problem with the stilts is if you fall you can't get back up without help," he explained. If the other performers were close by, they could quickly set him back up-right, and perhaps improvise a way to incorporate it into the action, but he remembered a performance at which he fell while nowhere near any other dancers. From thirty feet away, he exchanged a rapid glance with fellow dancer Mark Fucik, who had replaced Gaspard Louis in the role of Sandy,

one of the monk's followers. "Mark and I had a moment of performer te-
lepathy," Matt said. Without hesitation, Mark took the pole his character
had been using and threw it at Matt as if to attack while the demon was at a
disadvantage, and Matt seized it as if turning the tables, and clamored back
up on his feet, or rather his stilts, to continue the fight as if it were all part
of the story. Stage performers thrive on such moments of mutual improvisational problem-solving, and Matt, as he recalled the incident a decade
and a half later, clearly still savored it.

The thirty-minute documentary *Monkey and the Bone Demon*—the
film title drops the adjective "white"—is, among other things, an endearing snapshot of Matt in his heyday as a dancer, and of the pleasure and
playfulness of his and the company's hard work. The film captures too the
laughing camaraderie in the studio, and there is the always-sweet satisfaction in seeing an onstage hero and villain, in this case Benjamin Pring and
Matt Kent, having fun together offstage. Matt, like others in the troupe,
appreciated Ben's "fantastic disposition," the way he "almost always had a
smile on his face, and never said a bad word about anybody. We bonded
a lot on tour." Alas, although deeply admired by his colleagues, Ben didn't
want to be in Pilobolus for the long haul; he would soon choose to pursue
a career with Cirque du Soleil.

As for Alison, what we see portrayed of her in the documentary is mostly her art—and particularly her own version of the Pilobolus creative process. Without ever raising the issue *as* an issue, the film makes the case that
a studio situation presided over by only a single artistic director, if that director is the right person, can nonetheless achieve a strong and thoroughly
"Pilobolus" result. Mirra Bank had now captured on film two sides of the
Pilobolus dynamic, and after the conflicts seen in *Last Dance,* the short,
joyful *Monkey and the Bone Demon* feels like sunlight breaking through
cloudy skies.

4

From early in its existence Pilobolus had been interested in still photography, and in 2000 it began to create and publish an annual wall calendar
that showcased original photography of the troupe. The first in the series, a
calendar for the year 2001, relied on images supplied by the Joyce Theater,
but all but one of the subsequent calendars were created independently,
in collaboration with longtime friend and photographer John Kane. Back

in the 1980s, when John was in his thirties, he had gotten to know Moses and had photographed Momix, which he would continue to do, on and off, through the years. Soon after, he had met Robby, who had asked him to photograph Pilobolus, and he became the company's "unofficial official photographer."

John had been, in his youth, "the kid with the Polaroid Swinger"—the iconic white camera with a strap, easy to carry and easy to use, that had arrived in 1965 and become a commercial phenomenon—and his decades of photographic experience stretched back nearly as long as he could recall, as if he had received not only his first camera (a Christmas gift), but a certain gene, from his amateur-photographer father. The combination had colored the dirt roads of his rural small-town upbringing as an Italian American in Cheshire, Connecticut. By the time his images of Pilobolus had begun to appear on calendars, he had not only decades of photographic experience but a long familiarity with the company's aesthetic, the way Pilobolus tends to emphasize the human body as an artistic instrument and phenomenon unto itself—stripped, sometimes literally, of distractions, but endowed with a strange blend of the superhuman and the completely human.

Sidestepping the conventional impulse of dance photography, with its effort to capture the essence of live performance, the calendars were designed as original works, with poses conceived to distil and celebrate the Pilobolus sensibility. Like all examples of Pilobolus imagery, they benefited from the physical attractiveness of the dancers themselves, but as John has pointed out, Pilobolus is a great subject for a photographer "not only because of how they look but because of what they can do." His most iconic Pilobolus photos from the late 1990s and early 2000s feature the dancers against a solid white background (or, occasionally, a black one) and showcase their extreme flexibility, their seemingly anti-gravitational abilities to balance on and lift one another, and the witty visual effects created by the combinations of their bodies into, for example, a whimsical spiral, a human pinwheel, or a giant creature made of several performers. Whether clad in bright polychromatic unitards, monochromatic tights, or only dance belts, their costumes and their flesh tones stand out dramatically against the white or black backgrounds for a classic pop-art effect, with a touch of a circus sensibility and the vitality of what the French call *saltimbanques*. The images, used extensively for other marketing and media outreach beyond their appearances on the calendars, became a key component of the

Pilobolus identity, an encapsulation of its ideals that underscored that its essence is not motion but wit made physical through the human body.

The photo shoots took place in John's studio, which he had created in a converted cow barn by his house, on a farm that came up for sale in the late 1990s. When he moved there, photography was changing, and he chose to go digital, happy to be done with the darkroom: "I like to run outside. I like the sunshine. It was an organic, green move. No more chemicals." Green, too, for his palette, as his photography began to expand into the rolling green fields; but for several years, the Pilobolus shoots remained an indoor experience. The space would be, in Matt's words, "hot in the summer and cold in the winter. You walk in and there's old farm equipment. He was always very precise. He climbs up a ladder and sprawls on a beam and shoots down at you. Very DIY." The only Pilobolus director present would be Robby Barnett. "It was always Robby," said Matt. "Nobody else was involved. I would show up at John's—I was crazy at his photo shoots doing weird stuff to get a laugh." And, perhaps, to spark ideas. In the sessions, the dancers themselves came up with ideas, in an improv process similar to that used in the Pilobolus studio when making a piece, and with a parallel search for serendipity. As John put it, "Robby had a lot of great ideas visually, but they all did—a hive mentality." They simply "came up with stuff and tried to create it" and discovered that "sometimes the best images are the ones that you weren't looking for."

5

Early spring 2002. Rural Maine. Three dancers in a car together: Emily and Matt, and Matt's fellow dancer, twenty-three-year-old Ras Mikey C, on their way to Brooksville, the coastal town on Penobscot Bay, with a population of less than a thousand, in which Alison lived. Matt and Ras were to work with her on a new duet, the first Pilobolus piece to be made in Maine. It felt like driving forever, the kind of road trip in the era before GPS on which a traveler finally declares, as Ras did to his companions, "We are in the middle of *nowhere*"—and then a turn, and then another, and the sense of getting even further and further away from civilization. They had repeatedly put off eating, but as the journey stretched on they finally, starving, stopped at a little diner. By the time they reached, in the middle of the night, the old farmhouse in which they were to stay—an arrangement along the lines of what might years later be called "Airbnb"—they found nobody home, but a note on the door saying "Your rooms are upstairs," so they went up to the second floor. The next morning their hosts apologized for not being there to greet them: "Sorry, we had a bunch of lambs that were born in the middle of the night."

Ras had grown up in Northern Virginia, trained in dance, and attended the University of the Arts, where he had been selected to perform in a Momix ensemble piece. After his graduation in 2001, in need of a job, he had gone to a Pilobolus audition where he did some classically oriented moves, to which Jonathan said, "That's good, but can you make it look like you're being electrocuted?" (a reference to Gaspard's role in *Davenen*). Coming from a hip-hop background, improvisation came easily to Ras, and he got the job. Jonathan assumed things based on Ras's name, dreadlocks, and Rastafarian identity—Ras had to explain that he was from Virginia, not Jamaica. The directors, he would find, were "very New England–based" with a lack of sensitivity to certain aspects of culture: "Pilobolus is very 'United Colors of Benetton' and you fit into a part. I fit into an archetypal image the company had formulated. There was a lot of ignorance. Not that I blamed them. They lived in their bubble." Raised in the South, however, Ras connected with Matt and Emily. Or, as Matt put it, he and Ras "both grew up in the South where people are blatantly racist, and then moved to the North, where people are secretly racist. We both got that and bonded over it." Ras would become such great friends with Emily that he would refer to her as his sister.

As a performer he defied preconceptions, without super strength or movie-star looks but, as Matt says, "so charismatic you couldn't take your eyes off him." Ras replaced Ben Pring, and he couldn't really do the same things physically—nobody could—but Ras made it work. He worked hard to learn *Tsu-Ku-Tsu*. Matt would be tough with him but Ras respected the intense work ethic: "It was so great to have someone like Matt who would push me hard but know when to back off and let me get it. Matt is the reason I got good." He needed to be pushed but would rise to the occasion, and appreciated, too, the "maturity of the experience of the people who were in the company" who had been there before his arrival, not only Matt, but Otis, Renée, and others, from which he benefited.

Ras could be extremely blunt without hurting people's feelings, a trait Matt prized, and sometimes found hilarious, as when Ras tirelessly corrected Alison, who seemed unable to refrain from pronouncing his name as if it were "Ross" (it is pronounced "Ras" as in the first syllable of *Rastafar-*

ian). Yet it was Alison, of all the directors, Ras most admired and to whom he would give greatest credit for his own development: "What I learned most in Pilobolus, after studying so many years to be a dancer, I learned to be a human *first,* creating an environment for the audience to experience."

Once in Brooksville, Ras and Matt would go to a local gym to work with Alison and rehearse: a basketball-type gym, like a community center, with a rope hanging from the ceiling, a space about the size of Club Hall but with its wooden floor made of darker wood, and an older feeling. Emily would find things to do during the day, like yoga classes and grocery shopping, in a nearby town, Blue Hill, and then come by in the afternoon to see what they had done—but they were too exhausted to demonstrate. Their arms were dead. They were spending their days hanging by their hands from straps, their feet off the ground.

Alison had a growing interest in aerial concepts and an impulse to do something associated with the Victorian era, ideas she initially thought she might combine, perhaps putting Ras and Matt in powdered wigs and dresses.

"When we began," Matt recalled, "Alison told us we were going to be in drag, wearing seventeenth- or eighteenth-century period dresses. She loved to have me in drag. She loved that kind of naughty thing, but she also knew when to let go of something." When a premise wasn't working, Alison could dispense with it without any fuss, and soon the idea of drag got dropped. The intensity with which Matt and Ras had to work to accomplish the required physical feats—entirely off the ground and dependent on the muscularity of their upper bodies—created an indelible visual in itself, gritty and forceful, the polar opposite of drag's sly deceptions. In the end, with the two men bare-chested and clad in green pants that resembled combat fatigues, along with heavy boots, this new work would become one of the most strikingly masculine entries in the Pilobolus repertoire.

"As we started to develop material," Ras remembers, "Matt and I know each other so well we could push things without upsetting each other—getting more aggressive. She could see the implications. This is a black guy and a white dude stuck together. She realized that the inability of the two to escape each other was the angle to pursue."

In Alison's words, "It's about unexpected proximity. These two men never intended to be here together. They could be survivors from a war incident, marooned on a desert island, survivors of a plane crash. They have to learn to coexist."

In their real lives outside of the piece, everyone coexisted beautifully. When Emily offered to make a dinner at Alison and Eric's house, Alison thought it a lovely idea. "You do the cooking," she said, "and Eric will make the martinis." Emily made a vegetable risotto with the creamy sauce added separately so a nondairy version could be served to Ras, a vegan, and when she declared "dinner's ready" to the assembled group, an appreciative Alison replied "Oh, this is just wonderful. I need an Emily!" At which Eric, her perfect match, turned and replied mischievously, "Maybe *I* do."

The trip to Maine left Matt, Emily, and Ras with happy memories, and Alison with one of her best pieces. There were other effects, too. After weeks of doing pull-ups every day, Matt's upper body grew so much that he later thought that one of his costumes for another piece, a tank unitard that no longer fit, had shrunk. In reality, it hadn't; his side back muscles (sometimes referred to as "back abs") had grown much larger. "It's all upper torso hydraulics," Alison told the *Washington Post* later that year. "That whole illusion of float . . . it's all in the upper torso." She added that the demands of the piece initially made it almost impossible for Ras and Matt to get through an entire performance, but after months of work, they were both "cut like diamonds."

Prior to its summer premiere, however, the piece still needed a name. At an early performance in Philadelphia, where it was scheduled to appear directly after the program's intermission, a minor issue with the rigging caused a delay, so Alison, to keep the audience engaged, walked onstage and invited audience members to submit suggestions for a title, which she read through over martinis after the show. The winning entry, *Ben's Admonition,* came with an explanatory quotation. It refers to the pun popularly attributed to Benjamin Franklin, that he supposedly delivered as a warning at the signing of the Declaration of Independence: "We must, indeed, all hang together, or most assuredly we shall all hang separately."

Matt describes the piece's sensibility as "feeling like being in the middle of a void, but at the same time like two guys on a subway holding onto the straps, too close to the next guy, white and black; it escalates to a conflict. Finding yourself in a world where you're with the wrong person. You want to be separated but you need each other, like two convicts on a chain gang. At the end you just check out because there's nothing left." Paul Sullivan's mercurial score augmented the changing moods of the action, and Stephen Strawbridge's dark, somewhat foreboding lighting added to the sense of suspense and evoked an eerie completeness to the nonetheless unspecified setting.

"As a performer," adds Matt, "by the end of it you are in such pain it is kind of cathartic to pretend to 'hang yourself' at the end. It is a last extremely difficult move, because by then you're so exhausted, and you say to yourself: *Just this one more thing and it's over.*"

Despite the grueling nature of the piece—and the fact that Ras started to develop carpal tunnel syndrome from performing it—neither man had any regrets, only pride in the achievement. Their hard work paid off in rave reviews, best summed up by Jennifer Dunning's assessment in the *New York Times* that this "haunting" piece suggested that "Pilobolus can still blend narrative and acrobatic movement into a third thing that is pure metaphor." Dunning praised every aspect of the piece, and everyone involved with it, but "best of all" Ras Mikey C and Matt Kent.

6

On June 23, 2002, the *New York Times* published an article entitled "Within Pilobolus, Working Together and Pulling Away" in which writer Gia Kourlas revealed some of the tensions among the four artistic directors, noting that while Jonathan and Robby still worked in partnership, Alison and Michael each now chose to work alone. "It became power-brokering," Alison is quoted as saying of the earlier four-way collaborative, "and I don't have the patience for that." Similarly, Michael states that he enjoyed making *Symbiosis* "because I didn't have to run ideas by Jonathan and Robby. They couldn't reject them or run them down in front of anybody."

On July 12, Mirra Bank's film *Last Dance* opened in New York to highly positive reviews. It would go on to be shortlisted for an Academy Award and would win numerous awards and honors from film festivals, institutes, and foundations; but its release, coming on the heels of the *New York Times* piece, offered a further revelation of the contentious ways of Pilobolus, especially Jonathan, and of the company's infighting. The years-long decline in relations among the leaders of Pilobolus had become more public than ever before, a reality that did not bode well.

Yet if certain of the artistic directors had what seemed to be, more and more obviously, irreconcilable differences, elsewhere an opposite force was reaching its magnetic fulfillment. On July 27, a steamy hot day in Atlanta,

Emily and Matt, after five years of living together, finally married. The occasion was not without a touch of comic chaos. Only hours before the wedding, Matt discovered that his tux did not fit—and that nearly every man in the wedding party, whose tuxes had all come from the same local shop, had a similar problem. Fortunately, Matt's resourceful stage manager friend Alison Schwartz was on hand. "Get me some safety pins," she declared amid the panic, and proceeded to rig everyone's outfit to look good from afar—good enough for live theatre, which is, of course, exactly what a wedding is. Matt's dad, the Reverend Kent, performed the ceremony; the vows were exchanged; and to the great relief of Emily's family she rejoined the ranks of Godly respectability. And though Matt and Emily's future with Pilobolus may have looked uncertain, in the comedy-drama of their personal lives they had a new and very permanent contract.

TEN

Differences

1

Alison, having put Matt on stilts in *Monkey and the White Bone Demon* and had Matt and Ras hang from straps in *Ben's Admonition,* continued to take her performers further off the ground with her next endeavor, an aerial piece in which the dancers worked on silks. Made mostly at Jacob's Pillow and Washington Club Hall, it had a Romeo and Juliet theme, and Alison brought in an English professor as dramaturg ("a lady Shakespeare expert," as Ras put it) to help them analyze the play for a week. All the dancers had notebooks and were expected to behave like students, a tough sell for the intensely energized, movement-oriented troupe, many of whom had already encountered the play in high school. The dancers found the process exasperating, and, according to Ras, eventually Matt blew up and "made the lady cry." (Matt doesn't remember this, but says, "If that's what anyone remembers, I'm sure I did. In those days I made *everybody* cry, without ever trying to." One can imagine it: given his masculine, slightly rough voice and the intensity with which he declared his feelings, an expression of frustration could resonate as a personal attack—often to Matt's own bewilderment.)

Once the Shakespeare class had been dispensed with, Ras, Matt, and everyone else greatly enjoyed making the piece. Alison brought in two people to teach the dancers how to use the silks, an education far more to their tastes, and a skill not nearly as common among dancers then as it is now. "But then," according to Matt, "Alison just told them that we had enough information and made us figure out a bunch of stuff ourselves. She didn't want us to get stuck in technique or tradition. It worked." Although Matt wasn't a fan of every aspect of the piece, he loved the slow use of the silks and the economy of movement in those slow sections. Ras prized Alison's directorial wisdom: "Alison really worked with me to build more depth in my performance. She taught me how to hold the audience just by standing there, and to be more vulnerable, more generous."

The result, *Star-cross'd,* with music by Edward Bilous and Aki Nawaz, lighting design by Stephen Strawbridge, and costumes by Angelina Avallone, had its first public performance in May 2003 at the Bushnell Center for the Performing Arts in Hartford, after which the *Hartford Courant* declared it "a thing of remarkable beauty, grace, and athleticism." Its opening tableau, in which most of the troupe appears to be floating upside-down in midair, and its delicate final off-the-ground duet (the most exquisite of those "slow sections" that Matt admired) frame the piece with its two most memorable images.

Like all aerial works, *Star-Cross'd* also presented potential dangers, as became apparent the following month when the piece premiered at the ADF and an audience witnessed a frightening moment. According to a journalist who attended the Thursday performance, "Matt Kent's leg visibly trembled for several agonizing seconds, as he hung upside down between two pieces of fabric stretching from the fly space to the stage. His leg maintained enough tension in the fabric to keep him from plummeting. But asymmetry was noticeable on more than one occasion during Tuesday's repertory concert as well." Apparently it wasn't as scary for Matt as for the viewer; he did not recall this incident years later, and found the piece rarely frightening ("If anything went wrong you would just break character and hang on for dear life" he said with a laugh). Two weeks later, when Pilobolus returned to the Joyce for its annual summer season, Jennifer Dunning, writing in the *New York Times,* called *Star-cross'd* "sumptuous" and "a feast of big, soft swings about the stage on hanging lengths of silver-black fabric," praised its "gorgeous and teasing visuals," and declared the piece "an undeniable beauty."

At the end of the summer, Matt quit touring with the main company, but he planned to continue to work with Pilobolus Too. He and Emily bought a house and moved to Georgia in early fall, but Emily had to handle almost the entire process herself because by October Matt had been called back— his replacement had sustained neck injuries before ever going on the road, and needed time off. Matt agreed to fill in and went back on tour for what he thought would be a brief reprise. While in Budapest, however, just when he thought his extra tour of duty had ended, he stopped in an internet café, checked his email, and found an urgent message from Robby: Matt's replacement had returned to the company, gone away again for a week of physical therapy, and then never come back. Could Matt go to Macau (on the south coast of China, across from Hong Kong) and continue? Matt went, and would soon be touring with both Pilobolus *and* Pilobolus Too. He and Emily developed a running joke that they had bought the house in Georgia for her, not him.

They weren't always apart, however. Their work in Pilobolus Too would eventually give them the rare opportunity to perform together as a couple, and in the great Pendleton-Chase duets *Alraune* and *Shizen,* which by now were classics. Matt felt that Emily had in many ways a performance energy similar to that of Alison, and she also shared the statuesque, brunette look of Alison's years as a dancer. It all worked, as did the fact that Matt and Emily were a couple. The chemistry of these duets is, after all, the chemistry of lovers, and it's difficult to make them work without at least a hint of it. "The best performances are the ones that seem the most spontaneous," Matt explained, in regard to the two duets. "The visuals relate to the movement of nature. To be in sync with your partner takes on a different meaning—it isn't timed to the music. You have to be able to maintain a certain precision without being locked in by it."

As for his return to the main company, that had its stresses. He had hardly been gone, but in that brief interval the role of dance captain had been given to Renée, instantly reversing their relative places in the pecking order. Renée quite reasonably expected Matt to accept the change, and he soon did, but it took some adjustment. He also had to get used to new, younger colleagues, and at a few tense rehearsals he realized that he had again underestimated the power of his temper to intimidate others; he realized too, as he observed the new recruits, that he had forgotten how physically punishing one's first year in Pilobolus could be, as all prior physical limits are relentlessly pushed past. As he watched his younger colleagues evolve, he began to think differently about how best to relate to those around him—though it may not have occurred to him yet that now, at thirty-one, he too had entered a new phase of growing up.

One of those new recruits, Andy Herro, a strong, athletic young man with a background in football, tennis, and wrestling, as well as theatre, would come to be regarded by Matt as "a natural performer, and a natural leader, with charisma" and an abundance of positive energy. A Wisconsin native, Andy had, like many others, first seen Pilobolus on a video in a dance history class—the *Dance in America* show that contained *Untitled* and other early pieces. A friend who had auditioned for Pilobolus had encouraged him to audition too. He wasn't chosen immediately, but a few months later he received a call. He brought, along with his athleticism and theatre skills, a personal solidity and authenticity that radiated in his performances.

Another new recruit, Manelich Minniefee, replaced Ras Mikey C. Raised in North Carolina in a family of artists (his mother an actress, his father and younger brother both musicians), Manelich had gone to high school at the North Carolina School of the Arts, had proceeded to NYU's Tisch School of the Arts on a full scholarship, and after graduation had come straight into Pilobolus. In short, he was young, gifted, and remarkable; but, having been highly praised, he wasn't prepared for the culture shock of being relentlessly pushed during his first months with Pilobolus. What's more, he had arrived alongside the dancer who had dropped out, triggering Matt's return. All of this made it hard for Manelich to adjust. As Renée recalled, "He struggled with his own limits and with opening himself up to being pushed harder." His struggle, however, became a conscious one, to which he brought, over subsequent months, personal reflection and a deliberate effort to grow. Manelich would become a superb Pilobolus dancer and remain with the company for several years of phenomenal performances.

His onstage presence tended toward an intriguing balance, stoic but emotive, with an understated, seemingly effortless strength that radiated a power both physical and spiritual, a vitality beneath still waters. As for his offstage personality, it had other qualities that came to be prized by his colleagues, and especially by Matt Kent, who found him "candid, direct, quick to point out B.S., and very funny. One of those people I can't spend more than five minutes with before he has me laughing hysterically." Manelich also earned Matt's respect by embodying that highest of Pilobolus callings: "A partner that I totally trusted. He would want to go down himself before anyone else did."

2

One day Jonathan came into the studio and said, "I want to make a piece called Mega-*WATT!!!*" (his way of pronouncing, for effect, *Megawatt*). As Renée recalls, "Everyone got it right away. He wanted to make a high-energy piece. It was Jonathan trying to get us to go 'balls to the wall' for as long as we could."

In the early 1970s, Pilobolus had been called, by themselves and others, an "energy circus." Jonathan felt, however, that they had never fully lived up to the term, and he wanted to create a piece that would finally, truly, unmistakably be an energy circus. Work on it had already begun when Andy joined, and he found that the process involved, as he put it, "creating small sections of really tiring moves and then stringing them together." The dancers were given prompts to which they should improvise. One such prompt was *Fry like bacon*. Inherent in many of the prompts was the idea that there would be physical impact involved. For Renée, the project challenged the dancers "physically and emotionally"—because such an extreme physical challenge eventually tips over into emotion: "The essence of the piece was 'How far can you take your body physically? How far can you take a sexual energy or intensity?'" As answers to those questions continued to develop, one dancer, Jennifer Macavinta, had heart palpitations. Her doctors determined that the piece had become unhealthy for her to perform, and she had to bow out of it.

Jonathan had asked the dancers to bring in music that they liked. Unlike most Pilobolus pieces, in this case the music would come before the moves rather than being chosen afterward. The tracks selected had an edge that, together with the frenzied motion, lent *Megawatt* a dark sensibility, like a glimpse into a creepily hyperenergetic alternate reality, or a manic dystopian vision. That vision begins to unfold as the dancers make their snake-like entrance, flat on their backs, squirming into view headfirst but face-up, to Primus's "Here Come the Bastards" and soon builds into a tour de force in which dancers leap, fall, and roll with startling vigor, bounce off each other like pinballs, and indeed "fry like bacon"—and, in one of the piece's signature moves, flip themselves over backward and land standing in place.

Megawatt premiered on January 30, 2004, at the venue that commissioned it, Ruth Eckerd Hall in Clearwater, Florida. Matt felt good that he and Renée had "kicked ass" during its creation because so much of it came from improvs that they had done. The difficulty of performing the piece—

one of the most demanding in the Pilobolus repertoire, in terms of sheer stamina—didn't hit Matt as hard as it did some of the other dancers, because he had already been in Pilobolus for so long, and the difficulty was for him "a point of pride." As for Andy, new to Pilobolus, every time he had to perform *Megawatt,* "for the first year I wanted to vomit." But that didn't stop him: "What really kept you going was that Jonathan loved it so much. He would sit and watch it and laugh and be so happy, so *excited* to watch it." Indeed, for Andy, Jonathan's giggling childlike delight proved such an incentive that as a performer onstage "You're wanting energy to explode out of your fingers and out of your toes." He and the other dancers would perform it like conquerors, and elicit standing ovations.

Megawatt was the realization of pure intensity that Jonathan had sought for years—later referred to on the Pilobolus blog as a "sixteen-minute, six-dancer, twelve-mat energy circus performed to the hard, driving music of Radiohead, Squarepusher, and Primus"—and it became emblematic of his late phase. At its most powerful, *Megawatt* has, true to its name, a crackling electricity in performance that seems to transcend choreography, a half-illusory half-real sense of fiery superhuman energy, as if the performers are possessed. That energy had everything to do with Jonathan's fervent, gleeful goading-on of the dancers he both loved and relentlessly exhorted to fly higher, and alongside whom he so wished he could still be dancing. Its spark can be traced to the essence of his personality, from which came both the vitality and the difficulties he brought to the company, the exasperating challenges, sheer determination, and flashes of brilliance.

3

In January 2004, Itamar Kubovy joined Pilobolus as its first-ever executive director. He had no background in dance, nor in the management of a dance company, but he did have a background in theatre. The only child of scholar parents, he had grown up in New Haven, earned a Yale degree in philosophy (class of 1988), spent a decade in Europe doing work that included running theaters in Germany and Sweden, and had spent the past several years back in the US, adding a few directorial credits to his resumé, most notably a couple of John Guare plays and a codirector credit on the 2002 season finale of the hit television series *The West Wing.* He wasn't hired, however, to "direct" in the theatrical sense, but rather in the administrative sense. Or, to put it more bluntly, he had been charged with the assignment of saving Pilobolus from itself.

A few years earlier, in the late 1990s, Pilobolus's longtime agent Sheldon Soffer—the man who had insisted, back in 1980, that they not split up—had retired, and they had signed with IMG Artists, a move that increased the company's touring and overall activity. Pilobolus was making excellent new work, its dancers were superb, and business wasn't bad, but the behind-the-scenes dynamic between the four directors had reached the brink of collapse. They had tried everything to improve matters, even group therapy (with two different therapists), to no avail. With their ability to make business decisions paralyzed by relentless squabbling, they accepted their board's recommendation that they hire an executive director, an outsider who could come in and serve as their boss. Like so many groups whose origins had been colored by the late-1960s ideals of consensus decision-making and nonviolent anarchism, they had finally had to admit—perhaps later than most, after a valiant decades-long struggle to hold to their original methods—the need for hierarchy. Not surprisingly, it had taken more than two years of further argument mediated by an arts consulting firm, and six months of interviews with Itamar, the youngest candidate for the job, before they all agreed to hire him. As Robby later observed, they had at last made what would be their final decision as a group: to stop making decisions as a group.

Following Itamar's arrival, any number of fresh, sensible business decisions began to be made on a day-to-day basis, but many in and around the company felt a jolt when, to their way of thinking, a more "corporate" attitude began to take hold. Some dancers then in Pilobolus would later say that they saw from the moment of Itamar's arrival how he was going to "make Pilobolus more corporate"; others were taken by surprise; some felt Pilobolus was losing its soul. One dancer from these years summed up the feeling of several with these words: "It became codified as a 'family' rather than in the past when it had actually *been* a family."

In one small but telling example, the tradition of giving the dancers personally selected books as gifts—thoughtfully chosen based on the individual personalities of the dancers—was supplanted by a more materialistically generous but generic gift: everyone got an iPod engraved with their name. No doubt intended to show appreciation and a forward-thinking, technologically savvy attitude, and to suggest an exciting future for the company, for some this was instead an awkward moment, even though they recognized the gesture as having been meant well. A personally selected book, if chosen with insight, shows that the recipient is seen and valued as an individual, a thinker, and, in this case, an artist. This new, sleeker gift left one to wonder whether its recipients were now seen as a set of interchangeable employees—and that, of course, was the worry.

Regardless of any such minor cultural misfires, however, business began to improve. As for the long-battling directors, at least one dancer then in the company, Andy Herro, continued to find Jonathan inspiring, the artistic director with whom he got along best. Like others who saw past Jonathan's sometimes off-putting manner, Andy was neither offended nor threatened by him. Instead, he admired his passion: "Jonathan seemed like the last one whose heart was really in the company. He *loved* the dancers."

At the same time, Jonathan's judgment, both socially and artistically, could be erratic. In its original version *Megawatt* would remain a company favorite, but not long after its creation the desire for an evening-length Pilobolus work led to an attempt to develop the piece into a full-length show. Without benefit of plot, script, or a more nuanced or varied concept, the ill-advised *Megawatt > Full Strength* would be, not surprisingly, an exhausting failure, soon abandoned.

Despite blips of optimism in the first year after Itamar's arrival, the tensions within Pilobolus remained and morale continued to slip. As had been the case for as long as anyone could remember, the various artistic directors would give the dancers conflicting directions, and the performances would sometimes change based on which director was watching. But now the dysfunction had grown even worse. Jonathan and Alison would each ask the dancers about their experiences with the other director, looking for things to use against each other in their personal battle. Some of the dancers began to feel used themselves, and saw it much like the misuse of children in a divorce.

4

For her role as original inspiration and mentor, Alison was known as "the mother of Pilobolus." Moses and Jonathan had started the company, but it would never have happened without her. Through more than three decades of often emotionally charged situations, through joy and pain and much exhaustion, she had persevered with the group, and when she felt she could no longer function with her fellow directors collaboratively she had chosen to remain, even if from a distance, a part of Pilobolus, creating works for the company as a solo director, whether in Connecticut or Maine. Many of the best and best-reviewed pieces that had emerged from Pilobolus in the past several years had been hers, but in October 2005 it dismissed her, fired her, at the age of fifty-nine, in a bitter dispute that threatened to turn into a courtroom battle.

Years earlier, in the 1980s, a lawyer had explained to the directors of Pilobolus that as a nonprofit organization they were, in the eyes of the law, work-for-hire employees of their own company; that it was "Pilobolus" that owned their work, not themselves individually, and that they should sign contracts with one another to that effect, to protect the work. Jonathan and Robby agreed, Moses seemed open to the idea, but Alison and Michael refused, and the proposed contract went nowhere.

Alison's refusal to accept the idea that she might not legally own the work that she had made was, at that time, consistent with what many American choreographers believed. It wasn't until the resolution of the much-publicized legal dispute over Martha Graham's estate, at the beginning of the twenty-first century, that choreographers realized with a collective shock the extent to which work-for-hire laws governed the copyrights on the pieces they had created. In most cases, if they were collecting a paycheck from a dance company, even a dance company they had founded, the company (not the individual) owned the works. With the resolution of the Graham case, its attendant notoriety, and the arrival of an executive director at Pilobolus, the decision to ask all of the artistic directors to sign an agreement to the same effect—basically, the long-deferred agreement that had been abandoned two decades earlier for lack of consensus—was revisited, this time more firmly, as a directive. Negotiations quickly broke down.

Alison told several women close to her at the time (some in Pilobolus, some not) that she desperately wanted to *not* leave, that she was being pushed out. She was, quite rightly, immensely proud of her achievement with Pilobolus—she had earned, after all, a place in American dance history, one that she fully deserved—and she expressed real anguish about making the separation. Yet she would not compromise on the issue of ownership.

For an organization to present an employee with a stark choice of the kind Alison now faced is not always unreasonable, but it appears much harsher when the organization owes the original impetus for its existence in large part to that employee, who, nearing sixty, has spent the better part of a lifetime devoted to its success. Those looking in from the outside, and even many close observers, were upset and confused. Pilobolus dancers were puzzled by the claim that Alison's "distance" (living in Maine rather than Connecticut) somehow also posed a problem, given that it clearly hadn't hampered either her work or theirs; and it seemed an even flimsier criticism coming from a new executive director who himself wouldn't relocate from New York City to northwestern Connecticut. Some speculated that the dispute over rights wasn't the real crux of the matter but only the culmination of a personal power struggle between Jonathan and Alison that dated at least as far back as *Untitled;* others saw it as primarily a clash between Alison and Itamar. Robby, true to form, bore no ill will toward Alison but cast the situation in terms of a philosophical difference ("The very nature of collaboration, which is how we began, does not accept individual ownership"), one that left him—despite his pronounced preference for neutrality—aligned with Jonathan and Itamar. Michael pleaded passionately but hopelessly for Alison's cause, in a letter sent to the board.

Each side, or its representatives, accused the other of being impossible to negotiate with, and on this point both sides may have been telling the truth. It's hard to believe that Pilobolus really needed to give Alison an ultimatum and then fire her to protect its ownership of works that it claimed were already protected as the company's property by existing law. Yet to many of those who knew Alison well she had always had two contrasting qualities: brilliant flexibility in her creative process, and an absolute sink-her-heels-in refusal to budge if she made up her mind on an issue outside of the studio. What's more, in her adult working life she had never really had a boss. In her first job out of college, as a dance teacher at Dartmouth, she had been largely given carte blanche to do as she wished (with glorious results!) and then she had joined Pilobolus, and despite all the arguments there had never been a single individual who could simply overrule her in a nonnegotiable manner until now. Itamar, however, had not been hired as a mediator; he had been hired, with her consent, as a boss. In practical terms, when it came time to live with that reality, she couldn't accept it.

Whether inevitable or not, it happened: the board—what some would consider, essentially, Itamar's board—voted to dismiss Alison. She went public in an interview to the *New York Times* a few months later and cited the reasons for her departure as "artistic differences and sort of a mean-spirited power grab by the board."

Should she have left earlier, of her own choice? Perhaps, but it's hard to wish it: her final eight years with the company had produced marvels, and it is nearly impossible to imagine works such as *Tsu-Ku-Tsu, Monkey and the White Bone Demon, Ben's Admonition,* and *Star-Cross'd* springing into being without the specific concatenation of extraordinary dancer-actor-athletes who populated Pilobolus in those years, and whose particular ideas, experiments, and idiosyncratic gifts were brought forth by Alison's alchemy of director-as-catalyst, the same force that had brought forth Pilobolus itself.

Along the way, she changed her dancers' lives. Ras Mikey C feels that "Alison had the most impact on how I looked at what I was doing, then and now—my processing of movement." Gaspard Louis says of Alison, "We connected. She brought a certain awareness of each dancer, creating a slightly closer connection. Having her in the mix completed the group. Alison was the glue." For several dancers she remained not only a beloved mentor but one with whom they wanted to continue to work—and did, at least occasionally, outside of Pilobolus. "Alison is very nurturing," Rebecca Anderson Darling pointed out fondly, many years later, still a loyal friend; and then she added, with a chirpy laugh, "We're like two birds of a feather."

After a few years, a confidential agreement would be signed, and the only outward suggestion of its content would be the presence of a number of Alison's Pilobolus pieces (among them *Tsu-Ku-Tsu, Monkey and the White Bone Demon, Ben's Admonition,* and *Star-cross'd*) alongside her newer, post-Pilobolus works on her website and in performances that she would stage with a company of her own. She would go on. For example, in August 2007 her tendency to take Matt higher and higher into the air would reach its apex, literally, with him hanging from an excavator, thirty feet off the ground, above a Maine rock quarry in an outdoor piece called *Quarryography.* Still, that and other adventures must have seemed a world away in the difficult fall during which her long run with Pilobolus came to an end. Of the October 2005 meeting at an attorney's office in New York, at which the board voted—many by phone—to dismiss her, Alison later said: "It was clear how it was going to go, it was all arranged in advance." Before the final vote she rose, and complimented the chairman on his "nice choreography."

"And then as I went into the elevator I wept until I got out of town."

ELEVEN

Dreams and Silhouettes

1

By 2006, as she reached her mid-thirties, Renée knew she was nearing the end of her full-time performing career: "I felt like an old person in this company of younger people. I felt like the old lady a lot of the time." A new piece by Jonathan paired her with Andy Herro, with whom she loved to work. "To me Andy is primarily a performer and an actor," she explained, "and I understood the thought process because I think of myself as an actress more than a dancer. Physically and emotionally I could trust him. He pushed my buttons in more of a brotherly way, not to shoot me down but to egg me on. We would compete to one-up each other. Andy has a solid foundation to him." She and Andy wanted to create a piece about the life of a couple over many years, lovers with "a brotherly-sisterly kind of connection. The idea that you can tease each other, be in love with each other, fight with each other, hate each other, knowing that you're never going to separate, and you're going to go off into whatever else is next *together*. And when you find that connection with a person, you should hold onto it no matter what."

For logistical reasons, they made the piece in the local church hall rather than Club Hall, and they happened upon a small table and small chairs that became the setting. More character-based than many Pilobolus pieces, the concept evolved into one in which the male and female partners begin and end as elderly figures (Renée externalizing her feeling that she had become "the old lady") but morph back into younger versions of themselves as their history together is revealed. Renée gives a brilliant comic performance, perfectly in character even while standing upright on Andy's shoulders and balancing cheerfully as he continues to move, a sequence that provides a jaw-dropping mixture of Pilobolus derring-do and character-driven humor. (For Renée, the balancing act did not feel harder than other things she had done, and it didn't scare her. Early on in Pilobolus she had learned how to fall, recognizing the need to be like a cat always ready to land unharmed; but others remained in awe, including her costar Andy: "Renée was fearless, and the trust she had—!") Not all the moves were physically dangerous; some only risked one's dignity, as when Andy mooned the audience.

The piece, titled *Memento Mori,* had an uneven mixture of elements, but unmistakably among them a heart. As Renée said, "We were playful together and wanted to create that sense of playfulness in this couple, and show the audience to create it in life." She felt as if while performing it she lived it. And while not a Pilobolus classic, *Memento Mori* provides an excellent example of how even in many of its less-remembered works the company has regularly created strong, admirable theatre.

At the end of the summer Renée left the main company and became rehearsal director. Her final run at the Joyce in July elicited raves. In the *New York Times,* Jennifer Dunning praised her "hilariously deadpan" performance in *Memento Mori,* adding: "The duet brings out Mr. Herro's sleepy-lion charm and the piquancy and woman-warrior physicality of Ms. Jaworski." In the *Village Voice,* Deborah Jowitt took note of her role in Michael Tracy's latest, lighthearted piece, declaring, "Jaworski's terrific in *Aquatica,* as she is in everything—skilled as a dancer, subtle as an actress, fleet, strong, and able to minimize the effort that, say, brings her to stand slanted on a man's bent back, serene as he walks and turns. Sadly, this is her last season dancing with the company." *Dance* magazine wrote: "This, alas, marks the last Joyce season for the fabulous Renée Jaworski, a mesmerizing mover and consummate performer."

The transition to rehearsal director was difficult, not least because other veteran dancers had wanted it for themselves, and because, following on Alison's departure, it was a painful moment in the life of the company. On top of all this, Renée recalls, "Everyone on the road at the time was very young—twenty-one, twenty-two, fresh out of school—so part of the reason for keeping me on was that we had such a young company."

2

In its new, more business-focused mode, Pilobolus had increasingly taken on commercial projects, including television advertisements. A spot for the automobile manufacturer Opel (still owned, at that time, by General Motors) played only in Europe, but next came Hyundai, whose marketing firm had the idea that Pilobolus, given its skill at combining bodies into striking visuals, create the image of a car in silhouette. The result inspired praise as well as eventual imitation by other advertisers. More significantly, it attracted the notice of film producer Laura Ziskin, who had been chosen by the Academy of Motion Picture Arts and Sciences to produce the 79th annual Academy Awards telecast. She and the Academy came to Pilobolus with a question: "You made a car with shadows. Can you make other things with shadows?" If so, they wanted Pilobolus to make shadow images that playfully represented the films nominated for Best Picture.

Not knowing if they would get the job, but aware of the magnitude of the opportunity—a chance to appear on an Oscar telecast reaching tens of millions of viewers—Pilobolus directors and dancers immediately set to work in Club Hall with the windows covered in Duvetyne, a black fabric that blocked out the light from the freezing cold winter outdoors. With no template to work from, and feeling they had no idea what they were doing, they began to make demos. It all had to be figured out from scratch, and Jonathan, extremely impatient, frustrated his colleagues more than usual. While creating a shadow image of a giant high-heeled shoe to represent the film *The Devil Wears Prada,* Matt warned Jonathan that he shouldn't tell the performers to "roll out" of a complicated pose because they could get hurt. Jonathan agreed, then, when the time came, yelled "Roll out!" and when confronted, dismissed the issue. At one point Matt walked out in frustration. True to his character since childhood, mistreatment of others triggered his anger more than affronts to himself. Soon, however, he was back. The shadow performances—the other images included a little mini-van with a man chasing after it to represent *Little Miss Sunshine,* a gun to represent a James Bond film, and so on—were all videotaped. In order to get the complex poses precisely right and to avoid allowing the viewer to see small distractions along the way, the dancers were carefully positioned and videotaped in the finished pose and through the process of gracefully stepping back *out* of it; then the video was run in reverse, to make it look as if the dancers were stepping *into* the pose with flawless precision. The "performance" at the live Oscar telecast on February 25, 2007, was in fact a series of these pre-taped spots, and to further the Hollywood illusion of it happening live, the dancers were flown out for the show, where they walked the red carpet in Pilobolus style, as Tall Ladies and Fat Gnomes, and emerged from behind a curtain to take a bow during the live telecast. At one point during the show, its host, Ellen Degeneres, told the audience she had seen the dancers behind the screen: "They're naked!" Renée had perhaps the most entertaining shadow role of all, "impersonating" Ellen, or rather portraying a shadow caricature of her in a pre-filmed shadow skit for which Renée had studied Ellen's movement to prepare. The skit played off of one of that year's most infamous film titles, *Snakes on a Plane,* and depicted a shadow plane turning into snakes that devour the shadow-Ellen character as the real Ellen's voice is heard responding to the situation, as if ad-libbing over the microphone in the live telecast. Pilobolus also performed (live) at a party afterward.

The appearance on the Academy Awards would open a wealth of new opportunities for Pilobolus, mostly in the form of jobs for PCS (Pilobolus Creative Services), a branch of activity that existed alongside the company's two more traditional endeavors, its main touring company and its educational programs. Over the next couple of years, commercial gigs using shadows would be plentiful, and they seemed to herald a new era in which Pilobolus had a chance to become that rarest of entities, a dance company that could monetize its work, reap rewards, and thrive rather than endlessly struggle for survival. Behind the scenes, however, quietly at first, a much sadder aspect of its future had begun to emerge.

Toward the end of 2006, while still working on the shadow demos for the Oscars, Jonathan and Renée had had a private conversation in the lobby at Sonalysts Studios soundstage. He confided to her that he was ill with a form of myelofibrosis. He told her about the illness and then he said, "And it will kill me." She asked him how long it would be before that happened.

"I don't know," he said; and she replied, "OK. Thank you for telling me."

3

Michael Tracy's *Persistence of Memory* was created in the late spring of 2007, in the very hot environs of Washington Club Hall, which until 2010 had no air conditioning and was, as dancer Edwin Olvera recalled, "very punishing in hot weather." Edwin helped make the duet alongside the duo who would perform it in public, Manelich Minniefee and Annika Sheaff. He and Manelich "kept tagging back and forth with working with Annika," all three of them in great spirits, as they all liked each other and enjoyed working together, even though the piece was "incredibly physically demanding on Manelich," who suffered with neck and back problems.

When *Persistence of Memory* premiered in July at the Joyce, Deborah Jowitt noted in the *Village Voice* that "the performances by dark, muscular Minniefee, with his flying dreads, and slender, red-haired Sheaff make the duet sing." In this exquisitely paced love story, their tenderness and a sense of fragile retrospection bathe and temper the magnificent athleticism of the movement, as when, as Jowitt describes it, "he jackknifes into a shoulder stand with her balanced on the soles of his feet," or, "joined together, they cantilever out in perfect equilibrium." Opening and closing with one or the other dancer swiftly jogging backward in a circle, as if rewinding or unwinding, the piece makes clear its title and its nature as a time capsule, whether fictional or real, of a precious, fleeting love affair. Commissioned in memory of a woman who had died tragically young, it is arguably Michael Tracy's most moving work, in which his eye for lyricism and his seasoned dancer's ability to fuse together what amounts to an anthology of some of the best Pilobolus partnering techniques forges a flawless vehicle for its performers. *Persistence of Memory* toured successfully during its year or so of rotation in the Pilobolus program but quickly receded and joined the long list of Pilobolus works that have fallen out of the active repertoire. All but forgotten, it is thankfully preserved in a gorgeously filmed video that one hopes will one day break out of the Pilobolus archives and into the wider world again.

4

That spring of 2007 also saw the creation of one of those rare works that does stay in the repertoire. The chain of events that led to its creation had started more than a year and a half earlier, on a Monday morning, August 29, 2005, as Jonathan and Robby sat at a little café in New Preston drinking coffee. Itamar, who had driven up from New York City, walked in and said, "Do you realize what's happening in New Orleans?" Hurricane Katrina had caused the dams on Lake Pontchartrain to break and the parishes were being flooded. As they learned more, it all seemed apocalyptic, an eerie backdrop as the conversation turned to a matter closer to home: the precarious future of Pilobolus. The company's relationship with Alison had by this time completely broken down; Michael and Jonathan were not on speaking terms; Robby's interest in making dances had long since been depleted and he had stopped choreographing altogether for the past couple of years. What identity did the company have left, and what would motivate anyone to give it funds for further work? They felt that the essential feature of Pilobolus had always been collaboration but there wasn't any collaboration left. Consequently they decided they should bring in guest choreographers—lots of dance companies did that, but Pilobolus would do it in a different way than most. They would bring in collaborators not to choreograph *on* the company's dancers but rather *with* Pilobolus, as partners, adding their influence to the already idiosyncratic Pilobolus mix.

Rushes, the first entry in what would be called the International Collaborators Project, arose from a collaboration with choreographer Inbal Pinto and actor Avshalom Pollak, founders and artistic directors of The Inbal Pinto and Avshalom Pollak Dance Company, an Israeli contemporary dance company based in Tel Aviv. Still in their thirties at the time of their Pilobolus collaboration, they both had years of experience: Inbal (born 1969, in Israel) had studied graphic design before launching her career as a young choreographer in 1990; Avshalom (born 1970, in Israel) had trained as an actor and performed in many films, television programs, and theatre plays, including such classic roles as Romeo in *Romeo and Juliet,* Cassio in *Othello,* and Valere in *The Miser.* The two had begun working together in 1992; their partnership had already lasted for a decade and a half.

Robby had seen a performance of Pinto and Pollock's 1999 piece *Oyster,* an evening-length work filled with doll-like and puppet-like figures, described approvingly in the *Village Voice* as "part surreal vaudeville, part circus, and part toy store after midnight." In its range of both music and movement styles, it displayed an extreme eclecticism that suggested a potential match with the ever-morphing Pilobolus. Itamar and Robby flew to Tel Aviv, spent a couple of days with the pair, liked them a lot, and decided to invite them to collaborate on a piece for Pilobolus.

Initially it seemed advisable to have them work with veteran dancers who thoroughly understood Pilobolus, rather than the current touring dancers, who were younger and less readily available. This, and especially a larger idea being toyed with—that perhaps Pilobolus should, in general, have a separate group of "makers" while other dancers toured—both infuriated and depressed the dancers in the main company, who were understandably dispirited at the prospect of being cut out of the creative process. For the time being, however, the decision was made to convene a workshop of veteran dancers—Renée, Matt, Otis Cook, and Josie Coyoc, along with two of Inbal's dancers, Talia Beck and Andreas Merk—to develop material with Inbal and Avshalom.

At the end of the first day in the studio, Inbal left distraught (some say in tears). Robby called Renée that night: "Why are you guys being so horrible to her?" The dancers, however, as Renée pointed out, had simply done what they always did. They had been trained to take information and "chew it up and make it our own" and allow it to continue to evolve. "Inbal had not expected the Pilobolus method at all," Renée recalled. "She had expected to come and create a piece *on* dancers." Renée told Robby that Inbal did not seem to understand that this is the way Pilobolus works.

But—had there been anything else? What about Matt's way of challenging people, interpreted by some as "putting them in their place," letting them know that they aren't superior and are not in charge? When Robby called Matt, he received the same reply as from Renée but in a characteristically blunter form. Matt's recollection: "Robby said, 'You have to be nicer to Inbal.' It took me by surprise. And I said: '*You* have to stand up for the way we work.'" Whatever Robby said or did in his diplomacy with Inbal, it solved the problem. The next day she returned to the studio with a thicker skin, better able to work with the group. The piece would start as very free-associative and would evolve over the course of subsequent weeks.

Based on her aesthetic and her presentation, some found Inbal eccentric and idiosyncratic as both a personality and a director. Robby remained quiet. Matt, only present for the initial workshop and not the piece's later development, had no idea as to what would result or if it would be good. After that first workshop the piece moved into a second stage in which Inbal and Avshalom continued to develop it with the main company of then-current touring dancers—who were both relieved and excited to be included in the making of it after all, and, soon, thrilled by the experience. All told, *Rushes* would be made over the course of four or five nonconsecutive weeks. At the end of each day, Robby, Itamar, Inbal, and Avshalom would go home and discuss it. When one of the dancers, Jenny Mendez, sustained an injury during the process, Renée stepped in to take her place, both in making the piece and subsequently touring it, becoming the only dancer involved in all stages of its development (and, in true Pilobolus fashion, coming out of her "retirement" with lightning speed).

As the process of invention in the studio continued, it blossomed, met with an exhilarating sense of discovery by the eager troupe. Andy Herro recalled it with pleasure: "All of us who created *Rushes* just *love* Avshalom and Inbal. We had created such a connection. Robby was the best collaborator. He was willing to be more of a facilitator; he was willing to listen to their ideas. Avshalom and Inbal were also good collaborators with each other. Inbal was particularly good at editing."

Renée found Inbal to be more about the details, and Avshalom more the atmosphere, the sonic atmosphere, the music, while Robby worked with them on the larger shape. "It always had a Dali-esque sensibility, dreamstate, dreamlike, because that's where Inbal and Pilobolus overlap," Renée later explained. "The design of the costumes and the look of the piece is very Inbal. She started as an art student so she has a very visual approach. Inbal is a hands-on choreographer and Avshalom is quieter, more of an intellectual director, quiet in the studio. He spent hours talking with Edwin and intensely, privately working to create the character with the briefcase."

The man with the briefcase, also referred to as the traveler, originated by dancer Edwin Olvera, is central to the piece. In his work with various Pilobolus directors, Edwin had found that Jonathan would sometimes talk about the psychology behind the movement, but now, with Avshalom, who was an experienced actor himself, a whole new dynamic opened up. Avshalom encouraged Edwin to relate his character to someone, and Edwin thought of his father, who had been living like a hermit, in a basement in Chicago, for thirty years. Avshalom had Edwin crawl all over the floor. He would sit next to him and lower his voice and, as Edwin described it, "talk to you like telling you a secret, ask you what are you trying to do here, like theatre training. I had a wonderful bond with him."

The twenty-five-minute piece that resulted is, in Edwin's apt phrase, a "snow globe" in which is wrapped a solo (his role as the traveler), a trio (the other three male dancers), and a duet (the two girls). The piece would employ the music of Eddie Sauter, Miles Davis, John Blow, Dukes of Dixieland, and Arvo Pärt—and the sound of water. Its title *Rushes,* however, refers not only to that sound but to the cinematic concept of dailies, a.k.a. the "rushes" of a film in progress, or the "rushes" of this piece, which Robby and Itamar would review each night. When finished, it would elicit the highest of praise from one of Pilobolus's most devoted and longtime friends, Charles Reinhart, of the American Dance Festival: "A gem among gems!"

After a pre-curtain blast of rousing circus music, suggestive of a big, bright spectacle to come, the curtain goes up on an eerily anticlimactic image: a black stage (initially silent except for quietly persistent drips and gurgles of water) with a large circle of light on the ground and a bare light bulb above, and around the circle, twelve white chairs and six individuals: the Pilobolus standard, four men and two women. They are mostly dressed in black, reminiscent of the era of silent comedy, three of the men unified by a decidedly Chaplinesque look with black outfits, white shirts, and mustaches, the two women in black as well, and a short man with a big brown suitcase; the latter three figures are hunched over when they move, and their slapstick movement is a shuffle, not unlike the little-old-man shuffle of Tim Conway in television comedy skits of the 1960s or 70s. The movements of the six characters are mysterious as well as comic, for the choreography is not wedded to a clearly discernible theme or quantifiable "jokes" and the audience is provided few clues or cues to any larger meaning. We have entered into the surreal dream-logic of not making sense yet making sense, of inscrutable signals and buried emotion.

Ten minutes in, the hunched-over man with the suitcase (Edwin Olvera) takes a nap against a backdrop of cloth onto which is projected a film-dream that includes, among other things, images of chairs and of geometric pieces being shuffled. (The film is the work of yet another collaborator, stop-motion animation director Peter Sluszka, who, with a camera positioned above multiple planes of glass, had shot images of ink, water, and sodium bicarbonate as well as "photo cutouts, colored blocks, and branches" in order to create "controlled but hallucinatory transformations between the dream images.") This is succeeded by a sequence in which one of the three Chaplinesque men (Andy Herro) spins a tilted chair like a whirligig, a demonstration that segues into the entire troupe doing chair movements of various kinds to circus music (at last connecting back to the pre-curtain promise, now that any expectations have long since been forgotten or removed). This in turn gives way to a scene in which the two women, left alone and seated near the front of the stage, to the audience's right, watch as a "chair monster"—a pile of chairs with one human figure at their center, with the chairs on his limbs and so on—lumbers toward them, dragging itself onward to the point of collapse. Within another minute or two another change of tone arises, with suddenly delicate music and grace-ful slow movements as a woman (Renée Jaworski) is slid and lifted and danced with by three men; fallen chair-monster turns back into briefcase man, and the other woman (Annika Sheaff) crawls over to where he is standing on a chair, then climbs up him and drapes herself over him. As the rest of the troupe slide and reposition the chairs in a relay, he walks, with her body still draped over his shoulders, on the chairs: he steps from seat to seat as chairs are placed one in front of the next, again and again, just in time to continuously extend before him an ever-vanishing yet ever-replenishing walkway. It is an oddly exhilarating spectacle, and unexpect-edly touching, in part due to the fierce bucket-brigade conscientiousness, the determined support, on the concentrated brows and in every limb of the troupe members working with frantic precision to keep the chairs ap-pearing in front of the walker with his human cargo, and in part because of the change in this strange walker, who earlier, when hunched over with his briefcase, had walked with a sense of purpose (never specified) that seemed funny and vaguely pathetic, but whose purposefulness now, walk-ing upright carrying the weight of a woman in this bizarre but somehow vital spectacle of the chairs, reveals an unexpected dignity. He, and all of the manipulation of the chairs, comes to a stop with him standing on a chair under the bare light bulb. The woman on his shoulders swings her-self around in front of him and embraces him, still clinging to him. He is handed his briefcase. It is a perfect tableau, and in a note-perfect finishing touch, she reaches up and turns out the light.

5

November 22, 2007. The largest theater in Madrid, the awkwardly renamed Teatro Häagen-Dazs Calderón (the "Häagen-Dazs" having been inserted by the ice cream manufacturer that acquired it), with a seating capacity of two thousand. A dozen Pilobolus dancers, a mix of company veterans (Otis Cook, Josie Coyoc, and Matt Kent among them) and a few others with experience doing commercial work with Pilobolus, had been assembled to perform a corporate sponsored show between November 20 and 22. The program included *Megawatt* and an early shadow piece called *Love. Eat. Die.* Among those present to perform the latter was Emily Kent.

Over the first couple of days, pressure had mounted. As part of the same trip, Pilobolus had made a commercial for a wine company, Codorniu (sparkling wine), that also wanted them to do a performance in a wine cavern, a very cold cave, for a gala, and in his role as artistic director, Jonathan wasn't taking into consideration the needs of the dancers to make sure they would feel safe. To more than one observer, his aggressive behavior seemed to have grown worse in recent years: critiquing by simply demanding more, more, more ("You're not giving enough"), bullying his dancers and colleagues. At the same time, the increasingly corporate feel of Pilobolus had placed Jonathan in positions new to him, in which he felt compelled to deliver to the sponsors, the clients; and it had created an environment in which no one ever spoke up to the leadership to voice concerns. Matt would better understand these dynamics later, but at the time he found the disregard for the dancers intolerable. (The escalation of Jonathan's obsession with intensity also seems to have paralleled his knowledge of his own terminal illness. At the time of the Madrid performance, Matt was unaware of Jonathan's illness, and would not learn of it for several more months.)

The first night that Pilobolus performed, the commercial they had made played midway through the show and someone in the audience protested, which heightened the tension. Matt had warned that inserting such an overt product-placement style of endorsement might anger the audience, but the sponsors had wanted it and Jonathan had seemed, to Matt, "to cave to the rich people" for whom they were working, becoming a yes man. Others felt it too, but only Matt said it. It must have stung Jonathan, given his proud history of casting himself as a defiant rejecter of compromise.

Fifteen or twenty minutes before the next show, Jonathan came to Matt's dressing room and, in an obvious retaliation, lashed out at him, accusing Matt of not delivering the goods as a performer. Matt blew up. As Emily recalled, "Matt was furious that Jonathan was in his space while Matt was getting ready for a show." It violated a sacred rule. Matt's reply to Jonathan was along the lines of *"You can't come into my dressing room and call me an asshole and expect me to do the show."* And with that, Matt walked out, even as Emily and another dancer, Matt Thornton, urged him to come back. When he didn't, they each went out looking for him.

"I walked down the streets of Madrid to get him to come back," Emily later explained. "We could not do the show without him."

She found him in a little plaza, a circular area for pedestrians with a café in the middle of it, as, in the late afternoon light, other people walked around and went about their business. She begged him to come back. So he did: he stormed back into the theater and then, in a hallway to which the dressing rooms connected, he called the other dancers out and insisted that they witness as he confronted Jonathan. Much of his anger had been triggered by Jonathan's history of saying he would take safety into account, then not doing so; some of it had been triggered by his observation of insensitivity to others, as when Jonathan had told a female dancer she needed to lose weight and she was in tears. Now Matt made everyone hear what he had to say, and in front of them said "You guys have been telling me. Tell *him.*" And then he told Jonathan he was a bully, literally saying those words *"You are a bully"* to Jonathan, and he told others to do the same, to face Jonathan and say it, to his face. Of course the others were taken aback. Josie broke the tension by saying something that recognized that Matt meant well, an intervention that allowed the dancers to hurry back to their preparations for the show in the dwindling time that remained.

Somewhere amid the drama, Jonathan's wife JoAnne, understandably distressed, came in and yelled at Matt, but Emily told her to get out, that this was the performers' space in which to get ready and she couldn't be there—a shockingly uncharacteristic assertion from the mild-mannered Emily. (She would later be pardoned for this behavior thanks to a time-honored all-purpose excuse: she was pregnant, so how could she possibly be expected to control her emotions?)

Matt and Jonathan now faced off alone in Jonathan's room. Matt knew a moderator was needed so he called Itamar, apologized for interrupting his Thanksgiving—it was Thanksgiving Day in the US—and told him what had happened, saying "I completely understand if this means I can never work for Pilobolus again, but I could not look myself in the mirror if I let him treat people that way and didn't say anything about it." Itamar told them they both would have to work together, and he made Jonathan apologize to Matt.

Standing there after the call, Matt said to Jonathan: "I think of you as a mentor and here you are talking to me like this."

"If you think of me as a mentor," Jonathan replied, "then why don't you act like it?" and began, for a moment, to cry, then regained his composure.

The show went on, with Matt performing in *Megawatt.* As for the backstage drama that preceded it, Emily summed it up succinctly in retrospect: "It was the *worst.*" Matt later wrote Jonathan a letter of apology and tried to make amends. Jonathan wrote back that yes, they could work together again, but he listed a long set of conditions, or demands, as to how Matt should behave toward him in the future, that Matt should never get upset again, and so forth.

A few months later, in the spring of 2008, Jonathan and Matt worked together on the "human car" commercial for Ford Motor Company (Ford Canada), this time with Matt not as a dancer but as a creative director. The work took place in a giant warehouse set up with different areas for different purposes, such as one called "video village" where consoles and monitors allowed viewing of what was being shot and what had already been shot; it also had areas lit for filming, separate areas for catering, a couch area, and so on. Dark in some places, extremely bright in others, the space had an odd quality. Jonathan sought Matt out and, as Matt recalls, more or less pulled him into a corner—they stood off in a corner where it was dark. There Jonathan told Matt the secret that he had divulged to Renée much earlier, that he was dying. He stated the facts and then walked off, leaving Matt in a state of shock.

PART THREE

TWELVE

Shadows

On Saturday, July 19, 2008, I arrived back at my apartment in the early afternoon, from my first Pilobolus workshop. The guy who had left town the previous Sunday and the guy who came back were not quite the same. I stood in front of the mirror in my daylit bedroom thinking *you did it,* and a few minutes later, as I crossed my living room to the kitchen, I turned and happened to see my Pilobolus calendar on the wall and I suddenly choked up. At some point, either then or soon after, I wrote the following journal entry:

> Why was it such a moving experience? Here is one part of the reason (but only one part, there is more).
>
> An oversimplified but partial version would be that as the 98-pound weakling, last-one-picked-in-gym-class kind of kid, never athletic, I tended to internalize all the negative stuff anyone ever said about me and ended up with a fairly crummy body image and the feeling that anything to do with sports, physical activity, etc., was not for me. Basically, I wished I could be a spirit without a body. (This wasn't as sad as it might sound. I had loads of good stuff in my life—it was just the physical identity that was less than stellar.) As an adult I got much more comfortable with myself and eventually had a positive body image, but by then I had pretty much missed or disowned an entire area of life, or youth.
>
> Although I always thought sports were boring, dance is an entirely

different matter; I've always been all about art, expression, ideas, the spirit. At its best, dance manifests those things beautifully, gracefully, delightfully, with the human body. In Pilobolus I saw athlete-artists, a combination that is one-half my opposite and one-half my kindred, a proportion sure to draw me in. My fantasy image, I guess, is this: I imagine a guy who from early on felt totally at home in his body and pleased with physicality, and he is walking toward something, from quite a distance—while I, who from early on felt at home in my mind and in language, walk toward the same thing, but from the direction opposite. In the middle is the thing that draws us both: creative expression. There, at our mutual destination, we will meet and—what? Fail to connect? Or embrace?

I've been in awe of Matt Kent since the first time I saw Pilobolus twelve years ago, when he was starting out with the company. That was one of the greatest, most revelatory nights I've ever had in a theater, and all these years later this weeklong workshop ended with him embracing me in an intense hug.

Interestingly, the "fantasy image" I refer to in this passage had existed in my mind in various forms, at various times, long prior to the workshop and it hadn't been specifically Matt but more of a composite. Now, though, I wondered if I would ever see Matt and Emily again, or if this had all been merely one beautiful but transient spark.

2

That summer the shadow theme had found its way into new Pilobolus works, in an understated way in Michael Tracy's *Lanterna Magica* and in a central, much more self-conscious way in Robby and Jonathan's collaboration with puppeteer Basil Twist, *Darkness and Light*. The latter took an ambitious and significant step toward later shadow works, especially in its wise decision to display to the audience the dancers and lights behind the screen, and thereby underscore that the formation of the images takes place live in the moment; yet the piece itself felt overlong and humorless. *Lanterna Magica,* by contrast, showed Michael's ability to display a light touch even amid intense athleticism. Its concept, of a midsummer night's enchantments wrought by a lantern, arose one day when Edwin Olvera and the other dancers were rehearsing in the studio with Michael, improvising, struggling to find good material, frustrated by a lack of ideas. In the men's bathroom in Club Hall, on a shelf above the mirror to the left when one walks in, a lantern like a porcelain lighthouse sat alongside the paper towels. Edwin emerged from a bathroom break with a big smile and the lantern, and said, "Let's use this!" The other dancers were unenthusiastic but Michael said "Yes! Use that!" and they all continued to improvise. They stuck glow sticks, of the sort kept in a car in case of emergency, into the new prop to make it glow. (They would later have a different lantern made to use onstage.) The resulting piece, Edwin says, was "humorous and tender at the same time," a quality he often found in Michael's work. "In his pieces, you're going to do heavy lifting but it's going to be playful." Playful, lyrical, humane. As Michael said in the film *Last Dance:* "One of the great things about dance I find is that the dancers' bodies are always abstract and also they're always inherently invested with some kind of humanity."

In July, Pilobolus performed a shadow skit on *Late Night with Conan O'Brien.* Set to the Lovin' Spoonful song "Summer in the City," it portrayed a young girl's adventures in New York through silhouette images that ranged from a taxi, a park bench, and the Statue of Liberty to a playful dog, an elephant in the zoo, and, as punchline, a caricature of Conan O'Brien. In keeping with the show's standard live-to-tape process, the entire skit was performed live with a studio audience. As with the images created for the Academy Awards a year and a half earlier, the sudden convergence of dancers into a silhouette could charm the viewer, but now the dynamic transitions between the images, as the shapes of the dancers themselves quickly moved in and out of each scene in a rapidly shifting sequence, allowed the audience to take even greater delight in their artistry. The linked series of transformations, with its live mixture of playfulness, physical skill, and precision, was a harbinger of things to come.

3

Part of what Pilobolus had learned while making the pre-filmed pieces for the Oscars was that the "clicking into place" effect of seeing a group of dancers seem to magically and instantly solidify into a silhouette, an illusion originally created through the trickery of running the film backward, had real power. On a subliminal level, it is a key aspect of the enchantment, because, as Renée put it, "Everyone wants to believe it's that precise." Pilobolus had soon realized that it would be well worth learning to replicate the effect, to the extent possible, in live performance through sheer skill and relentless practice.

As the revenue-generating sideline of shadow-based projects expanded, each time a corporate client hired Pilobolus to create another miniature work, whether a shadow-themed commercial or another short shadow scene, Renée and Matt made it a goal to discover new techniques and narrative possibilities. As their store of ideas and images grew, they thought *We're going to have so much material we'll be able to make a show.* Eventually Itamar asked, over dinner, the question they had been anticipating: Did they think they could make an evening-length shadow show?

From the start, Renée and Matt both wanted to, as Matt would say, "smash it" and "shake this thing up"—meaning they wanted to radically expand on the choice made by Jonathan and Robby in *Darkness and Light* to allow the audience to see the shadow technique behind the scenes. They also knew they would need a collaborator "who could help knit this story and these weird Pilobolian absurd moments together." They found the person for that job in Steven Banks, the head writer for *Spongebob Squarepants*, the enormously successful animated television series for children, known for its surreal comedy. And, as Renée recalled, she and Matt had already developed the habit, when embarking on a shadow project, of using a certain term: "We would always say when we walked into the studio that we were going into Shadowland." Soon that word, along with a series of other elements, would enable a concept to take shape.

From their commercial work and their shadow skit on *Late Night with Conan O'Brien,* they already had a dog character (and a dancer, Molly Gawler, who was great at performing it) as well as a girl protagonist. They liked the idea of seeing a character transformed. Perhaps a girl turned into a dog, or a dog-girl? As they played with these and other images that they knew how to make well (for example, an elephant), the ingredients began to coalesce and point toward a story of a young girl transported to an alternate reality called Shadowland.

The collaborators on *Shadowland,* as the show would be called, were numerous, even by Pilobolus standards. Itamar, in a producer role, assembled all of the collaborators; he would also come in at certain points, infrequent and periodic, with his thoughts about the evolving show. Robby helped figure out the internal logic of the fantastic world they were creating, and to what point they could push the suspension of disbelief. Michael focused on what happened on stage at any given moment, zeroing in on details of movement, down to which way someone's feet should point. Renée and Matt were directors on the show as well, with all of their shadow-based expertise, and Renée would have a daunting simultaneous responsibility as a performer in the show during its evolution and debut. To all of this Steven Banks brought his knowledge of narrative structure and storytelling, and his long personal experience as a mime, so compatible with the Pilobolus mindset. He found himself in the midst of an entirely new manner of creation: "I had never worked like this before, because we're going in to start a show, there's no script, no outline, and five directors, honest to goodness directors . . . and everybody had their own say, in addition to the dancers. I call them 'dancer-actors' because in this they really were acting as much as they were dancing, also contributing heavily to it. So there wasn't one person [to whom you said] 'Well what do you think, Orson Welles?' This incredible collaborative."

Early on, Itamar, Robby, Renée, and Matt met Steve Banks at a bakery in New York near Union Square ("a tiny little place with really good coffee," as Matt recalled) to discuss narrative rules and possibilities. Steve asked the why and the how, the cause-and-effect questions, and he pushed the group to find the logic behind the choices. They started with a few rules. It was going to be a journey. The heroine, the dog-girl, always had to travel left to right. They made a decision to alternate between the screen (on which the shadows are seen) and the nonshadow elements; the audience, they decided, would get bored if they didn't see the human flesh, the human presence. As the concept evolved, they would have to negotiate the balance between coherent narrative and the desire to play with the surreal and abstract elements dear to Pilobolus, as well as, eventually, the question of an adult theatre experience versus a family-friendly or kid-oriented show.

Another crucial choice would be the music. Who to bring in as collaborator for that? With no dialogue in the show, the score and the songs would be extraordinarily important. Matt, with his early background in music and his longstanding interest in Pilobolus's musical choices, had a particular desire to find exactly the right person, and when he and Itamar first met with David Poe in a restaurant they immediately knew "He's our man." A folk-influenced, guitar-based American singer-songwriter with an impressive resumé as a producer and composer, David would contribute not only a number of witty and emotionally exact songs but also what Steve Banks called "an incredible score like a cinematic score . . . I had not heard of David Poe but man he just knocked it out of the park."

The music would, in Renée's phrase, "support the story through mood and metaphor" but not tell it directly (which would have been too heavy-handed). Renée and Matt worked closely with Steve to create scenes, episodes, that the girl would go through, and to find ways to convey the story and move it along. Given that even the song lyrics did not literally tell the story, the storytelling had to unfold almost miraculously, through the convergence of countless visual, musical, and theatrical details. One of the team's favorite shadow sequences, in which the dog-girl takes a car ride, provides a vivid example. The dog-girl, laughed at by those around her, is befriended by a guy in a Stetson and they drive through the night to a "road trip song" entitled "New Friends." As the scene begins, several performers turn into a car, and then the perspective rapidly changes to a view looking forward, as if we're in the backseat watching the driver with the hat—the "dharma bum," as Robby nicknamed him—and the dog-girl, in the passenger seat, interact. We see the car's rear view mirror and an air freshener shaped like a tree, and we see silhouette landscapes move by, including buildings, trees, and telephone poles. The driver rolls down his window, and in imitation the dog-girl rolls down hers—and then sticks her head out, and her tongue, as dogs always do. (Matt: "I remember thinking if we're making a show about a girl who's got a dog face she probably needs to ride in a car and stick her face out.") It became a moment at which every audience around the world laughed. Next, the driver smokes a joint, offers it to his passenger, and, to his frustration, she eats it. He offers her a sip of his soda and she jams her snout into the cup. Frustrated, he abandons her, even though she desperately wants to remain friends. The scene's humor and emotional texture (the friendship and its betrayal are poignant) are so well-calibrated, and the scene so absorbing, that one might fail to register the complexity and precision of the shadow work, in its many details: for example, the ingenuity with which the dog-girl is able to turn her head back and forth without losing the correct shape and profile, and the rapid and seamless change of perspective as the driver stops the car and the two get out.

Pilobolus did not invent the shadow theatre art form, but they were the first dance company to embrace it, to bring dance to it, and to thereby raise the level of physicality and invention behind the scenes and in front of the audience as well. With a process of constant challenge and problem-solving they combined elements in ways that had never been done before and took the form to a vastly greater level of complexity, with an impressive increase in both the number of moving parts and the ways in which those parts could be moved. Having long ago expanded the parameters of dance theatre, the company had found another theatrical form to merge into and redefine as well. They were again inventing, or at least reinventing, a physical language.

The lighting designer, Neil Jampolis, had been working with Pilobolus for more than thirty years, ever since Pierre Cardin had brought him in to improve the original troupe's presentation prior to their first Broadway run. He knew their aesthetic profoundly, having helped shape it; now he advocated on behalf of letting the subconscious have its way in the taletelling. He reminded them: "Don't lose Pilobolus." As Renée recalled, "He made us question everything, which was really a good role. . . . So while we were still playing with this new medium, everything that we have ever done goes into this and is connected. He was great."

It had been obvious from the start that Pilobolus would need a separate cast for this show, to enable its regular company of dancers to remain on tour as the already well-established version of Pilobolus. Most of the dancers brought in for *Shadowland* would be new, or largely new, but one trusted veteran, Mark Fucik, would be a key member of the team. Mark had joined the main Pilobolus company in 2001 with a background as a theatre major and, according to Emily, "Almost immediately he would bring to his roles a whole character that hadn't been there before. He came in at a slightly older age, closer to thirty, with a kind of maturity. He arrived with a kind of seriousness." Matt had found him complex and thoughtful, and loved working with him "because you always knew you were going to get something good. He was deep, there was a lot going on under the surface." And he was "Extremely strong. He would just get it done." Mark had performed in the main company until 2005, then had worked with Pilobolus on various projects and in various capacities. He returned to participate in *Shadowland* as dance captain and dancer, and to tour as part of the original *Shadowland* cast throughout its first two years. As a leader of the younger dancers in the cast, his experience and maturity would be important to the show's success on the road.

By the time summer rolled around again, the program for Pilobolus's 2009 season at the Joyce included *Dog-ID*, a new piece that was actually a rough draft of the opening section of *Shadowland*, performed by Mark, Renée, Molly, and the other *Shadowland* cast members. A bit overlong, with much good material but in need of further editing, it enabled its creators to experiment with how much the performers should be in front of the screen versus behind the screen.

That same July brought my second Pilobolus summer workshop, taught again by Matt and Emily, with a surprise addition: Jonathan. He had called Matt and Emily at nine o'clock the night before the workshop began and had informed them peremptorily that he had decided to co-teach it. He popped by, two or three times a day, throughout the week, and each time he sauntered into Club Hall, smiling, one could feel the energy become more complicated. He seemed to like me and to genuinely appreciate my ideas, and I could see and appreciate his many positive attributes, but the week would be, among other things, a window into the strained group dynamics that emanated from Jonathan's brash and at times mercurial manner. "You have to be able to look at the work that others in your group are creating," he told the attendees emphatically, "and, if it sucks, you have to be able to say *'That sucks!'* You're not saying that *they* suck, you're saying that *it* sucks." It was classic Jonathan: great advice in its recognition of the need to transcend niceties and offer the brutally honest criticism that leads to strong art; but horrible advice in its suggestion that insensitive language and a tone-deafness to the feelings of others is the way to get there. The tensions and contradictions inherent in this philosophy, and in Jonathan himself, had always reverberated around him, and still did. At one point Matt had to lunge with arms out like a referee between Jonathan and another workshop participant to prevent a fiery argument (the trigger wasn't that Jonathan had criticized someone's work but that a young man had dared to suggest that Jonathan had an ego). By Thursday, Matt and Emily had to gather and confer with the workshop group in secret, while Jonathan was detained elsewhere, in order to defuse the various tensions that had cropped up. It was, in short, a weird week—but by the end of it I knew that I had grown closer to Matt and Emily.

Eight days later, on August 1, from a sixth-row seat at the Joyce I watched a Saturday matinee that included *Dog-ID, Gnomen, Lanterna Magica,* and *Megawatt.* This was one of Andy Herro's last shows before leaving the company, and he had a noticeably strong stage presence. I did not know Andy but it had been interesting and impressive to see how he had developed, and he gave his all in this final run. In the concluding moments of *Gnomen* he emoted what seemed to me the stoic dignity of a soldier honoring a fallen comrade, and at the end of *Megawatt* he reached toward the

audience in the last moment before the lights went down, as if threatening to break the theatrical fourth wall, a gleefully demonic presence about to "get us" and perhaps pull us into his creepy world. I could sense why he was so well liked by his colleagues. Renée has since told me, "Andy left a mark on the company. He had such a good attitude. He attacked everything with everything he had. Intense to watch."

Another two weekends later came that blazing August afternoon—Sunday, August 16—on which Matt visited me in New Haven (lunch at India Palace, a stop at Atticus bookstore café) and I showed him my little first-floor apartment, shady with blinds drawn and lights off in a futile attempt to summon a sense of coolness, but in fact a steaming hot, unair-conditioned hotbox, for which I apologized as I stood in the alcove off my kitchen and he stood near my tiny kitchen table. He said, "Oh, don't worry, it doesn't bother me, I'm from Georgia." And there, as we both continued to stand in that quiet calm mixture of shade and crazy-high temperature, he recounted *Shadowland* for me, playing all the roles, with constant movement as he both demonstrated and explained the narrative, and I thought, *Matt Kent is performing a one-man show for me in my kitchen.* I loved it.

Five days later, on Friday, August 21, at Matt's invitation I attended the *Shadowland* tech rehearsal in Waterbury, Connecticut, before the show began its first European tour. In the giant hollowness of the empty theater, as one of a handful of individuals scattered among the center-front rows, I felt like both an insider and an outsider. I tried to remain meekly mute, if not entirely invisible, while the multiple creators focused intently on their work. The cast members were exhausted, but in each complete run-through—there were two that day—the show struck me as fabulous, with its abundance of rich imagery, humor, invention, and humane emotion. The centaur scene, with its graceful and delicate symbolism of sexual awakening, was performed with full nudity, though it was later decided not to present it that way publicly; instead, it would be performed, depending on the venue, either with dance belts or other, less revealing costuming. (When I later saw a version in which the dancers wore flesh-colored coverings, I felt that, ironically, the less revealing the costuming becomes, the more the audience is invited to *imagine* the bodies nude, which detracts from the naturalness and innocence of the scene.)

At the end of the afternoon I allowed myself to offer one comment to the directors as they conferred: "I could sit here and watch it another ten times." Michael Tracy's face brightened like that of a child who had received unexpected praise, and in retrospect I think I understand why he kept performing, touring, so much longer than the other founders: the applause from the audiences must have fallen on him like rain on an eager sunflower.

In September, *Shadowland* opened in Madrid, and it quickly became apparent that the intermission should be removed; this and many other changes were made. For the most part, audiences liked the show. People were intrigued, and would try to imitate the dog-girl silhouette. The agents, however, were saying that they didn't know how to sell it, that it was too dark to be a kid's show, and had nudity or near-nudity. Pilobolus discovered the real problem: these were their American agents, and it wasn't an American show. A European agent saw it and knew she could sell it. The odd freshness of the show and its medium (shadow-dance theatre with a twist) were not obstacles in the European market. The show eventually also obtained a more family-friendly sensibility, in part by giving the dog-girl more agency and clarifying the ending.

By December, Matt had become my dance-hero-turned-buddy. In those early days of our friendship he did most of the talking, an outpouring I encouraged by my insatiable interest in all things Pilobolus, but his energetic rush of thoughts into words would stop on a dime, like a whirlwind equipped with a pause button, if I wanted to put in a question or comment, to which he would listen with rapt attention. Even if the conversation were 95 percent his, I found that the next time we spoke, whether in two weeks or two months, he would say, "I've been thinking about what you said" and I'd ask, "What did I say?" and he'd recount one of the few thoughts I had offered, something I hadn't regarded as noteworthy and had completely forgotten, but which had resonated for him as a valuable insight and clearly mattered in the ongoing formulation of his own ideas. I had rarely, if ever, felt so heard, my ideas so valued, and all the more so because of the natural, casual manner of the affirmation.

4

On December 7, 2009, the cast of *Shadowland* performed a skit at the Royal Variety Performance, an annual tradition in England then already in its ninety-seventh year, attended by the Royal Family and subsequently televised to millions of viewers around the world. There Renée met the Queen, an experience recounted in a post Renée wrote for the Pilobolus blog:

> My first thought when we walked down the long entranceway to the Winter Garden Theater in Blackpool was that we were jesters and acrobats arriving in a Renaissance court. It was a beautiful theater with about 3,000 seats, balconies, and massive chandelier. The Queen sat in a box with four other people in the first balcony, stage left of center. At the end of our set, we bowed first to the audience, and then turned to bow to Her Majesty the Queen.

Renée and the dancers had created for the occasion a fantastic shadow tale of "a burglar stealing the royal crown from the Tower of London, and a young superhero who is half dog, half girl, and her sidekick, who chase him all over the country to rescue the crown." Because the piece was scheduled for early in the show, Renée had geared it toward lighthearted family fare, but she was nervous nonetheless "that we were somehow going to insult the Queen and all of England." The piece, with music by David Poe, went over well and elicited the desired laughs, as well as encouragement from the show's other performers in the greenroom backstage: Bette Midler, Whoopi Goldberg, Chaka Kahn, Miley Cyrus, and Lady Gaga. The truly royal encounter, however, still lay ahead:

> The Queen met us on stage after the show and was warm and grandmotherly. She asked us where we had been and where our company was going next. We had been instructed on etiquette before meeting her—don't speak until you're spoken to; address her as Your Majesty; say "ma'am" as in jam, not "mar'am" as in smarm; and do not extend your hand until a hand is extended towards you. I was *sure* she had reached her hand out to me when I extended mine, but then I wasn't so sure, and was frozen as we spoke, expecting guards to come and whisk me away. But all was fine—until she walked away and I realized I'd been barefoot the whole time that I talked to her!

Renée hadn't realized that meeting the Queen while still in her Pilobolus costume meant that she would be barefoot. Yet in retrospect it seemed a perfect Pilobolus detail.

5

In May 2010, the post-apocalyptic zombie horror television series *The Walking Dead* began filming its pilot episode in Atlanta, Georgia. Because zombies need to shuffle, the show's makers decided to bring in a movement coach. They wanted to find someone local to Atlanta, and they did, approaching Matt not through Pilobolus but through Facebook. At the time, he was working for Pilobolus only as a freelancer, so, happy for the solo gig, he said yes, and for three days, in a warehouse in Atlanta, he presided over a "zombie boot camp" with three hundred extras sent through in groups of about thirty at a time. His job was to train them and identify potential "hero zombies" for the director. (A "hero zombie" is one that will look good close to the camera, an extra who shows particular skill and can be placed more prominently than others; the idea is a variation on the filmmaking term "hero props" which refers to items that can be shown in close-up and still look convincing to the audience.) Matt treated the process as a massive workshop to tap into everyone's creativity and talked to the extras about "accessing their inner zombie" so that each could develop an individual approach within the parameters of zombie qualities outlined by the show's "bible" of background information. "You can't see very clearly but you can hear," he would explain, and then lead improvisational exercises in which, while a group of extras shuffled like zombies, he would quietly grab a chair and, while they weren't looking, throw it against a wall to make a loud noise to which they could respond. It was a little like a Pilobolus workshop but with a zombie motif. No one knew then how big the show would become, or that the addition of "zombie movement consultant" to one's resumé could become an impressive credit. "It was only a three-day gig," Matt recalled with a laugh, "but it was the most mileage I've ever gotten out of three days in my life."

6

Early on the morning of June 13, 2010, Matt received a phone call. "Something terrible has happened," Renée said through tears, and then, as so often happens in these situations, she struggled to gather the strength to say the next words. In that brief pause, frightening possibilities flashed through Matt's mind: Had Renée's daughter been in an accident? Had Robby collapsed while on his morning jog?

"Jonathan has died," she said.

He had been in Manhattan's Mount Sinai Hospital undergoing stem cell treatments for the myelofibrosis that he had been battling, and there had been complications. He was sixty years old.

They had, of course, known that this day would come; but as Renée told Matt, "I guess I just couldn't believe it was really going to happen."

Perhaps because Matt had needed to contemplate his own tangled emotional history with Jonathan, perhaps because he had grown up as the child of a minister (and thus in a home where, any time the phone rings, it might signal the death of a parishioner), or perhaps because he had come to feel a critical distance from his old mentor, Matt remained calm, and began to realize the extent to which those around him in Pilobolus had until now seemed to stave off the reality that had been so clearly impending. The same morning, not long after his phone conversation with Renée, I received a phone call at the office, from Matt.

Many, many of Jonathan's colleagues and collaborators, and especially the dancers he had mentored, would recall in vivid detail their experiences with him, how he drove them to new heights of achievement, inspired them, and changed them profoundly; and, in so many cases, above all else, how much they owed him.

As Matt would say in retrospect, and with respect, "He's still the guy who said 'You belong here.' I always felt I had a part to play, that he was going to pay attention to it. He had a way of paying attention to me in the studio that was very fortifying and rewarding."

In truth, despite all of their stark differences he and Jonathan had a parallel: their shared willingness to speak out, though in markedly contrasting ways. Matt had grown up with "the rebel Jesus" and a liberal Christian vision of social justice; his history of speaking truth to power from an early age had been encouraged by his father, who liked the fact that Matt would tell him whatever he thought, bluntly and without hesitation or fear. Jonathan too had encouraged Matt's questioning of authority and had brought out more of the side of Matt that some of those around him found intermittently off-putting, the directness that could, to Matt's surprise, upset them. Ironically it was that same willingness to challenge others that had ultimately led Matt to confront Jonathan himself. Yet, as he would readily admit, "I was so fond of him in so many ways."

Some who knew Jonathan remain grateful for specific gifts—Edwin Olvera, for example, credits Jonathan with teaching him to be a better public speaker and teacher—and others offer a more generalized appreciation. For some, there had never been any conflict or hesitation in their feeling for Jonathan.

"I *loved* Jonathan," Andy Herro declares instantly. "He made such good stuff. He had a heart. He was the heart of the company. He just loved creating work and he loved the dancers. Jonathan would say things that rubbed people the wrong way but he did it because he cared. He really wanted pieces to be great and wanted people to be happy."

As Andy recalled, Jonathan had a number of maxims that he shared in the studio. "Go when you go" meant that you must commit fully to whatever you're doing; "You have to play until you can play" meant that you must improvise long enough to become uninhibited; "Long muse, short fuse" meant that you should take a long time to play, but when it comes time to get down to business, don't be afraid to cut the weaker material. Or, to put it another way, "You have to create in the moment; you can't judge it in the moment."

Perhaps the dancer who remained closest to Jonathan to the end was Jamey Hampton, who had so revered Pilobolus from the start and had realized his dream of joining the company in the late 1970s. Through the decades the two had trusted each other with their vulnerabilities. A couple of days before Jonathan died, Jamey had received from him a very supportive, tender email.

At one point in the later years Jonathan had told Jamey, as he had said to many others, "I've learned that the only way you can succeed at this is to be *all in*. And now I'm all in." Jamey suspected that one of the reasons Jonathan had insisted on intensity in his later work was that he and the company had lost some of it when Moses left; if that is the case, he certainly reclaimed it.

Jonathan's final work, *Hitched,* began performances—dedicated to his memory—the month after his death, as one of the new works in that summer's Pilobolus season at the Joyce Theater. *Hitched* is a physical satire of marriage in which a bride and groom—played by two superb dancer-athletes, Eriko Jimbo and Chris Whitney, each costumed in wedding attire—chase and attack each other in a frantic burlesque battle as their garments are shed. The conflict escalates into a sort of vertical wrestling match that ends with the two participants tangled into a literal "wedding knot"—having become a single two-headed creature, functioning but dysfunctional, as they limp off into married life, each supplying one foot to walk with, and one of them backward, exhausted from battle but inseparable. Short, fast, hilarious, and entirely dependent on the indefatigable stamina of extraordinary performers, *Hitched* is pure Jonathan Wolken and a fitting punctuation mark—an exclamation mark, of course—to his theatrical vision, embodying several of his core values: his appreciation of brevity (a.k.a. "the sushi principle"); his love of humor and playfulness; and his overwhelming commitment, especially in his later work, to sheer intensity. It also embodies, perhaps consciously and perhaps not, the quality that for many of those who knew him, defined Jonathan himself, in that both the bride and the groom are relentless fighters, feisty, determined, and unable to relent; clearly they believe in battle to the end, and what they end up with is, however damaged, a symbiotic and still-functioning partnership. It could be read as a comic metaphor not only for marriage, but for Jonathan's temperament and his vision of collaboration—and of Pilobolus.

On June 16, on the blog that was then still a part of its website, Pilobolus had started a comment thread for individuals to post their remembrances of Jonathan. Among the first posts is this one:

June 16, 2010 at 6:16 am
Jonathan, in large dose, you altered my path, led me, pushed me, shoved me, pulled me, into who i am and what i do. how i think. thanks. Peace. I loved you. Say hi to Zappa for me.
i miss you.
matt kent

THIRTEEN

Partners

1

In April 2011, in an appearance arranged by Semmel Concerts as part of its marketing plan, Pilobolus's *Shadowland* troupe performed on one of Europe's most successful television programs ever, *Wetten Dass . . . ?* (the title of the show means "Wanna Bet?"). Pilobolus "killed it" with a brilliant performance, and *Shadowland* took off like a rocket, becoming a massive hit throughout Germany and neighboring countries. Eight months later the troupe's television success was reprised, and their fortunes given another boost, when the famous host of *Wetten Dass . . . ?*, who was to retire at year's end, included them in his highly rated "all-time favorites" retrospective special.

Over the next few years *Shadowland* continued its triumphant global march. In 2012 it had its Paris premiere at the Moulin Rouge and the troupe promoted the French run of the show with a superb performance on the television program *Le Plus Grand Cabaret Du Monde* with host Patrick Sébastien, in a skit in which the dog-girl discovers New York City (to the music of Alicia Keys) and then Paris (to the music of French chanteuse Zaz). A *Shadowland* DVD release followed in 2013, then a performance on the *BBC One Show* in March 2014, and the show's premieres in Australia and China that same year. *Shadowland* would ultimately play more than one thousand dates in over twenty countries in North America, Europe, Asia, South America, Australia, and the Middle East, as Pilobolus continued to develop its lucrative sideline of commercial shadow work, making dozens of bespoke shadow performances for clients around the world.

2

In July 2011, I participated in my third and best Pilobolus workshop, taught by Emily and Matt. Its colorful variety of lovable and eccentric participants could have come from, or inspired, a comic novel. Also in the mix were three recently recruited Pilobolus dancers. Somehow the group, and the week, had a combinational energy that allowed me, in my late forties, to let myself go ahead and be a bit more rough-and-tumble in my physicality and spontaneity, and I experienced a one-time-only, fully alive, joy-in-the-moment quality that I will always treasure. (Like the other workshops, most of the people in it were much younger than me, though I wasn't the only "older" person. Over dinner in an Italian restaurant, near the end of the week, one of the other participants, a woman named Jane who looked to be in her early fifties, and whom I had found inspiring in her determination to try every move and concept that we had been taught, told me nonchalantly that she was seventy. So much for my fortysomething daring! Here's to Jane, and to everyone like her.)

Pilobolus's roots had always been entwined with teaching, given its origins in Alison's classes at Dartmouth, and the various directors had taught assorted workshops over the years; but for most of its history, the Pilobolus educational outreach program had been patched together from whatever opportunities presented themselves, requests that came to Pilobolus from outside. In more recent years, Renée had worked with Jonathan on the groundwork for education program growth, and now there began to be a more concerted effort to formulate and offer what Pilobolus itself thought it should offer. Emily would become the person who would take charge of this program, develop it further, and gradually bring it to a broader level of success.

Emily teaches with a style and values that enable the workshops at their best to take the most appealing qualities of Pilobolus itself—the sense of fun and play, of communal bonding and shared achievement, of creative energy as liberation—and realize them as a natural empowerment, a force to discover and spread to others. Weight sharing techniques and certain concepts and practices that help elicit interesting improvisations are part of the teachings, as are exercises that provide a practical education in the nature of leadership, group decision-making, and invention. It can open onto an education in life—how to tap into a beneficial attitude, and how to get past inhibitions (as the early Pilobolus had to get past its own inhibitions, to transgress traditional assumptions about dance).

As the program evolved, so did its director. Emily began to find her voice and recognize her own calling amid the challenges and rewards of teaching and motherhood. To what degree to let individuals fend for themselves and to what degree, or when, to nurture? And in what ways? It soon became clear that these questions were part of her most meaningful work, and that like so many people, she had been partly distracted by the shapes society tells us our dreams should take. "For a long time I had a struggle within myself about teaching versus performing," she explained. "Performing, you get the applause and you get the kudos and the names in lights, that kind of feeling, so it can be very hard to feel that teaching is enough. I can see now that my strength lies in teaching. As a young dancer I sort of wanted it to be the other way, and that caused a lot of self-doubt and the 'Well, I guess I'm not good enough' kind of feeling, instead of just embracing the natural gifts I was given." Now that she loved what she was doing, she saw: "There's no reason to fight what's naturally you."

She had learned a lot about how to teach dance while in college, and only when she looked back, years later, would she see that "already then, at eighteen, I was doing what I was going to end up doing, which was going out and making shows for kids and teaching and performing. It was all right there."

In 2011 her role as education director, and her full embrace of it, still lay ahead, but at the end of that summer she and Matt relocated from Georgia to Connecticut again, this time more decisively. After years of working under contract as a freelancer, Matt had accepted a permanent position with Pilobolus.

3

Renowned for its ability to create whole universes with only the stripped-down human body on a bare stage, when Pilobolus chooses to use elaborate props or costumes, or to introduce video or other new media, it has an even greater need than most companies to justify those additions artistically. *Seraph* (2011) is among the Pilobolus pieces with the most explicit use of technology, an experiment in the use of two robotically controlled flying objects (small drones, each with four propellers) with only a single dancer—yet it's also among the most resoundingly humane pieces in the company's repertoire.

Conceived by Robby and Renée with several collaborators, it has a number of witty choices woven into its premise: it is, as Pilobolus has called it, "a pastoral fable"—but one built around robots; it can claim an unusual, not to say whimsical, identity as both a solo and a trio, depending on whether one counts the robots as dancers; and its use of classical music from the Romantic period—from a Schubert *trio,* appropriately—is dramatic in a way that becomes comic in its counterpoint to the actions onstage, especially the appearances and reappearances of the flying visitors. (For connoisseurs: the selection is Schubert's Trio No. 2 in E Flat, Op. 100, second movement: Andante con moto.)

Seraph provided an ideal showcase for dancer Matt Del Rosario, who, with his muscular body and laid-back Hawaiian vibe (as a native of the island of Lanai), his long black hair and half-Japanese, half-Filipino identity, channeled elements of his kind, spiritually thoughtful offstage personality to portray a gentle warrior with a wide-eyed compassionate curiosity, and even naivety, mixed with caution, physical acumen, and a readiness to defend himself—or to dive for cover in comic terror when the hovering saucers appeared threatening.

This protagonist, both noble and nimble, suggests a classic hero archetype: the male body liberated from the confines of gravity, a figure in pop culture that has morphed from Tarzan swinging through the jungle to Spider-Man swinging across a cityscape. The sense of nakedness and strength (like all superheroes in skintight costumes, Spider-Man is, visually, an opportunity for artists to draw a well-muscled, essentially nude male figure) as well as anti-gravitational freedom, litheness, airborne grace, and self-regulated power all amount to an ideal of male identity. An ideal in motion, perfect for Pilobolus. *Seraph* has at its center that type of figure, with comic touches (of fear, of bewilderment) that only make him more relatable and endearing. He enters the stage carrying a small flashlight and flickers it as if in parallel to his own flickering doubts or suspicions, as if on a potentially dangerous night patrol. That flickering light will soon meet the flickering lights of a mysterious object.

Most of the choreographic movement (for the human involved, rather than the robots) consists of runs, dives, and tumbles, deftly executed in response to, and in complement to, the movements of the drones—whose offstage pilots from the MIT Distributed Robotics Laboratory had to contend with the complex, daunting realities of controlling them throughout each rehearsal and performance. Unlike today's models, the robots had no sensors and couldn't self-stabilize. The newness of the technology made them highly challenging to manipulate—and to tolerate as costars. Their fast-rotating, sharp-edged little plastic helicopter wings would slice into their human dance partner when they bumped into him during practice sessions, leaving numerous small surface cuts.

The resulting piece, however, showed no such hardships. Exactly the right length at just ten minutes, *Seraph* is an unpretentious vignette perfectly edited. With an extremely simple movement vocabulary, no mime, and no excess motion, it maintains a sense of spontaneity as it demonstrates how dance can be made of nondance. And it evokes plentiful meaning.

A seraph is, in Christianity, an angel of the highest order in the celestial hierarchy. Often depicted as a child's head with three pairs of wings—two wings above, two below, and one on each side—a seraph is, along with other seraphim, a caretaker of God's throne, over which it hovers. The idea of multiple wings and hovering has, of course, obvious parallels with the drones, and, more subtly, the traditional association of seraphim with light and purity has, in the piece, a neat counterpart in the human-drone communications via blinking lights and the ultimately compassionate interactions that result. Another virtue with which the seraphim are associated is ardor, and certainly the ardent, pure, light-giving human depicted in *Seraph* meets the heavenly drones with the qualities they value; indeed, the fact that the piece's title is *Seraph* rather than the plural *Seraphim* (which would seem the more appropriate choice if one were naming it for the *two* flying robots) suggests that the piece's angelic namesake might be its human protagonist. The concept of ardor also resonates in a broader sense: to be held rapt in enthusiasm, in wonderment, living entirely at one with the moment, is to be in a divine state of grace. Not all theatergoers will get there via *Seraph,* but if met on its own terms it points beautifully and knowingly in the right direction.

Seraph premiered at the American Dance Festival on June 30, 2011 and in New York in July. Posters for the troupe's summer run at the Joyce Theater featured a John Kane photograph of Matt del Rosario standing with his face and upper body lit against a jet-black background, powerful arms folded as he gazes up warily at the mysterious glow of a flying disk hovering above him. The resonant image made him that season's face of Pilobolus, and gave *Seraph* a neatly emblematic entry in the John Kane Pilobolus iconography.

4

One day Martha Clarke—in her late sixties, white-haired but with the same old glint of mischief sparkling behind the eyeglasses that framed her wise eyes—was walking out of American Ballet Theatre, where she had been rehearsing a piece. As she passed a studio, she saw, through an open door, "this creature flying through the air with this raven blue-black hair and he finished the phrase and I stood at the door transfixed and I went to Herman Cornejo who I didn't know at all, had never seen him before, and I said, 'I love you.'"

The dark-haired, gravity-defying object of fascination, Argentine-born and entering his thirties, had been a principal dancer with ABT since 2003, and now Martha, "caught like a deer in the headlights by his brilliance," of course wanted to find a way to work with him. She had also long wanted to work with the great ballet star Alessandra Ferri, who had retired from American Ballet Theatre in 2007. That Martha should want to work with the finest dramatic dancers made sense given that her own artistic trajectory had traveled, over the years, toward increasingly narrative-based work. She turned to her bookshelf yet again, and to an old literary love, and considered Colette's novels *Chéri* and *The Last of Chéri* as possible inspiration. But would Alessandra and Herman mesh in the roles of Léa and her young lover Chéri? They did a workshop to test the idea. "The chemistry was instantly electric."

The two dancers, according to Martha, "contributed a lot to the making of *Chéri* because I'm not really a ballet choreographer." True to her long-ago mentor Antony Tudor, she acknowledged, "I care less about steps than what is emotionally truthful." With actress Amy Irving in the show's one speaking role, as Chéri's mother, and accompaniment from pianist Sarah Rothenberg's selection of works by Debussy, Mompou, Poulenc, and Ravel, *Chéri* premiered at the Signature Theatre in New York in December 2012 and a world tour followed.

The decade leading up to it had seen a reconsideration of Martha's long and distinguished body of work. She had unveiled a revised *Vienna: Lusthaus* in 2002 as *Vienna: Lusthaus (Revisited);* a new work, *Belle Époque,* two years later; a dazzling revival of *Garden of Earthly Delights* in 2008; and another new work, the award-winning *Angel Reapers,* two years after that. Perhaps the successful revival of *Garden of Earthly Delights* provided the most vivid reminder of her power as a creator of theatre. Although the original 1984 production had been a tremendous success, Martha updated and improved the show and further energized its ideas, dramatic movement, and overall choreography. She made much more and better use of aerial work from the early sequences onward; the Seven Deadly Sins sequence, intensified, evoked a far more horrific sense of human evil; and whereas the 1984 version depicted a man spinning in air as the introductory image to the section on Hell—one of the strongest images in the show—Martha shrewdly relocated it to make it the *final* image of Hell. (The show's final sequence still also involved the female serpent and the cello, and while extremely well done one does miss Martha's electrifying performance, the intensity of which remains my favorite element of the 1984 version.) The revived staging was also more effectively lit—beautifully lit at times in pale blue—and, in a lovely set of final images, as a light snow amid blue light falls on Adam and Eve, and they and the animals (played by bent-over humans) exit in the snowfall, an angel circles overhead; and the lyricism, after all the horror, offers a sense of divine grace.

Whereas one can trace some influence of Pilobolus in *Garden of Earthly Delights,* the sumptuous romantic drama of Martha's *Chéri* would seem much farther away, perhaps even a world apart. And yet it had sprung from another influence that had been there for Martha all along: "I think one of my previous lives must have been 1900," she mused, considering her repeated returns to that era. "I don't know how I found Colette or how she found me. Besides loving her writing, she loved animals, dogs and flowers and the countryside. As a woman she led a very wild love life, which is kind of what I was drawn to when I was a young woman . . . I found an identity with Colette." As she readily confessed, too, she had learned to accept, with the perspective of age, the loss of youthful passion—a central theme of *Chéri.*

5

The *Seraph* project with the MIT Distributed Robotics Laboratory had been only one among a profusion of collaborations that would characterize these years in Pilobolus, as the company created pieces with Pulitzer Prize-winning graphic novelist Art Spiegelman, musician Dan Zanes, Japanese choreographer Takuya Muramatsu of the Butoh company Dairakudakan, juggler Michael Moschen, Belgian-Moroccan choreographer Sidi Larbi Cherkaoui, Israeli author Etgar Keret, London-based Venezuelan choreographer Javier De Frutos, and, perhaps most inventively, the pop band OK Go.

The project with OK Go and its collaborator Trish Sie, renowned for choreographing the band's hugely popular videos (and also known to fans as the sister of lead singer Damian Kulash), revolved around the band's song "All Is Not Lost" and the creation of both an innovative music video and a related performance piece designed for Pilobolus stage shows. In the video, launched alongside the song's release as a single in August 2011, band members and Pilobolus dancers, outfitted in sea-green tights, created a kaleidoscope of images by rolling, sliding, stepping, or otherwise moving across a plexiglass surface positioned above the camera. According to Renée, it was in part "a love letter to Japan after the devastation of the tsunami" in that the song's message of hope was paired in the video with the use of the dancers' feet as shapes that form a "foot alphabet" or "foot font" of letters to spell out words and phrases (such as "spread love") in Japanese lettering as well as in English. A special interactive version of the video allowed viewers to send hopeful messages in multiple languages. In the stage version, Pilobolus dancers re-created the kaleidoscopic video, with audiences able to see both the activity of the dancers on the plexiglass surface and, alongside it, a simultaneous live feed from the camera beneath it. In its dual perspectives it amounted to a kinetic art piece about patterns, creation, and illusion. The video garnered a Grammy nomination for Best Short Form Music Video, and the live version was a consistent crowd-pleaser.

Trish Sie soon worked with Pilobolus again, invited back to help adapt her tango-themed video for OK Go's song "Skyscrapers" into a fast-paced, colorful Pilobolus stage piece. In that video, Trish and a male dance partner had tangoed their way across a series of vivid backgrounds, moving throughout Los Angeles (always from screen left to screen right, coincidentally the same direction as the dog-girl's movement in *Shadowland*). Renée recalls that it had been Robby Barnett's idea to try to make a live Pilobolus version, an intriguing challenge—done very quickly in five days, "a whirlwind but fun" (as was the piece itself, with its ever-changing backdrops and breathless costume changes). Renée and Trish struck up a friendship that led them to create a third Pilobolus piece, *Licks*, the concept for which took shape during a brief retreat that they spent, on Renée's birthday weekend, in a cabin in upstate New York; *Licks* would make dynamic use of string, rope, and the energetic music of Nortec Collective: Bostich & Fussible, who created new and remixed music for it.

As the cascade of collaborations poured onward, new influences led from one to the next. Thanks to his work on *Shadowland*, Steven Banks had become a trusted colleague, and Matt Kent decided to ask him for recommendations of people with whom Pilobolus might want to work. Steve, who is good friends with Penn Jillette, recommended the famous magicians Penn and Teller. An immediately appealing idea, it raised a fabulous question: What could a bunch of dancers do with a pair of hugely successful magicians? Like Pilobolus, they were known for quirky, playful, brilliant inventiveness in their field, and averse to clichés, so the possibilities seemed rich. Robby, Renée, and Matt flew to Las Vegas to work with Penn and Teller in a studio near The Rio, where the duo was performing. The pair would work with Pilobolus during the day and leave in mid to late afternoon to perform two shows at night. They were pros, and "they were so levelheaded about the whole thing," Matt recalled. As the group set about conceiving the new piece, it became apparent that the too-obvious—a dance piece infused with magic tricks—would be strained and silly, but that the opposite—a magic act that could *only* be accomplished with performers possessing the unique skill set of Pilobolus dancers—could be fresh and original. They settled on a Houdini-style escape theme and set to work.

All the while, always in the room as a consultant, was a gentleman in his late seventies who kissed the hands of ladies and seemed to have stepped out of the rat pack style of Vegas past, making an indelible impression on his new acquaintances from Pilobolus. Johnny Thompson, known to audiences for his comic magic act as the Great Tomsoni, was a legendary figure among magicians, the mentor and advisor extraordinaire, a living encyclopedia of magic-act history, strategies, secrets, and techniques. Revered by many, and clearly cherished by Penn and Teller, he quickly became cherished by Pilobolus as well.

As the escape theme took shape, the act became a combination of tricks that subjected the dancers to various humiliations and dangers: one is stuffed into a duffel bag, another locked in a box, two are chained almost-naked to a stripper pole, another is duct-taped to a chair, and a series of dramatic and surprising escapes unfold. Playfully titled <*esc*> (which is both the computer keyboard shorthand for the word "escape" and, appropriately, a visual representation of three letters "confined" between angle brackets), this nondance addition to the Pilobolus repertory would mostly delight audiences with its beguiling use of dancers as escape artists and its Swiss-watch-precise showcase of their skills in a new realm; but while brilliantly achieved, it also gave unsympathetic critics a chance to decry what some saw as Pilobolus's increasing embrace of slick, show-biz entertainment.

By now, the parade of distinguished names that had graced the list of Pilobolus collaborations, and the technological and pop-cultural accomplishments that had accompanied those pieces, had reached a point at which it did make sense to ask, not in the jaded tone of the more finnicky naysayers, but in a spirit of genuine concern: What was Pilobolus now, *without* guest artists, without show-business or high-tech elements, without giant props or screens or video monitors? Was Pilobolus to become a kind of corporate facilitator of artistic mash-ups? To what degree was another, more essential Pilobolus still there? As one dancer confided to me at the time: "We told the directors. Next year, no technology. Just bodies!"

Robby had read and been inspired by Leonard Barkan's book *Unearthing the Past: Archaeology and Aesthetics in the Making of Renaissance Culture*, a scholarly work that had intrigued him sufficiently that he decided to introduce it to his colleagues as the company returned to the studio in 2014 to create a new piece—this time, with no outside collaborators. He presented the book to them early on, then he stepped back. That wasn't unusual; Robby was known for his calm thoughtful silences, his quiet wise unobtrusiveness as a director. Now, though, his stepping back was a little different. For the past few years Renée and Matt had been gradually moving into the lead, preparing to take the artistic reins, and this piece would be Robby's last collaboration as he stepped further back and let the two of them take another step forward.

Entitled *On the Nature of Things*, after the ancient philosophical poem of the same name (*De Rerum Natura* by Lucretius), the new work that emerged had an operatic score adapted from Vivaldi and combined such influences as Renaissance sculpture, creation myths, imagery of legendary heroes wrestling, and the Adam-Eve-Serpent relationship. All of this coalesced into an intense dramatic trio, built on a single prop: a raised circular platform less than three feet wide that evokes a classical column or pillar, and provides an ingenious constraint as it delimits the action. The three dancers, nude except for dance belts, are the living classical statues who must balance together on it, in what Pilobolus called "a story about the birth of desire and its intertwined connection to shame and revenge." In its press notes on the piece, Pilobolus also pointed out that Lucretius "argued that physics and chance governed the world, rather than frightening godly powers." Physics and chance, in the form of athleticism and improvisation, certainly governed the Pilobolus process in the studio, and the company summoned, in lieu of frightening godly powers, an uncharacteristic and extraordinary display of gravitas. *On the Nature of Things* impressed audiences and provided a refreshing reminder that without flashy technology or famous collaborators Pilobolus could still make, with just bodies and brainpower, exciting and original new work.

On Tuesday, July 1, Pilobolus appeared at the Filene Center at Wolf Trap, in Vienna, Virginia, and the next day Sarah Kaufman, in the *Washington Post*, reviewed the "enthralling and frequently astonishing" performance, making the case for contemporary Pilobolus with an eloquent appreciation of *On the Nature of Things, All Is Not Lost,* and *<esc>*. Identifying the theme of the program as "how mystery prevails even in the face of absolute transparency" she noted with appreciation that the group had returned to its origins but expanded upon them "with inventiveness and complexity that is also wholly entertaining."

As always, the company headed into its annual summer season at the Joyce, but that year was particularly tough behind the scenes, stressful in terms of logistics, personal tensions, and communication, both within the company and between it and the theater. The factors were many, and they took a toll. The audiences still showed up in large numbers and left happy with what they'd seen, but after more than two decades of consecutive summer seasons at New York's greatest theater for dance, Pilobolus ended its longstanding tradition, as the Joyce's management and the Pilobolus management could no longer agree on terms. The break would provide the company with the opportunity to pursue, free from any agreements of exclusivity in the New York area, other venues at which it wanted to perform, and to experiment with performing in the city at other times of year; but to some observers—including this one—it seemed a sad choice and a loss. In all its particulars, of scale and shape and sensibility, the Joyce fit Pilobolus like a glove, and Pilobolus fit summer in New York the way sand, muscles, and sunshine suit a balmy day at the beach. In a smart bid to retain its usual summertime attendees, starting the following year the Joyce would fill the gap in its calendar with an apt alternative: Momix.

6

In the years during which I had taken my first three Pilobolus workshops I had stayed at an inn in nearby New Milford, a town with a pleasant green and a number of local shops. My first night there, the hot, deserted summer Sunday before my first workshop, alone and knowing no one, I had gone for a stroll to find a place to eat dinner. The tiny perfect restaurant I happened upon, called Salsa, with its fresh guacamole and other irresistible Mexican offerings, instantly became a cherished and often repeated part of my Pilobolus workshop experience. (In a subsequent year, and at the start of another workshop week, I headed to Salsa and my heart sank at the sight of its storefront empty, abandoned—and as I trudged through the streets looking for an alternative, my heart soared when I happened upon its new location! It had moved to a larger space, where it continued successfully for several more years.) The restaurant and its clean crisp ambiance resurface now as I recall a dinner that Matt and I had there a little later, in the summer of 2015.

That evening we talked about narrative genres, such as the western, science fiction, fantasy, film noir, and so on. Pilobolus had hit a financial bump and, predictably, it had been decided that the only thing to do was to conjure up a sequel to its biggest moneymaker, *Shadowland*. The new show's narrative, it seemed, might play with imagery from multiple genres, and over dinner Matt and I discussed my admiration for artists who know how to traipse happily from one genre to the next, whether in pop music (Blondie and its embrace of punk, disco, jazz, reggae, rap, and other categories beyond traditional rock), literature (Truman Capote's evolution through the Southern Gothic of his early works to the urbane satire of *Breakfast at Tiffany's* and the grim reportage of *In Cold Blood*), or the graphic novel (the French comic-art genius Jean "Moebius" Giraud, a visual master of chameleonic transformations in style and content). With regard to the latter, I told Matt about Moebius's whimsical penchant for jumping genres even from one page or one frame to the next, and how the absence of a transition can at times be the most striking transition of all.

The question of art versus entertainment, a question raised by the *Shadowland* shows and many of these brilliant artists' projects, seemed to fade in the face of sheer delight.

The prior year, under the auspices of Pilobolus and via his connection to Teller, Matt had worked on Aaron Posner's extraordinary production of Shakespeare's *The Tempest*. With Teller and, again, virtuoso illusionist Johnny Thompson to infuse the show with magic, Matt's primary responsibility had been the creation and choreography of Caliban, the half human, half monster son of a powerful witch, embodied in this case as a two-headed, four-legged creature of conjoined Pilobolus dancers Manelich Minniefee and Zach Eisenstat in a stunning partnered performance. As Renée says, "Pilobolus doesn't make dance pieces, it makes miniature worlds that exist on stage," and Matt took that lens with him to the entire *Tempest* project and worked on other aspects of choreography of group movement, with not only the two dancers but the actors, musicians, and other nondancers. He loved the project and especially loved Aaron and Teller's openness to collaboration. The show elicited raves, and Matt would be nominated for a Los Angeles Drama Critics Circle Award for his work.

Renée and Matt were both on top of their game, and for *Shadowland 2*, collaborating again with Steve Banks, David Poe, and Itamar, they would craft a playful tale of romance and a quest for a mystical bird, along the way dipping into various storytelling traditions. Midway through the new show's development, the original *Shadowland* finally made its US debut. That premiere, in November 2015 at the NYU Skirball Center—a.k.a. The Jack H. Skirball Center for the Performing Arts, an 850-seat theater owned by New York University—wasn't as momentous as one might have hoped; after playing to half a million people around the world, the show's remarkable freshness and innovations had by now been imitated repeatedly by others and seen by millions on TV. Looking back on its success and the bumps along the way—the various changes of cast, the waves of profits, and the ripple effects of having a hit in Europe—Renée would see the experience as one in which "there was a lot of learning about how to scale a business, how to run multiple tours at the same time, and where to allow growth and where to hold onto the smallness of things and the quaintness of not being part of a giant corporate entity." That smallness and quaintness, even when served to a global audience, remained central to the Pilobolus appeal. In the end, *Shadowland* "did great things for the company, and we learned so much about storytelling." It would continue to tour, more modestly, in the US.

Shadowland 2 wasn't technically a sequel but an entirely separate story, well-crafted and charming, marketed as a new installment in the same Pilobolus shadow genre, and when it premiered in Germany the following July it proved a solid success in Europe, with a surprise bonus at home: it elicited a better audience response in the US than the original.

That fall Pilobolus underwent a generational change. With the retirement of Robby Barnett and Michael Tracy, Renée and Matt were named artistic directors, the first individuals after the founders of Pilobolus to hold that title.

FOURTEEN

Branches

1

One of the gifts of art is the sense of being fully alive—a gift I recalled as I reread, with pleasure, these lines from Virginia Woolf:

> But it was summer now. She had been waked by the birds. How they sang! attacking the dawn like so many choir boys attacking an iced cake.

Dance, and its permutations in movement-based theatre—with its inherent physicality, its athleticism, the pulsing breathing human life-force out of which it is composed and with which it is enacted—ideally suits the transmission of that gift, that sense of being fully alive.

Those vivid words from Woolf appear in her novel *Between the Acts,* a book that also contains a passage in which "magnificently straight" trees "suggest columns in a church . . . an open-air cathedral, a place where swallows darting seemed, by the regularity of the trees, to make a pattern, dancing, like the Russians, only not to music, but to the unheard rhythm of their own wild hearts."

And so, leaping forward three-quarters of a century from that marvelous prose, and its birds like outdoor artists of motion in a space defined by trees, we come to *Branches.*

In 2017, Jacob's Pillow, the renowned dance center and festival located in the Berkshires of Massachusetts, had a new director, Pamela Tatge, who had been appointed the previous year. In one of her first acts as director she had commissioned Pilobolus to create a new work for the center's outdoor stage, with the bucolic landscape as real-world backdrop. Renée and Matt, given the plum opportunity to deliver on their new identities as fully fledged artistic directors, wanted to bring Jacob's Pillow the vitality it sought, and to avoid making what is sometimes derisively known as "plop art"—work touted as "environmental" that has simply been "plopped down" in a designated location without the artist having genuinely responded to the surroundings. Pilobolus's own bucolic setting provided a perfect way in: they informed the dancers that they would be making a piece about having a dialogue with nature, and then took the troupe to Steep Rock, a nature preserve of almost one thousand acres, located, like their Club Hall rehearsal space, in Washington Depot. There they walked through the woods, on the same trail on which Matt would sometimes go for hikes with Robby and where Renée often walked her dog. Afterward, they and the dancers returned to the studio to get to work.

The award-winning nature documentary *Planet Earth II* had made its way across the ocean, from the BBC to US television, with its innovative use of drone technology that enabled much closer camera shots of animals: "These amazing shots of the animals," as Matt later said. "You could see their personalities." Renée and Matt were fascinated and influenced by it. In the studio, the dancers began to embody animal personas and behaviors, which quickly led to both comic and physical invention. The highly accomplished musician David Van Tieghem, brought in as sound designer, became another influence. He seasoned the soundscape with samples of nature sounds, such as wind and water, so that the music was rarely "only" music. He had worked with Pilobolus on another piece not long before, and Renée and Matt knew that David had roots in 1980s electronic music; but they were startled to learn, when he mentioned it offhandedly, that he had worked with David Byrne and Brian Eno on the 1981 album *My Life in the Bush of Ghosts,* parts of which are used in the Pilobolus classic *Day Two* that Renée and Matt had, of course, performed in and later directed, countless times through the years.

The nineteen-minute piece that premiered on the Jacob's Pillow "Inside/Out" stage did full justice to its setting in the Berkshire hills and merged fresh energy and classic Pilobolus sensibilities. Six dancers—this time, in a departure for Pilobolus, an equal number of male and female—descend from the trees and emerge from the surrounding greenery, wearing only flesh-colored shorts or leotards that suggest naked creatures. A series of

seamlessly linked vignettes imply that they are birds (we hear the prominent sound of rustling feathers and witness their flocking) or, at other
times, some ambiguous, unidentified type of mammals. Comic and lyric
elements alternate and overlap but never cancel or upstage one another,
and the effect is light in the best way, graceful and unpretentious and perfectly paced. A crowd-pleaser from its first performance, *Branches* would
become a solid part of the Pilobolus repertoire and exist in multiple forms.
An excellent filmed version, in its original Jacob's Pillow setting, employs
overhead shots with cameras attached to drones, the better to amplify the
sense of lyricism and landscape. *Branches* would also make a successful
transition to indoor performances, with much work on the lighting—
which had to be brighter than anticipated, to replicate what the sun had
accomplished outdoors.

The same year would see a fruitful collaboration with virtuoso banjo
player Béla Fleck and his wife and frequent musical partner Abigail Washburn. That piece, *Echo in the Valley,* would premiere at the American Dance
Festival alongside *Branches;* and the following year Pilobolus would premiere its first female trio, *Warp & Weft,* as well as an experimental comic
piece, *Eye Opening.* All four had their merits, but *Branches* would be the
most frequently performed over the coming years.

2

An idyllic spring day, Saturday, May 25, 2019. The weather had already,
the day before, become gorgeous, fairytale perfect, the mood superb, as
it would continue to be throughout the Memorial Day weekend. On that
pristine afternoon, I attended a reception for John Kane in Washington Depot, Connecticut, in connection with a small exhibition of his photographs
of both Pilobolus and Momix, installed in handsomely enlarged versions
at the Judy Black Memorial Park and Gardens, a small, elegant public space
with a modest shell-like building that serves as a gallery and can be opened
onto the impeccably landscaped area in front of it. I had written about John
and several of the works in this show in an essay published by the *Paris
Review Daily* nine days earlier, on May 16, entitled "Visual Magicians in the
Hills of Connecticut," which began as follows:

In the hills of northwestern Connecticut there is a portion of the
state, a rural and rural-suburban region, that I refer to as "Pilobo-

land": it includes Washington, New Milford, and other nearby towns, and has long been home to two of the world's most celebrated dance-theatre companies . . . Pilobo-land, however, is more than a place; it's also the overlapping worlds, on stages and in minds, that its creators create. Just as Vladimir Nabokov dubbed his cherished intangible possessions "unreal estate" one might, in regard to Pilobolus and Momix, speak of "surreal estate." It's a place where landscape becomes dreamscape, where the rural and the theatrical are both strikingly pictorial, and no photographer has captured them more artfully or faithfully, through multiple decades, than resident John Kane, a selection of whose work is now on display in the heart of the territory it documents.

Within the parameters of a small number of images chosen from thousands that he had taken over the years, John had selected a representative sample. In one of my favorites, Jun Kuribayashi holds his form straight at an antigravitational forty-five-degree angle while grasping a curved metallic bar that Matt Del Rosario, turned away from him, holds behind his own curved body. Against a stark white background, with nothing to distract from the geometric lines of the spare, crisp image, the configuration evokes a bow and arrow, hammer and sickle, sundial (the indicator on a sundial is called a *gnomon,* and Jun's impressive angle in the photo mirrors a pose from *Gnomen*), a more modern timepiece, or all of the above, while also evoking the strength, fragility, and beauty of the human form. It's perfect Pilobolus, and perfect John Kane, as it demonstrates how precisely the lines and curves of the human body can be delineated and, in turn, delineate ideas.

An offbeat image from 2007, of Renée doubled over vertically, held aloft over Andy Herro's raised right arm as he gazes off to the side with an ambiguous stare, was another unforgettable shot that had been taken against a neutral backdrop, while others reflected the diverse settings of later series. The calendar for 2008 had been photographed in an abandoned factory ("It was *freezing* cold," Andy had told me. "Forty degrees outside and snowing") whereas for the 2010 calendar John had photographed Pilobolus outdoors in its Connecticut surroundings. One of these latter images, with a vibrant green and red palette, stood apart for its serene absence of athleticism: a Pilobolus dancer, Jenny Mendez, ensconced in a pile of apples that seem to embrace her in abundance as she lies on a bed of grass, with only

her face, its closed eyes and apple-red lips, and her arms visible. As I wrote in my *Paris Review* essay, "She embraces herself, and perhaps, symbolically, the apples, the universe, and life itself. It's a picture that can at first seem less impressive than those that entail acrobatic feats, but its stillness and its emphasis on sensibility reveal that the essence of Pilobolus and Momix is not dance, not choreographic movement or motion, but the marriage of wit and physical sensuality. Here, stillness itself becomes the theme, sensibility is everything, and the longer one stares at this vision of a dancer at rest, the stronger it grows, until one comes to cherish the cherishing it endorses."

My observations on specific photos had pleased John, and he had added a large blow-up of the article, poster-size, off to the side of the exhibition, to provide context for visitors. Now, to celebrate and honor John's long-standing collaborations with both Pilobolus and Momix, the reception would feature a unique gift: an on-site performance by the two companies in collaboration, up close for the gathered audience of a few dozen friends and local admirers. Behind the scenes, when the idea had been raised, everyone had been receptive, Renée and Matt as well as Moses and Cynthia, and Cynthia had thought they might want to make use of some costumes that Momix had on hand but hadn't used: black hoop skirts that had a buoyant quality. Rather than bring in young Pilobolus dancers from the current company, Renée, Matt, and Emily had decided that they would perform as well as co-create, with longtime Momix dancer Steven Ezra as the fourth member of a quartet. It was something of a family affair, as Renée, of course, had begun her career working for Moses and Cynthia, and Emily had long ago babysat their now-adult daughter; and Moses had recently been back in the Pilobolus studio, at Renée and Matt's invitation, as they prepared to revive *Day Two.*

The quartet for John Kane's reception was, as Emily said, "like a little fruity dessert—light and frivolous," perfect for the festive occasion. In a playful variation on the Pilobolus "tall ladies" concept, the performers would enter the grounds of the small park as a pair of two-person-tall figures, with all of them—the men as well as the women—clad in the black hoop skirts. Because the hoop skirts were not nearly as long as the dresses of *Untitled,* the effect was very different: the "stacking" of the women atop the men did not conceal the men but covered only their upper bodies, and made a two-story person, with two hoop dresses one above the other, or in Emily's phrase, "a kind of bulbous, caricature-like shape," like a double bell; it resembled a toy figure or doll with the sensibility of a novelty item. Because of their buoyancy, the skirts would glide, and frequently made the dancers look as if they were floating. The four dancers had worked out an amusing sequence of movements and flips (the skirts also flipped over well) staged to a suitably cheery, old-timey song, "Canoe" by Kat Edmonson.

Afterward, once Renée and Matt had dispensed with their hoop skirts, Matt introduced the next piece—he was in fine form in his playful, energetic calling out to the audience—and the two of them demonstrated, with Matt blindfolded, a short portion of a duet they had been developing in the studio with their current dancers for a work-in-progress called *Tales from the Underworld*. Then, as a finale, Steven Ezra performed *Man Fan*, an excerpt from Momix's show *Botanica* that involves the unfurling and billowing of an enormous white cape that dwarfs its wearer and resembles a giant sail, and evokes an ethereal voyage: a lovely vision to see under, and against, a perfect blue sky on a glorious May afternoon.

The reception then continued with mingling and visiting, and Matt introduced me to Moses and Cynthia. Moses was "on" in the best way, delightful, chatty, witty, forthcoming, telling anecdotes. When I mentioned the long-ago May 1971 video of the original *Pilobolus* trio, and the brief interview that had accompanied it, he said "Good thing it's brief—my smartass college-age self"—but as I stood listening to him I had already been struck by the extent to which I was seeing the same person fifty years later, with the same rapid-fire wit and insouciance. He mentioned that he was seventy (though I, like everyone else, thought he looked nearly twenty years younger) and that he needs people around him who are "reliable" and "realistic" like Cynthia, to help keep him earthbound, or—he hesitated, seeking the right word. "Tethered to the earth," I said, and he said, "Yes, tethered, that's the word, because otherwise I'm off to Alpha Centauri." At another point he mentioned that he feels that the flowers and the sun and the wind, the elements of nature, "don't get credited enough" as creators of the arts. He talked about his compulsion for taping. He spoke with affection to Renée of the fact that seeing her always reminds him of the Momix show *Baseball* from her time with the company, and that his recent return to the Pilobolus studio in Club Hall to consult with her and Matt on the revival of *Day Two* had been "therapeutic" for him. Matt had told me, separately, that Moses had thoroughly enjoyed seeing the rehearsal of *Day Two*, during which he had chuckled quietly and leaned over to Matt to say, with a sly smile, "I need my mushroom tea." Moses had also remarked to Matt, with pleasure, that as he watched the dancers they seemed as if they were the same ones from thirty years ago, the past playing out for him again before his eyes.

When we spoke of the book I was writing—this book—and I told him that I thought Pilobolus was a wonderful story, he said, "It's also about American history. You could fill the whole book with *that*." It was a comment that would stay with me, as my research continued and I became increasingly aware of the influence of the times on the early Pilobolus.

3

As I spoke with Moses I had a vivid picture in mind of his Momix work, from having seen the company perform twice in the preceding year, both at the Joyce Theater and at a preview of their newest show, *Alice*, in Torrington, Connecticut. The summer show at the Joyce had been an impressive overview. With no backdrop other than a black curtain and occasional projections, and no videos or other multimedia elements; with no sets; with a theatrical universe made entirely of dancers, costumes, music, light, and occasional props, the show deftly strung together a "greatest hits" of seventeen short pieces with very rapid transitions between them—lights fade, music fades, then almost immediately the lights go back up.

There were pieces based heavily on optical illusions and others based primarily on mood, some built around props and others more heavily focused on costuming and movement (whether that of a fan dance or a whirling dervish). In the ultimate prop piece, *Dream Catcher,* the rocking giant metal sculpture central to the piece somehow, surprisingly, does not upstage the two fantastic dancers who use it—which is what makes the whole thing ingenious. Of the illusionary pieces, *Paper Trails,* based on a prodigious use of white paper, unspooled and crumpled and transformed, struck me as the most interesting with its slow build and increasingly, overwhelmingly surreal mood, brought to a fine, witty culmination. *If You Need Some Body* displayed the antic comedy-skit side of old Pilobolus taken to a looser, even kookier extreme, with all the Momix dancers paired with lightweight mannequins to double the number of "performers" onstage and create a hilarious high-speed finale to the music of Johann Sebastian Bach. But the best piece, and the one that got the most ardent, unrestrained applause, was the male solo *Table Talk,* in which the only prop is a table. You can't beat the sheer excitement of seeing a dancer perform jaw-dropping, awe-inspiring moves in rapid succession, in a tour de force solo replete with humor and the moment-to-moment suspense of not knowing what he'll do next.

I noticed that Moses liked to bring in world music, and world dance and culture in general, but then morph, repurpose, or redeploy these elements in a vision particular to Momix. I noticed too that Momix is like a different flavor of Pilobolus. If I had to name that flavor I might call it "Pilobolus goes to the candy shop" but I wouldn't mean that as a putdown. Or perhaps rather than "candy shop" I should say "toy shop." Given his love of nature and his love of invention Moses blends the natural and the artificial; he draws inspiration from flora and fauna, sunlight, moonlight, and landscapes, and he builds a series of toys. What's more, as he said long ago, in the film *Moses Pendleton Presents Moses Pendleton,* he sees the human body itself as a toy: "Most people don't know how to enjoy their bodies. It's the greatest toy we have. I think for me that's what dance is about . . . and if you have that attitude, I think your body will dance no matter whether it's sitting, drinking coffee, making cappuccino, taking a shower, or dancing."

All of these influences and more had informed Momix's most recent endeavor, the suitably trippy *Alice,* loosely based on *Alice in Wonderland.* It had its official premiere in February 2019 in Italy, the country that had always most avidly embraced Momix and in which the show would continue to play throughout the year. A brief article in the *Corriere di Verona* described *Alice* as "a fantastic game built with surreal paintings and choreography" and quoted Moses as saying, "I see *Alice* as an invitation to invent, to fantasize, to subvert our perception of the world, to open up to the impossible. The stage is my hookah, my mushroom, my rabbit hole." Indeed it is, and to criticize Momix for being "lightweight" is like going into a toy store and complaining that they don't sell philosophy books. If its shows inspire awe more than empathy, with a slightly more circuslike quality than Pilobolus, they nonetheless tap into and elicit a sense of wonder, pleasure, magical life, and humor, and make the world a little richer, brighter, and more beautiful for the effort; and beauty always has depth for those who contemplate it deeply.

4

In a promotional photo released that spring, three figures cross Eighth Avenue in Manhattan in a parody of the famous cover image for the Beatles album *Abbey Road*. From left to right, they are a Pilobolus "tall lady" and two individuals strolling like comic hipsters in black hats and sunglasses (Renée and Matt). To the upper right, the marquee of the Joyce Theater reads: PILOBOLUS, with the dates "June 11 thru 29." In an accompanying online video clip, the tall lady—portrayed (in the upper half) by dancer Heather Favretto—makes good use of her height as she places the letters of the Pilobolus name on the marquee, without need of a ladder. The photo and video were the perfect accompaniment to the announcement: Pilobolus was "coming home" to the Joyce for a summer run, with a program of favorite pieces spanning the company's history.

Over the five years since Pilobolus had last appeared at the Joyce Theater, there had been changes in management at both organizations. Pilobolus had brought in an excellent general manager and CFO, Daniel Ordower, who, upon hearing that the Joyce had a new program director, reached out. With different personalities in place, negotiations were easier, and soon an agreement was reached and the homecoming announcement made.

At the theater, longtime Joyce employees approached Renée and Matt with great warmth, happy to see the two of them arrive now as artistic directors, having watched them from their beginnings as dancers. These were people who worked on the technical side and had also been young when Renée and Matt were young performers. "You grew up together, in a way," Matt explained. "Renée had performed there with Momix at the age of twenty-one." These were the people who, a quarter-century earlier and through the following years, had been standing in the wings with towels, ready to block the dancers from crashing offstage when they came sliding off at high speed from their most crowd-pleasing encore, or, as Matt put it, "They're the people who caught us naked when we slid across the stage in *Day Two*." They had known, observed, and assisted Pilobolus from all angles, had seen the company through all its phases in those years, and had seen everything, good and bad, that had happened. To them, Pilobolus *had* come home.

The current dancers, who had never performed at the Joyce, were excited, too, with the recognition that this was no ordinary engagement but their turn to become, in at least a small way, a part of Pilobolus, Joyce, and

American dance history. For some, to perform at the Joyce had been a life-long dream; but they were also excited to go there for another reason: they knew it was a clear statement that Pilobolus was moving in a direction that was true to itself. Renée and Matt had decided that for their restaging of *Untitled* they would invite the original "tall ladies"—Alison and Martha—to return to the studio to help fine-tune it. Alison politely declined, but Martha chose to accept.

Renée had performed *Untitled* for the first time seventeen years earlier, in 2002, on the Joyce stage, with Jennifer Macavinta, a colleague who she felt brought an elegance and a "visual designer" mindset and "always kept the big picture in mind right from the beginning." Renée knew and loved the piece: "It encompasses the best of what Pilobolus can do, nonverbal storytelling and character building, and has so many different levels that resonate, back and forth between narrative and abstraction. The movement is the theatre and the theatre is the movement." But, as she also knew from experience, "It is one of the most complex pieces to perform. The way that the legs and upper body [of the two female dancers] work, and trying to maintain this character while maintaining your balance, it's very hard. It's like doing magic, where you don't want the audience to see the work that's going into it behind the facade."

To have Martha return to Club Hall to revisit this classic was a special pleasure. More than a decade earlier, at Robby's invitation, Martha had taught Renée her brilliant Crowsnest solo *Nocturne* so that Renée could perform it at the American Dance Festival, which she did, in June 2008, as part of a Pilobolus program that played to a full house. Renée had greatly enjoyed the rehearsals with Martha, liked getting to know her, and had been struck by her intelligence, and her clarity as a director. Now Martha brought to the restaging of *Untitled* not only the understanding of one who had helped create it, but the flexibility and freedom of a director with a lifetime's experience questioning and revising her work. She asked the dancers repeated questions, to tailor the piece for them; she proposed changes freely; and as Renée later explained, "Martha looked at *Untitled* and saw ways to make it better." For Renée, who found this inspiring, it reinforced that "the story came first." In one of the most noteworthy improvements, the fight sequence between the two "suitors" became stronger and more dynamic, bolstering the energy of the piece's latter half.

Another guest in the studio had a much quieter presence. Accompanying Martha was a well-liked middle-aged man with dark curly hair and glasses, a cheerful face, and an easy laugh: her son, David Grausman, long a successful jazz pianist. As a little boy he had traveled the world with her, streaked through *Walklyndon* and sung for the silk merchants in Kyoto; now, in a hushed tone, so as not to presume, he asked Matt if it might be permissible for him to stay and watch the rehearsal if he promised to remain in the background, unobtrusive. Matt told him that of course he should sit right up front with them, as their guest. David thanked him and confided his reason for wanting to watch: "It's just that it reminds me of my childhood."

Moses's visit to the studio to consult on *Day Two* was less revisionist than Martha's approach but equally pleasurable, as he clearly relished the experience of seeing the piece again from his present vantage point. *Day Two* has a trancelike quality, and an element of that energy is required of the performers, along with a certain presence. As Matt points out, "There's a confidence that you have to have in order to perform it; you can't be un-sure that it's cool. You're not playing for applause or feedback. You're bring-ing the audience into another world that is primitive—and also modern, because of the music—a futuristic retro ritual." Today *Day Two* is both "fu-turistic" and "retro" in another way as well: after four decades, it's a docu-ment of an earlier time even as it continues to lead new audiences into a vision that still feels forward-looking. "The best way to direct it," accord-ing to Matt, "is to get people to respond authentically. 'Stop watching the video, you're not that person.' It has to be customized for the person doing it." Matt compares it to technique versus sparring, in martial arts. "The goal is to make it feel like the technique is part of the epic story you're telling." Moses approved.

For that summer's two alternating programs at the Joyce, along with *Untitled* and *Day Two*, a half dozen other "greatest hits" were drawn from the five decades of Pilobolus. All told, the selection would include, from the 1970s, *Walklyndon* and *Untitled*; from the 1980s, *Day Two*; from the 1990s and 2000s, *Gnomen*, *Symbiosis*, and *Rushes*; and from the 2010s, *On the Nature of Things* and, for the first time at the Joyce, *Branches*. The lat-ter served as a perfect overture to summer, and there were plenty of New Yorkers who still recalled that for a very long time summer in New York had meant the pleasure of seeing Pilobolus at the Joyce. Ticket sales were fine, and, in the same domino effect that has benefited Pilobolus ever since its founders played the Bordeaux Festival in 1973, sold-out crowds became more frequent as word of mouth spread. Closing night was packed.

On the afternoon of Saturday, June 29, the final day of the run, a matinee performance of *Walklyndon* had incorporated a number of small rainbow flags in honor of gay pride. (The next day was World Pride Day, the fiftieth anniversary of Stonewall, and the city was already filling with weekend celebrants.) Midway through the piece, in the tradition of early Pilobolus, a pair of giddy streakers raced across the stage waving rainbow flags. This got an extra laugh, but most of the audience wasn't in on the best part of the joke: the streakers were Renée and Matt, and they hadn't told the dancers what they were planning. (Matt and Emily's nine-year-old, Sammy, in the eighth row, loved it.)

A little later, Matt, his street clothes back in place, stood with me on the sidewalk in front of the theater, and as we talked to each other a pair of women on their way out from the matinee—they looked to be in their late fifties or so, two intelligent, well-educated, well-read New York women— paused and politely interrupted us. "Are you the director, one of the directors?" one of the women asked Matt. "I'm sorry to interrupt, but we just want you to know. We've been coming to see Pilobolus from the beginning, and this season was the best *ever*. You got *everything right*. It was perfect."

They weren't the only ones who thought so. That night, a sold-out house offered thunderous applause as *Day Two* and the slides-as-bows ended both the evening and the run. After the show, a backstage toast. And gifts for the dancers: photos from the performances, as keepsakes, and, in a revival of an old tradition that Renée and Matt had appreciated in their own earlier years, each dancer was given a book, chosen especially for him or her in light of the artistic directors' knowledge of that dancer's tastes and interests.

FIFTEEN

Life

1

The one thing everyone in Pilobolus always agreed on was the desirability of a rural setting, and a half-century later the company's New England landscape still carries, as if in the freshness of its air, an idea of freedom, and of connection to nature and to one another. "There's something about historical buildings that relates to nature—the wood from which old houses were made, the use of the natural world and its cycle—that speaks to me as an artist," says Renée. "The give and take that happens between nature and humans. I feel much more inspired when I'm around it. Waking up to the sounds of birds. It gives me a sense of calm and contemplation."

Matt adds: "It's like Thoreau, *Walden*. It's the green, it's the small town, it's interacting with the community. It's a *pace* thing."

The influence of the setting finds its way into the work in a manner indirect or, sometimes, literal; for example, the branches used in *Shadowland* were taken from trees outside Washington Club Hall. Now, however, in a new decade, amid an unanticipated set of challenges, the natural landscapes have taken on another dimension.

As 2020 began, Renée, Matt, and Emily, along with their colleagues in managing Pilobolus, Kirsten Leon and Anna Bate, entered the year with hope, ambition, and some concern. Near the end of 2019, Itamar Kubovy had announced his resignation after sixteen years as executive director, having effectuated the transition of Pilobolus to a new generation. In the wake of his amicable departure the board and staff had deliberated as to whether to hire a successor into the same role or to reinvent the position—but then a third option had occurred to them. Itamar had initially been hired because Pilobolus had four artistic directors who couldn't work together; now it had two artistic directors who could, with a long and effective track record of doing so. With that realization, the full responsibility of leading Pilobolus would be returned to the artists. On January 1, Renée and Matt were in charge.

It wasn't an easy assignment. Pilobolus had always been a small number of individuals working extraordinarily hard to create a wildly outsized cultural impact, and despite some flush periods over the years (which enabled, for a time, expansions of various kinds) it had never maintained large financial reserves or enjoyed the long-term security of a major endowment. To stay viable, the company that Renée and Matt had inherited would need a big, successful tour. They immediately began to devise one. With Pilobolus's fiftieth anniversary coming up, it seemed the perfect time to put together a celebratory show that they decided to call *The Big Five-OH!* As they began, one could almost hear Jonathan's ghost in the background, exhorting as he had in life: "Well, then, who's going to save Pilobolus? Well, I guess it's going to have to be you!"

The staff members had begun to reorganize themselves and their tasks, rethink their priorities, determine the likely program for the anniversary tour, and establish an impressive and growing list of bookings for it, when suddenly, in March, they, like the rest of the world, were stopped in their tracks. The unthinkable had arrived: a global pandemic. Like other theatre companies deprived of the ability to tour, they improvised online offerings, particularly in the form of livestream events, often in partnership with other institutions. Jacob's Pillow kicked off its own livestream series with a Pilobolus evening that featured a screening of the filmed version of *Branches* followed by a conversation with Renée and Matt, and attracted thousands of viewers from around the world. Pilobolus educational programs for its community were offered in abundance, most of them in free livestreamed classes taught indefatigably by Emily, Renée, and Matt; and among these, Emily's class for middle-aged and older adults, *Connecting with Balance*, developed into a project that the company decided to market as a streaming video series; months later it would become the subject of a segment on *CBS This Morning*. And near the end of 2020, for the first time in almost a decade, the company produced a wall calendar for the coming year, once again in collaboration with John Kane.

All of these efforts were energetic and meaningful, but the most impressive pandemic-era Pilobolus achievements arose from using the need for public safety as grist for theatrical innovation. In the horrific summer of 2020, rather than abandon the locally based "Five Senses Festival" that it had initiated and headlined in the past couple of years, Pilobolus morphed its contribution into an "art safari" in which attendees would remain within the safety of their cars while driving through a landscape of live outdoor Pilobolus-conceived performances, its soundtrack available through their car radio. In the first half of 2021, while most live performances continued to be postponed, Renée and Matt assembled four dancers for a quartet show that could be performed outdoors (and socially distanced) at a few venues; by that summer they had modified their "art safari" concept, now separated from the local festival, to create a post-vaccination version in which attendees again drove through a scenic landscape, in this case Sunny Meadow Farm in Litchfield, Connecticut, making stops where they could get out of their cars to safely observe an entirely new set of performances that Renée and Matt had conceived as a thematically unified program.

Bloom: A Journey, as it was titled, consisted of four parts. The first, "The Ferryman," staged on a pond and the embankment alongside it, featured the American jazz and "vintage pop" singer Kat Edmonson with dancers Casey Howes and Jacob Michael Warren (the ferryman of the title) in a scenario set to two songs: "The Waters of March" by Antônio Carlos Jobim, which Kat sang on the shore while Jake and Casey did a gravity-defying duet in the canoe, probably the first time Pilobolus dancers have negotiated their balancing act on a body of water; and "No One Is Alone" by Stephen Sondheim, sung as a duet between Kat and Jake and danced as a trio by Kat, Jake, and Casey. The counterintuitive combination of Sondheim and Pilobolus might seem a risky one, but the strong performance—arranged by Rob Kapilow and played by longtime Pilobolus friend and collaborator Paul Sullivan—along with Jake's unexpected but seamless transition from dancer to vocalist, made it work, as did Kat Edmonson's world-class professionalism as both singer and emcee, welcoming audiences to the journey.

From here audiences returned to their cars and drove a short distance into the woods to stop at the second station, "The Rugged Countryside," built around another musical guest, multi-instrumental musician Stuart Bogie, wearing Pan-like horns and accompanied by nymphs and satyrs embodied by Pilobolus dancers. He also had many additional horns of the musical kind—two saxophones, an alto sax, a trombone—and musicians to play them; as well as an androgenous young Pan-in-training who shared his mischievous, magical tendencies. (For some observers, this younger Pan, played by eleven-year-old Sam Kent in horns and a skirt, stole the show as he conducted audience participation in the clanging of gongs.) The third piece, "Far and Wee," followed another short drive and beckoned attendees onto the sunny hillside of an apple orchard, where the results of a community dance project with individuals ranging from preteen to octogenarian took the form of a spring pageant with dancing fabrics, accompanied by the Litchfield Choral Union. The music consisted of Rob Kapilow's original settings of two classic poems by e. e. Cummings ("in Just-" and "i thank you God for most this amazing") on either side of a performance of "Whither must I Wander" (a work by Ralph Vaughn Williams, with lyrics from *Songs of Travel* by Robert Louis Stevenson), the latter arranged and conducted by the Litchfield Choral Union's musical director Jonathan Babbitt. As a ritual of spring it was lovely, and the clear contrasts to the equally ritualistic piece that had preceded it (deep in the woods versus out in the sun; wordless instrumental soundscape versus a community of voices raised to convey verbal poetry) lent a satisfying internal balance to the *Bloom* journey's sequence.

The final piece, "The Legend of the Wendigo," took the audience back into the woods, and though it too had a ritualistic underpinning, its concept made a dramatic turn of a different kind. Throughout its long history Pilobolus has usually created movement first and added music later, though it would sometimes make exceptions, as when it worked with OK Go or when it chose, for *Bloom,* to build pieces around musical collaborators Kat Edmonson, Stuart Bogie, and Rob Kapilow. For *Bloom*'s final segment, however, Renée and Matt chose neither of these options; instead, "The Legend of the Wendigo" was based on, and accompanied by, a spoken-word narrative, a single human voice speaking truth and wisdom. That compelling voice belongs to Darlene Kascak, a storyteller at the Institute of American Indian Studies, based in Pilobolus's hometown of Washington, Connecticut. With the help of sound designer and composer Ben Sollee, Renée and Matt wove together Darlene's telling of a traditional myth about the Wendigo, fearsome creatures that have insatiable, cannibalistic appetites, with her personal recollections of life as an American who is a member of an Indigenous people. The piece fuses myth, memoir, cautionary tale, consciousness-raising, education, and physical movement into an affecting whole, both timely and timeless, that in just ten minutes in a wooded setting, with dancers in thick animal-like costumes topped by animal-skull heads, brings the audience through an illustrated monologue that leaves them changed.

The structure of *Bloom: A Journey,* with its outdoor setting and drive-through logistics, necessitated a grueling schedule of eighteen perfor-mances a day for five consecutive days and limited the number of individu-als by whom it could be seen, but its innovations were not lost on those who did see it. A review in the *Hartford Courant* declared that "*Bloom* is what theater and dance needs to be now that it's back" and the show met with warm appreciation from those lucky enough to attend it. Perhaps a subtler significance could only be detected by those closest to its creators: with its reconsideration and elevation of the role of music and environ-ment in its works, as well as its shift in sensibility, it seemed to broaden the Pilobolus palette and reflect a fresh, increasingly distinct artistic signature from Renée and Matt.

2

What is Pilobolus? I've often thought of it as a dance company that never stops reinventing the meaning of the word *dance.* I love its refusal to set-tle on a single identity—which makes me think again of Bowie, Capote, Moebius, Blondie, the kind of artists I most value, known for their endless reinvention and eclecticism. Eclecticism, for Pilobolus, includes the pre-sentation, within a single program, of multiple short pieces with different sensibilities. But—is *reinvention* the right word? Jasper Johns, when asked about his longtime collaboration with Merce Cunningham and how he re-sponded to the latter's perpetual reinventions, replied, "I did not think of reinvention but of the unfolding and exercise of an inner language." Like-wise Pilobolus—its long-ago genesis influenced in part by Merce Cunning-ham's original thinking—continues not so much to reinvent itself but to unfold and exercise an inner language, in its case one embodied in a physi-cal movement vocabulary that has now spread throughout and beyond the dance world.

A global phenomenon begun by a handful of mildly eccentric friends, Pilobolus has become the guardians (or conduits? stewards?) of a precious energy. Among that energy's ingredients are a sense of fun, play, mischief; audacity; and of getting past inhibitions of different kinds. The not infre-quent pun titles that exemplify the spirit of Pilobolus, the willingness to be goofy and (maybe) profound at the same time; the visual invention and visual metaphor, with two or more levels at once; the acute observations of the natural world, transmuted into visual play; the combination of sensual athleticism and wit in an equation that begets joy. Creative energy as a liberating and inspiring force.

The navigation, or negotiation, of a space between art and show business, and also between high and low senses of humor, drama, narrative, and cultural tastes. And because Pilobolus traffics in the "oddness of poetry" (for, as most good poets know, poems require a certain oddness), it follows naturally that Pilobolus often produces enigmatic rituals and oneiric fantasies. Wrapped deep within all of this is Moses's long-ago concept of the body as "toy" and the related ideas that emerged from a countercultural moment a half-century ago, one that enabled Pilobolus to become part of a revolution in how one sees the body and its artistic possibilities—human sculpture and defying the usual parameters of gravity, weight, movement; and a new sense of flight added to the already-existing sensibilities of flight in dance.

New Yorker film critic David Denby wrote in 2000: "The most striking element of visual rapture is the sight of sublime bodies flying through the air. Eroticism has been transformed into airborne athleticism." He wasn't talking about Pilobolus; he was reviewing the first *X-Men* movie. Yet those two sentences put me in mind of Pilobolus, whose seemingly super-heroic dancers perform live, without the aid of computer-generated film effects, and with a proximity and reality that can make them, for many observers, even more breathtaking to behold.

As suggested by Denby's reference to "eroticism," another common denominator between the two spectacles is the sheer joy of looking at a great body radiating vitality, sexiness, and exuberance. Never merely beautiful bodies, however, an image of the "ideal" Pilobolus man or woman might start with a mischievous gleam in the eyes and smile of a person with a well-muscled, heroic body—to which is perhaps added a colorful costume that suggests the look of a daredevil, or, in some ways more daring, no costume at all. One thinks not only of desire but of *love* as a combination of humor, risk, vulnerability, heroic or brave achievement, trust, connection, bonding, synthesis or symbiosis, the comic and romantic, all entwined.

Pilobolus, in its long evolution, has been a collective in the 1970s, a dance company from 1980 into the early 2000s, an entity that flirted with becoming something broader, both more corporate and more amorphously an "arts organization" in the new century, and, most recently, a self-styled "rebellious dance company" that stopped short of leaving behind its past as it now embarks on still another rejuvenation of its identity. The other "C"—beyond collective, company, and corporation—is community, and Pilobolus has grown a large one over the course of its existence. Beyond being a sensibility, an energy, a set of ideas, a symbol and embodiment of certain ways of thinking about art, life, education, movement, and humanity, it is also a set of specific individuals, in various configurations—and a bunch of people, works, performances, and experiences for which I have great love, admiration, and gratitude.

Andy Herro's favorite Pilobolus memories are those of overcoming adversity in the moment, whether during a performance or outside of one. He recalls a time that he and his colleagues were in Arizona with no props or costumes (the items had not been delivered, due to inclement weather) and they put together an entire program in one morning, based on pieces that required minimal costuming, and performed it that night. Solving problems together. As he told me, "You can get mad, you can fight, you can swear, but you can't quit. That's the greatest thing about Pilobolus. We're going to work together. We're going to find a solution." That sentiment might seem ironic given some of the clashes and departures in the company's history, but Andy is right that mutual achievement is the heart of Pilobolus. Its story is one of glorious success in the face of the human tendency to give up—on oneself, on one's colleagues, on the possibilities of each new day.

As for the foolish idea that art requires conflict and combustion, personal battles and suffering, I recall a conversation with Lee Harris about the earliest days of Pilobolus, when those four young men set in motion something larger and more lasting than themselves. "I'm an extremely nonconfrontational person," he explained, and told me that back then he didn't see any confrontational qualities in Jonathan, and that he didn't leave Pilobolus because of any conflicts. He emphasized the way things worked in those days: "Ego was *not* involved in the creative process." It's a purity of process to which, it seems, Renée and Matt have attempted to return Pilobolus.

And it is only now, nearly a decade and a half after first seeing *Rushes,* that I realize that its memorable finale—in which bright white chairs are rapidly slid one after another to form an ongoing walkway, ever-emerging but ever-tenuous, for the figure stepping from one to the next—represents, for me, a vision of human civilization. All of that energetic movement and determination to get those chairs in place, in time, becomes an eloquent symbol of the collective work of a society to sustain a situation in which each fragile individual can take one step after the next through life, often carrying another fragile individual in one's arms, without crashing to the ground.

3

———

I've called Pilobolus and Momix "visual magicians" but I give my highest marks to *life's* magic tricks—as when people step off a Pilobolus calendar and into my life, and the "puppyish" young guy on stage turns into a teacher and then a best friend. Or the way my love of *Gnomen,* with its sensibility of brotherly alliance that transcends (or bonds) gay and straight, has entwined itself through my life, allowing its ease with the human—and its energetic grace that can still make my eyes mist up—to last through the years.

I'm far from the only person over whom life and Pilobolus have together cast a spell. When Renée recounted for me, nearly a quarter-century after the fact, her experience of seeing Pilobolus for the first time (we were speaking by phone; she was at an airport, about to fly back to Connecticut from some Pilobolus business out west), I was touched by what I suddenly heard: the voice of an excited young fan, reliving a moment of pure joy, the happiness as fresh as if she hadn't already risen to the level of artistic director of the very company she was describing, as if she were still in awe of the magic of that first time she sat in the audience; as if she hadn't already learned every detail of how that magic is made, and hadn't already lived, time and again, so many of the inevitable ups and downs and day-to-day challenges that chip away at even the best of dreams-come-true. It was the voice of a perpetually young (but wise!) woman, born to be exactly who she is, where she is.

In October 2021, Pilobolus launched its fiftieth anniversary tour, *The Big Five-OH!* The program, conceived as a "remixed retrospective," opened with a revived and revisited version of *Megawatt,* Jonathan's bravura "energy circus," which Renée rather ingeniously saw could be repositioned as a lead piece rather than kept in its traditional role as a finale. For the first leg of the tour, Renée and Matt had also prepared long-overdue revivals of the sublime *Shizen* and the comic solo from *The Empty Suitor,* as well as a new shadow piece and, of course, longtime favorite *Day Two.* As the tour proceeded into 2022, those pieces would gradually be joined by *Untitled, On the Nature of Things,* and *Branches,* as well as "The Legend of the Wendigo" from *Bloom,* now staged for indoor performance as *The Ballad,* for which Pilobolus hired native tribal members to be designers. Another two new pieces would be added in 2023 for the tour's final months and its New York run at the Joyce that summer: *Awaken Heart,* a quartet made with Pilobolus veteran Gaspard Louis, and *Noctuary* (initially called *Evening Song*), a sextet made with veteran dancer Derion Loman and his choreographic partner Madison Olandt, with a sound score by Jad Abumrad, best known for creating *Radiolab* and the award-winning podcast *Dolly Parton's America.* With a growing list of bookings that expanded as the pandemic receded, the two-year tour heralded the healthy return of Pilobolus.

4

The perennial question for Pilobolus, as for most artists, remains. The life-force and its beautiful vitality—How to get it into a theatre piece, a dance, a book—a work of art? In any celebration of life there is an antagonist, even if invisible, and that enemy is the death-impulse in all its forms: apathy, negativity, depression, aggression, or actual death itself. A well-made work of art, like a well-lived life, must offer alternatives.

On a Saturday morning in early May 2017, as I watched a Pilobolus "open rehearsal" for friends and supporters at which fragments of two new works in progress were shown—both presentations spirited and vibrant, each in its own way—I jotted down a phrase, three words that had popped into my head: "Let's make stuff." The words seemed to me, in that moment, to encapsulate the impulse behind Pilobolus.

I enjoyed so much about that day: the way the cool spring morning turned sunny by noon; my talk with Matt after the event and our midday stroll in Washington Depot with nine-year-old Owen; and a feeling that caused me, a little later, to dash in my notebook a poem-like list of phrases. "Everything just right / A perfect May moment / Blue skies and my love for Matt and Emily"—the kind of emotion that, poured onto a page, would make a terrible poem but is irreplaceable to the person who lived it. Next on the list was this question: "How to capture such happiness, of the kind that has so many invisible, non-material dimensions, in a concrete construct of words?"

I now see that this question echoes the "perennial question" mentioned above. But the key to its answer lies in the same three words I had jotted down as I watched the dancers perform the lively "rough draft" fragments. For at its most basic, in the end, Pilobolus—and I, and perhaps you too—are really about that one essential, positive human impulse: *Let's make stuff*.

ACKNOWLEDGMENTS

My friend and colleague Liz Pelton told me long ago that I should write a book about Pilobolus, at a time when I was not yet ready to do so; but she, and the idea, persisted. My friend Jessica Rostow has shared and enabled many of my Pilobolus-related excursions, from the first night we saw Pilobolus—and onward throughout the subsequent quarter-century. Many of my other friends, loved ones, and admired colleagues, too numerous to name, have also encouraged me: I hope I've let each of you know how much you mean to me.

This book itself is my acknowledgment of Pilobolus, its admirable creators and contributors, and the people I most cherish there. I thank Matt, Emily, and Renée for their friendship and inspiration, and for so much else that has made this book possible: it would not exist without you. I thank John Kane and Jonathan Sa'adah for their extraordinary photographs. I thank my literary agent Gail Hochman, University Press of Florida editor-in-chief Stephanye Hunter, and the UPF staff, for their vital roles in bringing this book into the world.

Finally, and with deepest gratitude, I thank my parents, who loved me and believed in me, and who, in a great and beautiful tradition, selflessly gave me opportunities that had not been given to them. I will love them forever.

PILOBOLUS DANCERS
THROUGH THE YEARS

The inventors of *Pilobolus* (the dance)

Steve Johnson • Robert (Moses) Pendleton • Jonathan Wolken

The inventors of Pilobolus (the company)

Robert (Moses) Pendleton • Jonathan Wolken • Robby Barnett • Lee Harris
Alison Chase • Martha Clarke • Michael Tracy

Dancers who joined subsequently

Jamey Hampton • Georgiana Holmes • Robert Faust
Carol Parker • Peter Pucci • Cynthia Quinn

Guest dancers who worked with Pilobolus in the late 1970s and 1980s

Kammy Brooks • Daniel Ezralow • Dom Blumenfeld • Phil Catchings
Elisa Monte • Judy Hendin • Helen Heineman • Sarah Rudner
Richard Korngut • Carolyn Minor • Lisa Dalton

Dancers who joined from 1984 onward

Jude Woodcock • Austin Hartel • Josh Perl • Tim Latta
Jack Arnold • Jim Blanc • Rick Merrill • Amy Spencer
Adam Battelstein • Kent Lindemer • John Mario Sevilla
Vernon Scott • Rebecca Jung • Sebastian Smeureanu
Darryl Thomas • Peter Francyk • Rebecca Anderson
Mark Santillano • Matt Kent • Gaspard Louis • Trebien Pollard
Tamieca McCloud • Josie Coyoc • Rebecca Stenn [Pilobolus Too]
Emily Kent [Pilobolus Too] • Otis Cook • Benjamin Pring

Renée Jaworski • Ras Mikey C • Mark Fucik • Jennifer Macavinta
Andrew Herro • Manelich Minniefee • Matthew Thornton
Jenny Mendez • Jun Kuribayashi • Edwin Olvera • Jeffrey Huang
Annika Sheaff • Christopher Whitney • Winston Dynamite Brown
Matt Del Rosario • Eriko Jimbo • Nile H Russell • Jordan Kriston
Shawn Ahern • Benjamin Coalter • Mike Tyus • Derion Loman
Sayer Mansfield • Antoine Banks-Sullivan • Teo Spencer
Nathaniel Buchsbaum • Jake Warren • Heather Favretto
Krystal Butler • Zach Eisenstat • Quincy Ellis
Isabella Diaz • Casey Howes • Paul Liu
Hannah Klinkman • Zachary Weiss • Marlon Feliz

Shadowland players not included above

Molly Gawler • Damon Honeycutt • Lauren Yalango
Beth Lewis • Christopher Grant • Derek Stratton
Roberto Olvera • Maddy Landi • Kingsley Ibeniche
Magic Distephano • Victoria De Renzo • Jared Doster
Christina Doboz • Alex Lieberman • Ariana Nakamine
Justin Norris • Morgan Houghton • Keith Kaplin • Klara Beyeler
Neva Cockrell (*Shadowland 2*) • Mistral Hay (*Shadowland 2*)
Michael Johnston (*Shadowland 2*)

Artistic Directors 2016–onward

Renée Jaworski • Matt Kent

BIBLIOGRAPHY OF SOURCES

This book is based on my own experiences and observations, on my friendships and conversations with people in and around Pilobolus, and on print, online, audio, film, and video resources both public and private.

I am grateful to every individual who kindly spoke with me about Pilobolus during the writing of this book, whether briefly or at length, whether formally or informally, whether on the record, off the record, or (most often) a mixture of the two. I particularly wish to thank Mirra Bank, Robby Barnett, Alison Chase, Martha Clarke, Ras Mikey C (Michael Courtney), Rebecca Anderson Darling, Daniel Ezralow, David Grausman, Jamey Hampton, Lee Harris, Andrew Herro, Renée Jaworski, Steve Johnson, John Kane, Emily Kent, Matt Kent, Alice Kitchel, Gaspard Louis, Tim Matson, Edwin Olvera, Moses Pendleton, Charles L. Reinhart, Jonathan Sa'adah, Paul Sullivan, and Jude Woodcock.

The sources of all direct, attributed quotations in the book, whether derived from my own interviews or from elsewhere, are included in the bibliography below. In the case of individuals quoted from my own conversations, their names appear in the first section along with the dates on which we spoke. I do not, however, include dates of conversations with my friends Renée Jaworski, Emily Kent, and Matt Kent, with whom I speak so frequently that our friendship is, happily, like a single perpetual conversation.

Another important source for this book is the unpublished series of Pilobolus interviews conducted in 2004 and 2005 by Lesley Farlow and Norton Owen for the New York Public Library for the Performing Arts. These conversations, part of the library's ongoing project to compile an oral history of dance, focus primarily on the company's origins and early years. Because the interviews were intended solely to document the recollections of the participants, they are not strictly accurate in all details, but the collective total of 355 pages of transcripts, when cross-referenced and fact-checked against other sources, proved extremely helpful in my research. These interviews are listed below under "Unpublished sources quoted or consulted."

My gratitude to the New York Public Library for the Performing Arts and its excellent staff also extends to their assistance in enabling me to watch several videos of Martha Clarke's theatrical works and to view Joyce Chopra's film *Martha Clarke Light and Dark.*

Three other important films, *Moses Pendleton Presents Moses Pendleton* (1982), *Monkey and the Bone Demon* (2001), and *Last Dance* (2002), are identified and quoted in the text.

I am grateful to Dartmouth's Rauner Special Collections Library for digitizing and making available to me a number of rare early films and videos of Pilobolus. My description of the December 29, 1971 performance of Pilobolus at The Space is based on my viewing of a film of it that, while imperfect, is an invaluable record of the event, and has remained more or less buried for nearly half a century.

My friends at Pilobolus gave me extraordinary access to private video archives of the company's performances through the years, as well as to their own deep knowledge and directorial experience, to enable me to describe Pilobolus works with greater accuracy and precision.

Individuals quoted from interviews conducted by the author

Mirra Bank, March 17, 2019

Martha Clarke, October 13, 2019 and May 23, 2020

Ras Mikey C (Michael Courtney), March 10, 2019

Rebecca Anderson Darling, November 19, 2018

Daniel Ezralow, December 12, 2020

Jamey Hampton, January 22, 2020

Lee Harris, October 2, 2019 and October 12, 2019

Andrew Herro, February 12, 2019

Renée Jaworski, ongoing conversations

Steve Johnson, August 16, 2020

John Kane, March 1, 2019

Emily Kent, ongoing conversations

Matt Kent, ongoing conversations

Alice Kitchel, February 9, 2020 and email of February 10, 2020

Gaspard Louis, October 5, 2019

Edwin Olvera, January 20, 2019

Charles L. Reinhart, October 10, 2020

Paul Sullivan, March 16, 2019

Jude Woodcock, March 24, 2019 and July 26, 2020

Unpublished sources quoted or consulted

Barnett, Robby, "On the Genesis of Pilobolus," an essay that Pilobolus provided to media contacts, of which portions appeared in "Pilobolus: A Creature of Organic Dance in Motion," an interview by Dennis Coleman in connection with a Pilobolus appearance in Australia, *Ballet-Dance* magazine, September 2008. Full text courtesy of Pilobolus.

Barnett, Robby, and Tracy, Michael, "An Oral History of What Makes Pilobolus, *Pilobolus*," a private presentation at a Pilobolus Board Retreat on April 23, 2016. Transcript courtesy of Pilobolus.

Farlow, Lesley, interview with Alison Chase, November 13, 2004. Transcript of a sound recording made for the New York Public Library for the Performing Arts as part of the "Oral History Project, Dance Division, New York Public Library" (Performing Arts Research Collections: Dance).

Farlow, Lesley, interview with Moses Pendleton, June 22 and 28, 2004. Transcript of a sound recording made for the New York Public Library for the Performing Arts, see above.

Farlow, Lesley, interview with Michael Tracy, June 29, 2004. Transcript of a sound recording made for the New York Public Library for the Performing Arts, see above.

Farlow, Lesley, interview with Jonathan Wolken, March 22, 2005. Transcript of a sound recording made for the New York Public Library for the Performing Arts, see above.

Owen, Norton, interview with Robby Barnett, June 1, 2004. Transcript of a sound recording made for the New York Public Library for the Performing Arts, see above.

Owen, Norton, interview with Martha Clarke, February 25, 2005. Transcript of a sound recording made for the New York Public Library for the Performing Arts, see above.

Pendleton, Moses, 2010 commencement address at the University of the Arts.

Published sources quoted or consulted

Anderson, Jack. *The American Dance Festival*. Durham, NC: Duke University Press, 1987.

Anderson, Jack. Obituary, Murray Louis. *New York Times*, February 1, 2016.

Arnott, Christopher. "Pilobolus' Tranquil, Transfixing 'Bloom' at Sunny Meadows Farm in Bridgewater." *Hartford Courant*, July 23, 2021.

Barnes, Clive. "Dance: Pilobolus Images." *New York Times*, March 6, 1976.

Bennetts, Leslie. "Dream Imagery of *Vienna: Lusthaus*." *New York Times*, April 23, 1986.

Brown, Chip. "Martha Clarke's Passion for the Past." *Washington Post*, September 3, 1986.

Burnham, Emily. "Brooksville choreographer to debut new show in Orono." *Bangor Daily News* (Maine), November 15, 2010.

Carman, Joseph, Steven Sucato, and Wendy Perron. "He Said/She Said: Dancers and Choreographers Talk about the Role of Gender in their Lives and Work." *Dance Magazine*, November 2005.

Christiansen, Richard. Review of Pilobolus. *Chicago Tribune*, September 1, 1978.

Croce, Arlene. "Getting It All Together." *The New Yorker*, March 18, 1985.

Croce, Arlene. "Prose Into Poetry." *The New Yorker*, December 19, 1977.

Croce, Arlene. Review of Crowsnest. *The New Yorker,* June 15, 1981.

Croce, Arlene. "What You See Is What You Get." *The New Yorker,* April 5, 1976.

Denby, David. "Dazzled." *The New Yorker,* July 24, 2000.

Dunning, Jennifer. "Imagery and Emotional Quirks, Shown in Any Order." *New York Times,* July 3, 2003.

Dunning, Jennifer. "Moses Pendleton, Choreographer and Product of His Time." *New York Times,* December 27, 1989.

Dunning, Jennifer. "No One Ever Said Friendship Was Easy." *New York Times,* July 9, 2002.

Dunning, Jennifer. "Pilobolus at the Joyce . . ." *New York Times,* July 19, 2006.

Dunning, Jennifer. "Pilobolus in New Type of Extravaganza." *New York Times,* December 17, 1988.

Dunning, Jennifer. "Yes, Pilobolus Has a Mother Too." *New York Times,* July 18, 1996.

Editorial. "El fracaso de Pilobolus" ("The Failure of Pilobolus"). *Processo* (Mexico), January 22, 2000.

Garmey, Jane. "Where Nothing Changes. Ever." *New York Times,* September 23, 2009.

Gussow, Mel. "Clarke Work." *New York Times,* January 18, 1987.

Gussow, Mel. "Stage: 'Garden of Earthly Delights.'" *New York Times,* April 5, 1984.

Hyde, Nina. "From New York." *Washington Post,* November 11, 1984.

Interview with Moses Pendleton. *The Class of 1971 Newsletter,* Dartmouth College, Fall 2014, p. 4.

Jaworski, Renée. "Performing for the Queen." Pilobolus blog, December 21, 2009. (Blog no longer online; text courtesy of Pilobolus.)

Job, John. "puh-LOB-o-liss!: How a Handful of Dartmouth College Stoners Started a Revolution in Modern Dance." *Austin Chronicle,* March 2, 2001.

Jowitt, Deborah. "Dancing on Strings." *Village Voice,* April 29, 2003.

Jowitt, Deborah. Review of Pilobolus. *Village Voice,* July 18, 2000.

Jowitt, Deborah. "Rock and Roll Circus." *Village Voice,* July 17, 2007.

Jowitt, Deborah. "Take a Bite." *Village Voice,* July 16, 2006.

Jowitt, Deborah. *Time and the Dancing Image.* Berkeley: University of California Press, 1989.

Kaufman, Sarah. "Martha Clarke Has Made a Career of Movement. Now She Cherishes Stillness." *Washington Post,* September 27, 2014.

Kaufman, Sarah. "Pilobolus's Naked Display of Magic." *Washington Post,* July 2, 2014.

Kisselgoff, Anna. "A Monkey Saves a Monk, Who Thereby Is Made Wiser." *New York Times,* July 5, 2001.

Kisselgoff, Anna. "An Evening of Transformations by Momix." *New York Times,* December 29, 1989.

Kisselgoff, Anna. "Dance: New Group from Dartmouth." *New York Times,* December 31, 1971.

Kisselgoff, Anna. "Dance: Pilobolus Climbs High." *New York Times,* November 25, 1977.

Kisselgoff, Anna. "Day Two: A New Creation by Pilobolus." *New York Times,* December 21, 1981.

Kisselgoff, Anna. "Not Ballet, Not Acrobatics, But Pilobolus!" *New York Times,* November 20, 1977.

Kisselgoff, Anna. "Pilobolus Dancing Its Way to Togetherness." *New York Times,* March 5, 1976.

Kisselgoff, Anna. "The Yin and Yang of Adam and Eve." *New York Times,* July 11, 2001.

Kourlas, Gia. "Within Pilobolus, Working Together and Pulling Away." *New York Times,* June 23, 2002.

Kramer, Jane. "Letter from Europe." *The New Yorker,* April 5, 1982.

Larcen, Donna. "New Pilobolus Dance Soars with Innovation." *Hartford Courant,* May 11, 2003.

Macaulay, Alastair. "Cunningham and Johns: Rare Glimpses into a Collaboration." *New York Times,* January 7, 2013.

Matson, Tim. *Pilobolus.* New York: Random House, 1978. Includes unattributed introductory essay.

McDonagh, Don. "Dance Fans Reap a Bonus in Park: Spirited Pilobolus Troupe Stages Witty 'Monkshood.'" *New York Times,* September 3, 1974.

McDonagh, Don. "Dance: Gymnastics Transcend Stunts." *New York Times,* April 17, 1973.

McDonagh, Don. "Pilobolus Thrives at Home in Washington." *New York Times,* January 22, 1978.

"Narghilè, funghi e la tana del coniglio : Momix reinventano la storia di Alice" ("Hookah, mushrooms and rabbit hole: Momix reinvents the story of Alice"). *Corriere di Verona* (Italy), November 16, 2019.

Nixon, Amy Ash. "Natural Calling." *Caledonian Record* (Northeastern Vermont and Northern New Hampshire), February 25, 2017.

O'Connor, John J. "TV: Pilobolus Style Is Unusual Dance." *New York Times,* May 4, 1977.

O'Connor, John J. "TV: 'Pilobolus and Joan,' Solid Visual Achievement." *New York Times,* July 1, 1974.

Parry, Jan. "Martha Clarke, Director and Choreographer, on *Chéri.*" *DanceTabs.com,* September 28, 2015. https://dancetabs.com/2015/09/martha-clarke-director-and -choreographer-on-cheri/.

Pendleton, Moses. "A Postcard from MOMIX Artistic Director Moses Pendleton About the Company's Upcoming Season at The Joyce." *Dance Enthusiast,* July 20, 2018. https://www.dance-enthusiast.com/features/postcards/view/Postcard-MOMIX -Artistic-Director-Moses-Pendleton-Season-Joyce.

Perron, Wendy. "Martha Clarke: Between Terror and Desire." *Dance Magazine,* October 2000.

Pilobolus. "In memoriam Jonathan Wolken." Pilobolus blog, June 16, 2010. (Blog no longer online; text courtesy of Pilobolus.)

Pilobolus. Q&A Interview with Peter Sluszka. Pilobolus blog, January 18, 2010. (Blog no longer online; text courtesy of Pilobolus.)

Pilobolus. "The Sushi Principle." Pilobolus blog, June 24, 2010. (Blog no longer online; text courtesy of Pilobolus.)

Pranzatelli, Robert. "Visual Magicians in the Hills of Connecticut." *Paris Review Daily,* May 16, 2019. https://www.theparisreview.org/blog/2019/05/16/visual-magicians/

Rahner, Marc. "Q&A: Innovative Dance Troupe Founder of Pilobolus Chats About Flexibility, Creativity." Interview with Jonathan Wolken. *Seattle Times,* October 21, 2007.
Reardon, Christopher. "Keeping Pilobolus Safe for Democracy." *New York Times,* July 11, 2004.
Rich, Frank. "The Stage: 'Vienna,' from Martha Clarke." *New York Times,* April 21, 1986.
Rizzo, Frank. "Pilobo Loss." *Hartford Courant,* August 6, 2006.
Smith, Amanda. "New York Notebook: The Pils Move Forward—Or Backward?" *Dance Magazine,* 2006.
Smith, Dinitia. "Martha Clarke's Midlife Dream." *New York Times,* July 23, 1995.
Sommers, Pamela. "Philobolus" [sic]. *Washington Post,* October 10, 1979.
Teachout, Terry. "Dancer Alert: Pilobolus Holds an Open Audition." *New York Times,* June 28, 1998.
Tobias, Tobi. "Entangled Bodies, Gymnastic Feats Highlight Pilobolus NYC Dance." posted on Tobi Tobias's blog at *ArtsJournal,* July 17, 2007. https://www.artsjournal.com/tobias/2007/07/entangled_bodies_gymnastic_fea.html.
Traiger, Lisa. "Pilobolus, Monkeying Around." *Washington Post,* June 15, 2001.
Traiger, Lisa. "Pilobolus: Stretching the Limits of Modern Dance." *Washington Post,* December 6, 2002.
Wakin, Daniel J. "Pilobolus Suffers Bitter Breach Over Rights to Choreography." *New York Times,* July 24, 2006.
White, Edmund. "Nabokov: Beyond Parody." In *The Burning Library.* New York: Knopf, 1994.
Woods, Byron. Review of Pilobolus at the American Dance Festival. *Indy Week* (North Carolina), June 18, 2003.
Woolf, Virginia. *Between the Acts.* New York: Harcourt, 1970 [London: Hogarth Press, 1941].

Video interviews

American Dance Festival, video interview with Moses Pendleton, unidentified and not dated but almost certainly July 1981 (in the Dartmouth archives; digitized and provided to the author by Dartmouth). From the video's content it is clear that it was taped at the American Dance Festival around the time of the first performance of *Day Two.*
American Dance Festival, video interview with Martha Clarke, 2013.
Jaworski, Renée, and Matt Kent, "Pilobolus *Shadowland*" livestream conversation with Steven Banks, a Pilobolus online event sponsored by the Quick Center on May 7, 2020.
Jaworski, Renée, and Matt Kent, "Pilobolus Origins" livestream interview with Ann Wolken and JoAnne Torti, a Pilobolus online event, March 28, 2022.
Olvera, Edwin, video interview with Emily Kent, Winter 2017. Posted online by Pilobolus.

Quinn, Joan Agajanian, interview with Daniel Ezralow, *Beverly Hills View,* recorded July 14, 2017; accessed online via Daniel Ezralow's website (ezralowdance.com) in October 2020.

Reinhart, Charles L., interview with Martha Clarke, "Fridays at Noon"; event streamed live on November 6, 2015, retrieved July 10, 2017.

Signature Theatre, video interview with Martha Clarke, posted on November 7, 2013 to promote the production of *Chéri* at that time.

Stahl, Lesley, "The Magic of Pilobolus," CBS *60 Minutes,* February 2004.

University of North Carolina Public Television in conjunction with the American Dance Festival, interview with Alison Chase and Michael Tracy, 1997. Part of a documentary on Pilobolus that focused on four works performed at the ADF in Durham, North Carolina that year.

Winer, Linda, interview with Martha Clarke, "Women in Theatre" video, February 2007/ June 2007.

INDEX

Abumrad, Jad, 259

Aeros, 127, 160

Ailey, Alvin, 40

All Is Not Lost, 229, 232

Alraune, 70–71, 75, 91, 128, 149, 181

Anaendrom, 51, 58, 60

Anderson, Rebecca (later Rebecca Anderson Darling): background, 122; described, 13, 141, 160; and Alison Chase, 189; and *Aeros,* 127; and *Last Dance,* 142–43, 146–47; and *Orangotango,* 136–37; and *Tsu-Ku-Tsu,* 154

Aquatica, 191

Arcane Collective (company), 112

Ashe, Chris, 63

Aubade, 40, 60

Austin, Lyn, 97, 103

Avallone, Angelina, 153, 165, 180

Awaken Heart, 259

Babbitt, Jonathan, 254

Bach, Johann Sebastian, 244

The Bad Plus (band), 8

The Ballad (a.k.a. *The Legend of the Wendigo*), 254–55, 259

Bank, Mirra, 141, 146–47, 160, 164, 167, 177. See also *Last Dance* (film); *Monkey and the Bone Demon* (film)

Banks, Steven, 208–9, 230, 234

Barkan, Leonard, 231

Barnes, Clive, 71, 75

Barnett, Isaac, 101, 108

Barnett, Lincoln, 21

Barnett, Robby [Robert Morgan Barnett]: background, 21–22, 43; described, 13, 41, 79–80, 107–8, 139–40; joins Pilobolus, 35,

36–39; in early Pilobolus, 43–44, 51; and Martha Clarke, 41, 53–55, 76, 78–80, 98; and Susan Mandler, 74, 80, 101; in Crowsnest, 79–80, 86, 88; returns to Pilobolus, 101; and photographers, 43, 63, 168, 173; and creation of Pilobolus works: and *Monkshood's Farewell,* 61, 63; and *Gnomen,* 128–33; and *On the Nature of Things,* 231; and *Rushes,* 194–97; and *Shadowland,* 208–10; and *Sky-scrapers,* 229; and *Untitled,* 67–68; personal views: on early Pilobolus, 32, 51; on changes to Pilobolus, 86, 185; on clashes between directors, 127, 143, 188; retires, 231, 235

Bate, Anna, 251

Battelstein, Adam, 137, 149

BBC One Show (television program), 221

The Beatles, 55, 246

Beck, Talia, 196

Ben's Admonition, 173–77, 179, 189

Between the Acts (Woolf), 236

The Big Five-OH! (tour), 252, 258–59

Bilous, Edward, 180

Blanc, Jim, 129

Blaska, Félix, 73, 79–80, 88

Blondie (band), 8, 85, 233, 255

Bloom: A Journey, 253–55, 259

Blow, John, 197

Bob Marley and the Wailers (band), 84

BodyVox (company), 112

Bogie, Stuart, 253–54

Bone, 75

Bonsai, 83

Bosch, Hieronymus, 60, 97–98

Bowie, David, 255

Branches, 236–38, 248, 252, 259

Brundibár (Krása-Hoffmeister), 141
Byrne, David, 88, 90, 237. *See also* Talking
  Heads (band)

Cameo, 60, 66
Camerlo, Humbert, 89
Capote, Truman, 233, 255
Cardin, Pierre, 59, 73–77, 97, 211
Carson, Johnny, 102
CBS This Morning (television program), 252
Chaplin, Charlie, 83, 198
Chapman, David M., 93
Chase, Alison Becker: background, 18–20; as
  teacher at Dartmouth, 18–23, 29, 32–33;
  meets Martha Clarke, 41; joins Pilobolus,
  54–57; and Moses Pendleton, 23, 53, 55,
  81–82, 83–84, 86, 93–95; in the film *Moses
  Pendleton Presents Moses Pendleton*,
  93–95; as choreographer-director, 108,
  164–67, 175, 180, 189; and creation of
  specific works: and *Untitled*, 65–68; and
  Alraune, 70–71; and *Shizen*, 75–76; and *A
  Miniature*, 86–87; and *Televisitation*, 102–3;
  and *Aeros*, 127; and *Orangotango*, 136–39;
  and *Tsu-Ku-Tsu*, 150–54; and *Monkey and
  the White Bone Demon*, 164–67; and *Ben's
  Admonition*, 173–77; and *Star-Cross'd*, 179–
  80; clashes with other directors, 127, 139,
  140, 177, 186–89; separation from Pilobolus,
  186–89; forms own company, 189; *Quarryography*, 189
Chase, Eric, 18, 60, 84, 87, 95, 137, 166, 176
Cherkaoui, Sidi Larbi, 229
Chopra, Joyce, 87
Ciona, 54, 61, 64, 65, 74, 75
Clarke, Martha: background, 40–41; described,
  57, 76, 88, 105, 227, 228; and Robby Barnett,
  41, 53–55, 76, 78, 88; meets Alison Chase, 41;
  joins Pilobolus, 54–57; brings son David on
  tour, 58–59; reflections on Pilobolus, 53, 54,
  56–57, 77; and creation of specific Pilobolus
  works: and *Monkshood's Farewell*, 60–62;
  and *Untitled*, 65–68 (and restaging of, 247);
  and *Wakefield*, 77–78; decides to leave
  Pilobolus, 77–78; forms Crowsnest, 79–80;
  and *Nocturne* (Crowsnest), 78–79, 247; in
  film *Martha Clarke Light and Dark*, 87–88;

solo works: *Chéri*, 227–28; *The Garden
  of Earthly Delights*, 97–99, 228; *Vienna:
  Lusthaus*, 103–5, 227; later works mentioned
  (*Angel Reapers, Belle Époque*), 227–28. *See
  also* Crowsnest (company)
Clarke, Shirley, 40
Cocteau, Jean, 73, 78
Colette, 227–28
Connecting with Balance, 252
Cook, Otis, 123, 165, 166, 174, 196, 199; and *A
  Selection* and *Last Dance*, 142–43, 147–48;
  and *Symbiosis*, 161–63; and *Tsu-Ku-Tsu*,
  151, 152
Cook, Ray, 20, 35
Cornejo, Herman, 227
Corriere di Verona, 245
Costello, Elvis, 131
Courtney, Michael. *See* Ras Mikey C
Coyoc, Josie, 142, 166, 196, 199, 201
Croce, Arlene, 6, 71–72, 75–76, 87, 105–6
Crowsnest (company), 79, 81, 82, 86, 87–88,
  97, 98, 247
Cummings, e. e., 254
Cunningham, Merce, 19, 20, 40, 255
Cyrus, Miley, 216

Daily Telegraph (London), 55
Dairakudakan (Butoh company), 229
Dance (magazine), 105, 191
Dance in America (television program), 61, 74,
  75, 99, 120, 182
Darkness and Light, 206, 208
Darling, Rebecca Anderson (*née* Rebecca
  Anderson). *See* Anderson, Rebecca
Dartmouth, 16–36, 40; Hopkins Center, 19, 21,
  29, 31; Webster Hall, 21, 29, 43–44, 60; goes
  fully co-ed, 51
Davenen, 160, 174
Davis, Miles, 197
Day Two, 4, 10, 100, 102, 111, 113, 132, 160, 162,
  237, 259; described, 91–92; making of, 88–
  93; revival in 2019, 242, 243–44, 246, 248,
  249; "slides" as curtain call, 92–93; viewed
  as classic work, 105–6, 159
Debussy, Claude, 109, 227
Debut C, 109
De Frutos, Javier, 229

Degeneres, Ellen, 193
Del Rosario, Matt, 225–27, 239
Denby, David, 256
Dennis, Robert, 68
De Rerum Natura (ancient poetic work), 231
di Prima, Diane, 37
Dog-ID, 211, 212
Dorfman, Carolyn, 160
Dorr, Nell, 63
Duet 92, 120
Dukes of Dixieland (band), 197
Dunning, Jennifer, 109, 177, 180, 191
Dupond, Patrick, 81

Echo in the Valley, 238
Edge, The (a.k.a. Dave Evans), 112
Edmonson, Kat, 243, 253, 254
Eisenstat, Zach, 234
Elfstrom, Robert, 93
Elysian Fields (a.k.a. Olympic Dances), 128
Empson, William, 137
The Empty Suitor, 83, 120, 259
Emshwiller, Ed, 64
Eno, Brian, 4, 88, 90, 93, 100, 237
Eriko Jimbo, 219
<esc> (Pilobolus work), 230–31, 232
Espace Cardin (theater), 73, 79
Eto, Leonard, 150–53
Evening Song (a.k.a. Noctuary), 259
The Eve of Samhain, 73, 75
Eye Opening, 238
Ezra, Steven, 242, 243
Ezralow, Daniel (Danny), 83–86, 89–90, 95, 110–12

Fashion Aid, 111
"fat gnomes," 101–2, 193
Faulkner, William, 68
Faust, Rob, 86, 89–90, 101
Favretto, Heather, 246
Femme Noire, 160, 164
Ferri, Alessandra, 227
5 by 2 Plus (dance company), 83
Fleck, Béla, 238
Fracci, Carla, 81
Franklin, Benjamin, 176
Fucik, Mark, 166, 211

Garden of the Heart, 149
Gawler, Molly, 208
Geisel, Theodor Seuss (pseud. Dr. Seuss), 13, 37
Geode, 38, 60, 69
Giobbi, Lisa, 101, 102–3
Giraud, Jean (a.k.a. Moebius), 233, 255
Gish, Lillian, 63
Glazer, Susan, 157
Gnomen, 3–4, 5, 13, 15, 129–33, 212, 239, 248, 258; described, 3–4, 130–31; making of, 129–33
Goldberg, Whoopi, 216
Goodman, Donna, 36
Gorky, Arshile, 97
Goya, Francisco, 79
Graham, Martha, 40, 135, 187
Grausman, David, 41, 58–59, 60, 77, 87–88, 247–48
Grausman, Philip, 40–41, 60, 87
Great Performances: Dance in America (television program). See Dance in America
Guerin, Isabelle, 81
Gussow, Mel, 98

Hampton, Jamey: in Pilobolus, 80–86, 88–90; in Momix, 110–12; and origin of Momix name, 84; and Crowsnest, 88; friendship with Jonathan Wolken, 219
Harbison, John, 128
Harris, Lee: background, 22, 35; joins Pilobolus, 35–36; and early Pilobolus, 33, 36–39, 42–44, 51–59, 64; leaves Pilobolus, 57–58; on the Pilobolus method of composition, 42–43, 257
Harrison, Wallace, 19
Hartford Courant, 180, 255
Hawkins, Alma, 19
Herro, Andrew: background and presence, 181–82, 212–14, 239; and Megawatt, 183–84; and Memento Mori, 190–91; and Rushes, 197, 198; and Jonathan Wolken, 186, 219; on Pilobolus, 257
Hersey, John, 103
Hilmer, Lucy, 93
Hiroshima (Hersey), 103
Hitched, 219–20
Holland, Phil, 110

Holmes, Georgiana, 83
Horst, Louis, 40
Howes, Casey, 253
Humphrey, Doris, 135
Hunt, Linda, 77

"in Just-" (Cummings), 254
Institute of American Indian Studies, 254
Integrale Erik Satie, 80–81, 89
Irving, Amy, 227
ISO (company), 111–12
"i thank you God for most this amazing"
    (Cummings), 254

Jacob's Pillow, 179, 236–38, 252
Jagger, Mick, 109
Jampolis, Neil Peter, 109, 211
Jaworski, Renée: background, 155–60;
    described, 10–11; as performer in Momix,
    157–60; first time seeing Pilobolus, 159,
    258; auditions for and joins Pilobolus, 160;
    and directors of Pilobolus, 161; and Jona-
    than Wolken, 161, 193, 217–18; and Martha
    Clarke, 247; and Matt Kent, 164, 251–52;
    as workshop instructor, 10–11; praised
    as performer, 191; and Academy Awards
    performance, 193; meeting with the Queen
    of England, 215–16; describes Pilobolus
    works as "miniature worlds," 234; named
    artistic director, 235; and return to the
    Joyce Theater, 246–49; and restaging of
    Untitled, 247; as leader of Pilobolus with
    Matt Kent, 251–55, 258–59; and creation
    of Pilobolus works: and *Bloom,* 253–55;
    and *Branches,* 236–38; and *Megawatt,*
    183; and *Memento Mori,* 190–91; and *On
    the Nature of Things,* 231–32; and *Rushes,*
    196–97; and *Shadowland,* 207–11, 234–35;
    and *Shadowland 2,* 234–35; and *Symbiosis,*
    161–64; and collaborations with OK Go
    and Trish Sie, 229–30; and other works,
    165, 225, 242–43, 259
Jillette, Penn, 230
Job, John, 89
Jobim, Antônio Carlos, 253
Johns, Jasper, 255

Johnson, Stephen, 16–18, 21–23, 24, 29–35, 82
Journey to the Hindbrain (dance piece by
    Sarasvati), 120, 125
Journey to the West (book), 165
Jowitt, Deborah, 64, 106–7, 153, 191, 194
Joyce, James, 120
Jung, Rebecca (Becky), 122, 129

Kafka, Franz, 64
Kahn, Chaka, 216
Kane, John, 167–73, 226–27, 238–42, 252
Kapilow, Rob, 253–54
Kascak, Darlene, 254
Kaufman, Sarah, 232
Keaton, Buster, 83
Kent, Emily Milam (*née* Emily Milam):
    background and college years, 123–27; and
    Matt Kent, 123–27, 134–36, 148–49, 173–76,
    177–78, 180–81, 199–201; as dancer with
    Pilobolus, 148–50, 181; as workshop instruc-
    tor and educator, 7–8, 10–11, 223–24; and
    Pilobolus-Momix collaboration, 242–43;
    and Ras Mikey C, 173–76; and author, 7–8,
    10–11, 212, 259–60
Kent, Matt (John Matheson Kent): back-
    ground, 117–21; described, "intensity" of, 7,
    142–43, 179, 181; psychology and personal-
    ity, 117–19, 215, 218; and Emily Milam Kent,
    123–27, 134–36, 148–49, 173–76, 177–78, 180–
    81, 199–201; first time seeing Pilobolus, 120;
    auditions for Pilobolus, 121–23; early experi-
    ences with Pilobolus, 126–33; seen as young
    dancer by author, 5, 6; as dance captain,
    164; as performer, 165, 166–67, 180, 242–43;
    in the film *Last Dance,* 142–43, 147–48; in
    Pilobolus Too, 180–81; and photo shoots,
    173; as workshop instructor, 7–15, 212; as
    consultant for *The Walking Dead* (televi-
    sion series), 217; nominated for Los Angeles
    Drama Critics Circle Award, 234; named
    artistic director, 235; and return to the Joyce
    Theater, 246–49; and restaging of *Day Two,*
    243–44, 248; as leader of Pilobolus with
    Renée Jaworski, 251–55, 258–59; and Ras
    Mikey C, 173–77; and Paul Sullivan, 133; and
    Jonathan Wolken, 13, 121, 128–29, 139–40,

200–202, 212, 217–18, 220; friendship with author, 7–10, 12–15, 205–6, 212, 214, 215, 233, 259–60; and creation of specific Pilobolus works: and *Ben's Admonition*, 173–77; and *Bloom*, 253–55; and *Branches*, 236–38; and *<esc>*, 230–31; and *Gnomen*, 128–33; and *Megawatt*, 183–84; and *Monkey and the White Bone Demon*, 165–67; and *On the Nature of Things*, 231–32; and *Orangotango*, 136–38; and *Rushes*, 196; and *A Selection*, 142–43, 147–48; and *Shadowland*, 207–11, 214, 234–35; and *Shadowland 2*, 234–35; and *Star-Cross'd*, 179–80; and *Tsu-Ku-Tsu*, 151–52, 154; and other works, 242–43, 259

Kent, Owen, 11, 259
Kent, Sam, 249, 254
Kent, Scott, 119
Keret, Etgar, 229
Keys, Alicia, 221
Kisselgoff, Anna, 39, 44, 71, 75, 92, 112, 163, 166
Kitchel, Alice, 24–29
Klezmatics (band), 160
Kourlas, Gia, 177
Kramer, Jane, 95
Kubovy, Itamar, 13, 184–88, 194–97, 201, 251–52; and creation of *Shadowland*, 208–9, 234
Kulash, Damian, 229
Kulka, John, 8–9
Kuribayashi, Jun, 239

Labèque, Katia, 79
Labèque, Marielle, 79
Lady Gaga, 216
Lanterna Magica, 206–7, 212
L'Après-midi d'un faune (ballet), 109
Lar Lubovitch Dance Company, 83
Last Dance (film): making of, 141–48, 164; reception, 177; as influence on author's perceptions of Pilobolus, 9, 10, 13
Late Night with Conan O'Brien (television program), 207, 208
Lee, Riley Kelly, 75
The Legend of the Wendigo (a.k.a. *The Ballad*), 254–55, 259
Lennon, Julian, 109
Leon, Kirsten, 251

Le Plus Grand Cabaret Du Monde (television program), 221
L'histoire du Soldat (theatrical work), 77
Licks, 230
Limón, José, 40, 135
Lindemer, Kent, 122
Loman, Derion, 259
Los Angeles Times, 111
Losick, Vic, 146
Louis, Gaspard: background, 122–23, 127; and making of *Gnomen*, 129–33; in *Last Dance*, 142; in *Tsu-Ku-Tsu*, 151–52; and other Pilobolus work, 165, 166, 189, 259
Louis, Murray, 19, 32–34, 38, 55, 61, 122
Love. Eat. Die., 199
The Lovin' Spoonful (band), 207
Lucretius, 231–32

Macavinta, Jennifer, 163, 183, 247
Malmstrom, Bud, 118–19
Mandler, Susan, 74, 80, 112, 140
Marley, Bob, 84
Martha Clarke Light and Dark (film), 87–88
Martin, John, 19
Matson, Tim, 77
McDermott, Joan, 64
McDonagh, Don, 53, 60, 65
Mee, Charles, 103–4
Megawatt, making of, 183–84, 186, 199, 201, 212–14, 258
Megawatt > Full Strength, 186
Melrose, Claudia, 17
Melvin, Mark, 159
Memento Mori, 190–91
Memoirs of a Beatnik (di Prima), 37
Mendez, Jenny (Jennifer), 196, 239, 242
Merk, Andreas, 196
Merrill, Al, 24
Midler, Bette, 216
Milam, Emily. *See* Kent, Emily Milam
A Miniature, 87
Minniefee, Manelich, 151, 182, 194, 234
MIT Distributed Robotics Laboratory, 226, 228
Miyake, Issey, 111
Moebius. *See* Giraud, Jean
Molly's Not Dead, 101–2

Momix (company): origin of name, 84; as touring vehicle for Alison Chase and Moses Pendleton, 86; as quartet, 110–12; redefinitions of name, 110; reconfigured in late 1980s, 109–10, 112; and Pilobolus, 113, 158, 238–39, 242–43; in 1990s, 157–59; works noted or discussed, 158, 243–45

Momix (solo), 84–86, 94

Mompou, Frederic, 227

Monkey and the Bone Demon (film), 164–67

Monkey and the White Bone Demon, 164–67, 179, 189

Monkshood's Farewell: making of, 60–63; as popular piece, 65, 71, 74, 75; in the evolution of Pilobolus, 91, 94, 106; later influence, 98, 101, 128

Morgan, Barbara, 135

Morrison, Van, 131

Moschen, Michael, 229

Moses Pendleton Presents Moses Pendleton (film), 93–95, 135, 245

The Mothers of Invention (band), 36. *See also* Zappa, Frank

Muramatsu, Takuya, 229

Murray, Jan, 55

Nabokov, Vladimir, 137–38, 239

Nawaz, Aki, 180

New Yorker (magazine), 6, 71–72, 75–76, 95, 103, 105–6, 256

New York Times: feature coverage, 71, 75, 76, 142, 177, 188; reviews (1970s), 39, 53, 60, 64, 65, 71, 74, 75; reviews (1980s), 98, 105, 109, 112; later reviews, 163, 166, 177, 180, 191

Nijinsky, Vaslav, 36, 109

Nikolais, Alwin, 17, 33–34, 55, 61, 122

Nirvana (band), 8

Noctuary (a.k.a. *Evening Song*), 259

Nocturne (Crowsnest), 78–79, 247

Nortec Collective: Bostich & Fussible, 230

O'Brien, Conan, 207, 208

Ocellus, 42–43, 52, 71, 74, 75; in photos, *48–50*

O'Connor, John J., 64

OK Go (band), 229, 254

Olandt, Madison, 259

Olsen, Solveig, 159

Olvera, Edwin, 193–94, 197–99, 206–07, 219

Olympic Dances (a.k.a. *Elysian Fields*), 128

On the Nature of Things, 231–32, 248, 259

Orangotango, 136–39, 164

Ordower, Daniel, 246

Oyster (dance theatre work by Pinto and Pollak), 195

Pagliaccio, 71, 75

Paris Review Daily, 238

Parker, Carol, 86, 89, 100

Parker, Robert, 99, 105

Parsifal (Wagner), 95

Parson Nibs and the Rude Beggars, 84

Pärt, Arvo, 197

The Particle Zoo, 120, 129, 159

Paul Taylor Dance Company, 83–84, 85

Peaslee, Richard, 97, 103

Pendleton, Nelson (father of Robert [Moses] Pendleton), 23, 25, 94–95

Pendleton, Robert (Moses): background, 23–29, 94–95; described, 16–17, 23–29, 44, 109, 243; identity crisis of, 25–26; and Alice Kitchel, 24–29; summer of 1969 in San Francisco, 26–27; belief in "free love" ideals, 27–28, 53; and Alison Chase, 23, 53, 55, 81–82, 83–84, 86, 93–95; clashes with Jonathan Wolken, 82; purchases Victorian house, 80; leaves Pilobolus, 112–13; philosophical influence on Pilobolus, 17, 53, 245, 256; and creation of Pilobolus works: and *Pilobolus* (trio), 16–18, 29–32; and one-legged solo in *Monkshood's Farewell,* 61, 62; and *Untitled,* 66–68; and *Alraune,* 70–71; and *Shizen,* 75–76; and *Momix* (solo), 83–86; and *Day Two,* 88–93, 243–44; and *Debut C,* 109; and creation of works outside Pilobolus: project for the Paris Opera, 80–81; *Moses Pendleton Presents Moses Pendleton* (film), 93–95, 245; and Momix (the company), 109–12, 157–58, 243, 244–45. *See also* Momix (company)

Penn and Teller, 230–31. *See also* Teller

Perl, Josh, 103

Perlmutter, Donna, 111

Persistence of Memory, 193–94

Piazzolla, Astor, 138

Pilobolus (book by Tim Matson), 77
Pilobolus (company): formation, 29–37; early
    public performances, 36–39; origin of
    name, 17–18, 31; method of composition,
    42; shared house in Norwich, Vermont,
    43; moves to Connecticut, 60–61, 64–65;
    expands to a sextet, 53–57; at Fringe Festival
    (Edinburgh, Scotland), 55; at Bordeaux Fes-
    tival (France), 56; makes Broadway debut,
    75–76; and Olympics (Winter 1980), 83–85;
    decides to hire new dancers and continue
    as a company, 86; undergoes financial
    crisis, 112–14; relationship with American
    Dance Festival, 54, 62, 68, 78, 88, 93, 102;
    relationship with the Joyce Theater, 134,
    232–33, 246–49; company identity, 51, 71–72,
    105–7, 255–58; and importance of rural
    setting, 251; and wall calendars, 6–7, 167–73;
    clashes between directors, 127–28, 139–40,
    143, 146–48, 177, 185–89; hires executive
    director, 184–86; disputes over ownership
    of work, 100–101, 187–89; Academy Awards
    telecast, 192–93; creation of shadow images
    and related works, 192–93, 206–16, 221,
    233–35; PCS (Pilobolus Creative Services),
    193; educational outreach program, 223–24;
    summer workshop, author's experiences
    with, 7–15, 205–6, 212, 223
Pilobolus (trio), 16–18, 29–39, 52, 243
Pilobolus and Joan (film), 64
Pilobolus on Broadway (television special), 100
Pilobolus Too, 149, 180–81
Pinto, Inbal, 195–97
Planet Earth II (documentary), 237
Poe, David, 209, 216, 234
Pollak, Avshalom, 195–97
Pollard, Trebien, 123, 128–33
Pontois, Noella, 81
Posner, Aaron, 234
Poulenc, Francis, 227
Prélude à l'après-midi d'un faune (orchestral
    work), 109
Primus (band), 183, 184
Prince, 109
Princess Margaret, 55
Pring, Benjamin, 142, 151–52, 165–67, 174
Processo (newspaper), 138

"pseudo-parody to disarm criticism" (literary
    theory), 137–38
Pseudopodia, 69–70, 71, 75, 159, 160
Pucci, Peter, 86, 100

Quinn, Cynthia, 86, 89, 100, 102, 107, 135, 158–
    59, 242–43

Radiohead (band), 184
Radiolab (radio program), 259
Ras Mikey C (Michael Courtney), 151, 173–77,
    179–80, 182, 189
Ravel, Maurice, 227
Redford, Robert, 60
Reinhart, Charles, 54, 78, 88, 102, 197–98
Reinhart, Stephanie, 78
Rejoyce, 120
Renelaugh on the Randan, 75
Return to Maria La Baja, 101
Rich, Frank, 105
Robbins, Jerome, 59
Roland, Ashley, 110–12
Rothenberg, Sarah, 227
Rushes, 194–99, 248, 257–58

Sa'adah, Jonathan, 43
Sante, Jude Woodcock. *See* Woodcock, Jude
Santillano, Mark, 122; and making of *Gnomen,*
    129–33, 135, 159
Sarasvati, Bala, 119–20, 125
Satie, Erik, 80, 89
Sauter, Eddie, 197
Schickele, Peter (a.k.a. P.D.Q. Bach), 59
Schiele, Egon, 103
Schubert, Franz, 225
Schwartz, Alison, 178
Sébastien, Patrick, 221
A Selection, 141–43, 146–48, 160, 165
Sendak, Maurice, 141–43, 146–48
Seraph, 224–27, 228
Seuss, Dr. *See* Geisel, Theodor Seuss
Sevilla, John-Mario, 122
Shadowland: making of, 208–12, 214–15;
    and Royal Variety Performance, 215–16;
    international success of, 221; creation of
    sequel, 233–35; US debut, 234; referenced,
    229, 230, 251

Shadowland 2, 233–35
Shakespeare, William, 162, 179, 234
Sheaff, Annika, 194, 199
Shizen, 75, 91, 93–94, 128, 181, 259
Sie, Trish, 229–30
Simpson, Tommy, 149
Slavenska, Mia, 19
Sluszka, Peter, 198
Soffer, Sheldon, 86, 185
Soft Cell (band), 95
Sokolow, Anna, 41
Sollee, Ben, 254
Solo from The Empty Suitor, 83, 120, 259
Sondheim, Stephen, 253
Songs of Travel (Stevenson), 254
Sowell, Ashley, 119–21, 125
Spiegelman, Art, 229
Spyrogyra, 51, 52, 54
Squarepusher (band), 184
Star-cross'd, 179–80, 189
Steinberg, Morleigh, 110–12
Stenn, Rebecca, 137, 149
Stevenson, Robert Louis, 254
Stodelle, Ernestine, 135
Strawbridge, Stephen, 153, 176, 180
Sugarhill Gang (rap group), 84, 85
Sullivan, Paul, 85, 86–87, 101, 133, 166, 176, 253
"sushi principle" (Pilobolus teaching), 14, 69, 220
Symbiosis, 161–64, 177, 248

Tales from the Underworld, 243
Talking Heads (band), 4, 88, 90, 91, 93, 100
"tall ladies," 66–68, 193, 242, 246, 247
Tamiris, Helen, 40
Tatge, Pamela, 236–37
Taymor, Julie, 112, 162
Teachout, Terry, 142
Televisitation, 103
Teller, 230, 234
The Tempest (Shakespeare), 234
Thanksgiving improv, 37–38
This Is Not a Play! (play), 138
Thomas, Darryl, 122
Thompson, Johnny, 230, 234
Thoreau, Henry David, 251
Thornton, Matt, 200

Time Out (magazine, London), 55
Titus (film), 162
Tonight Show (television program), 102
Torti, JoAnne, 139, 201
Tracy, Michael: background, 20, 21–22; invited to join Pilobolus, 51, 57–58; described, 108, 140, 215; continues to tour in 1980s, 86, 101, 102; positions on crises in Pilobolus, 113, 187, 188; and difficulties with Jonathan Wolken, 127, 139, 143, 177, 195; meets filmmaker Mirra Bank, 146; and creation of specific Pilobolus works: and *Aeros,* 127; and *Lanterna Magica,* 206–7; and *Persistence of Memory,* 193–94; and *Shadowland,* 208–9; and *Solo from The Empty Suitor,* 83; and *Symbiosis,* 161–63, 177; and *Untitled,* 67–68
Trio No. 2 in E Flat (Schubert), 225
Tsu-Ku-Tsu, 150–54, 160, 164, 174, 189
Tudor, Antony, 40, 227
Twist, Basil, 206

U2 (band), 112
Unearthing the Past (Barkan), 231
Uno, Dos, Tray, 164
Untitled: making of, 65–68; restaging, 247–48; in Pilobolus repertoire, 71, 73–75, 259; referenced, 69, 77, 91, 106, 109, 128, 132, 182, 188, 242

Vagabond, 75
Van Tieghem, David, 237
Village Voice, 153, 191, 194, 195
Vivaldi, Antonio, 231

Wakefield, 75, 77–78
Walden (Thoreau), 251
The Walking Dead (television series), 217
Walklyndon: making of, 37; expanded for six performers, 54, 62; and streaking, 59, 248, 249; referenced, 5, 38, 42, 52, 71, 139, 149, 159, 248
Warp & Weft, 238
Warren, Jacob Michael, 253
Washburn, Abigail, 238
Washington Post, 84, 105, 111, 153, 176, 232
Wetten Dass . . . ? (television program), 221
White, Edmund, 137–38

Whitney, Christopher, 219–20

Williams, Ralph Vaughn, 254

Wolken, Ann, 22, 44

Wolken, Jonathan: background, 22; described, 17, 13, 76, 184, 186, 218–20; contrasted to Robert (Moses) Pendleton, 44; as workshop instructor, 13–14, 212; as director, 128–29, 143, 147, 183–84, 186; and "sushi principle," 14, 69, 220; and other directorial maxims, 219; and first meeting with Matt Kent, 120–21; and Katia Labèque, 79; and Maurice Sendak, 143; and love of Frank Zappa, 36–37, 139–40, 220; personal clashes: with Martha Clarke, 77; with Moses Pendleton, 82; with Matt Kent, 200–202; with other directors, 67–68, 139–40, 143, 146–47, 186, 188, 195; and creation of Pilobolus works: and *Gnomen,* 128–29, 133; and *Hitched,* 219– 20; and *Pilobolus* (trio), 17–18, 29, 31; and *Pseudopodia,* 69–70; and *A Selection,* 143, 146–47; and *Megawatt,* 183–84; terminal illness, 193, 200, 202, 217–18; final work, 219–20; as posthumous influence, 252

Women Who Run with the Wolves (Estés), 162

Woodcock, Jude, 99–103, 107–8, 122, 129, 160

Woolf, Virginia, 236

X-Men (film), 256

Yorinks, Arthur, 141, 143

Zanes, Dan, 229

Zappa, Frank, 36–37, 139–40, 220

Zaz, 221

Ziskin, Laura, 192

Photo by Elizabeth Foxwell

ROBERT PRANZATELLI is the author of a number of essays published by the *Paris Review* and other literary journals. His writings include portraits of visual creators (among them Belle Epoque artist Lucien Métivet, French comics genius Jean "Moebius" Giraud, and contemporary Belgian graphic novelist Max de Radiguès), essays on literary figures (Vladimir Nabokov, Truman Capote), and a number of stories and poems. He is a longtime staff member of Yale University Press.